LONDON
ENCOUNTER

SARAH JOHNSTONE

D1053620

London Encounter
1st edition – May 2007

Published by Lonely Planet Publications Pty Ltd
ABN 36 005 607 983

Australia	Head Office, Locked Bag 1, Footscray, Vic 3011
	☎ 03 8379 8000 fax 03 8379 8111
	talk2us@lonelyplanet.com.au
USA	150 Linden St, Oakland, CA 94607
	☎ 510 893 8555
	toll free 800 275 8555
	fax 510 893 8572
	info@lonelyplanet.com
UK	72–82 Rosebery Avenue, Clerkenwell London EC1R 4RW
	☎ 020 7841 9000 fax 020 7841 9001
	go@lonelyplanet.co.uk

This title was commissioned in Lonely Planet's London office and produced by: **Commissioning Editor** Clifton Wilkinson **Coordinating Editors** Kyla Gillzan, Kate James **Coordinating Cartographer** Joshua Geoghegan **Layout Designer** Evelyn Yee **Senior Editors** Helen Christinis, Katie Lynch **Managing Cartographer** Mark Griffiths **Cover Designer** Nic Lehman **Project Manager** Sarah Sloane **Thanks to** David Burnett, Amanda Canning, Sally Darmody, Jennifer Garrett, Michelle Glynn, Amanda Sierp, Stephanie Pearson, Celia Wood, Wendy Wright

Photographs by Lonely Planet Images and Doug Mckinlay except for the following: p101 Richard Bryant/Arcaid/Corbis/APL; p31, p164, p199 Amanda Canning; p152, Matt Carr Photography/Photolibrary; p174 BBC; p53, p103, p132 Sarah Johnstone. **Cover photograph** Commuters on Platform at London Underground Station/Up The Resolution (uptheres)/Alamy.

All images are copyright of the photographers unless otherwise indicated. Many of the images in this guide are available for licensing from **Lonely Planet Images:** www.lonelyplanetimages.com.

ISBN 978 1 74059 747 0

Printed through Colorcraft Ltd, Hong Kong.
Printed in China

Acknowledgement London Underground Map © Transport for London 2006

Lonely Planet and the Lonely Planet logo are trademarks of Lonely Planet and are registered in the US Patent and Trademark Office and in other countries.

Lonely Planet does not allow its name or logo to be appropriated by commercial establishments, such as retailers, restaurants or hotels. Please let us know of any misuses: www.lonelyplanet.com/ip.

HOW TO USE THIS BOOK

Colour-Coding & Maps

Colour-coding is used for symbols on maps and in the text that they relate to (eg all eating venues on the maps and in the text are given a blue fork symbol). Each neighbourhood also gets its own colour, and this is used down the edge of the page and throughout that neighbourhood section.

Shaded yellow areas on the maps are to denote 'areas of interest' – be that for historical significance, attractive architecture or a strip that's good for bars or restaurants. We'd encourage you to head to these areas and just start exploring!

Prices

Concession prices can include senior, student, member or coupon discounts. Meal cost categories are listed on the Quick Reference page on the inside front cover.

SARAH JOHNSTONE

Sarah Johnstone came to London on a short
break, and a decade-and-a-half later finds herself
entrenched there. She thinks that *almost* qualifies
her as a 'Londoner', but she's still not sure. Having
studied journalism as part of a Bachelor of Arts
back in Queensland, she's seen many sides of
the English capital while working on a range of
magazines, including *Business Traveller* and Virgin
Atlantic's in-flight magazine *Hot Air*. She's completed a Master of Science at the London School
of Economics, worked at Reuters and had a few
articles published in the *Independent on Sunday*, *Guardian*, *Observer* and
Times. She's been writing guides for Lonely Planet for the past five years.

SARAH'S THANKS

Sincere thanks to all the usual suspects who accompanied me on nights
out and provided me with tips. I don't mean to sound unnecessarily
ungrateful but, as always, space is tight, time is short and my brain is fried
by this juncture. You know who you are anyway. Cheers.

THE PHOTOGRAPHER

Doug Mckinlay has been a photographer for 20 years, having started out
as a stringer in exotic war-zone locales from Cambodia to El Salvador. His
travel and news images have appeared in publications such as the *Times*,
the *Independent*, the *Guardian*, the *Mail*, *Conde Nast Traveller*, *Maxim*, the
Observer, *High Life*, *CNN Traveller* and Lonely Planet guidebooks.

Our Readers | Many thanks to the travellers who wrote to us with helpful hints, useful advice and interesting anecdotes.
Bianca Barbaro, Kathy Belpaeme, Jason Brown, Pablo Contestabile, Bryan Cronk, Brent Kendall, Tracey Seslen, Melanie
Simunovic, Mark Westerfield.

Send us your Feedback | We love to hear from travellers – your comments keep us on our toes and help make our books
better. Our well-travelled team reads every word on what you loved or loathed about this book. Although we cannot reply
individually to postal submissions, we always guarantee that your feedback goes straight to the appropriate authors, in time
for the next edition – and the most useful submissions are rewarded with a free book. To send us your updates – and find out
about Lonely Planet events, newsletters and travel news – visit our award-winning website: *lonelyplanet.com/feedback*.

Note: We may edit, reproduce and incorporate your comments in Lonely Planet products such as guidebooks, websites and
digital products, so let us know if you don't want your comments reproduced or your name acknowledged. For a copy of our
privacy policy visit *lonelyplanet.com/privacy*.

Buses on Ludgate Hill, with St Paul's Cathedral (p18) in the background

CONTENTS

THE AUTHOR	**03**
THIS IS LONDON	**07**
HIGHLIGHTS	**08**
LONDON DIARY	**31**
ITINERARIES	**37**
NEIGHBOURHOODS	**42**
>SOHO & COVENT GARDEN	46
>BLOOMSBURY & FITZROVIA	62
>MARYLEBONE & REGENT'S PARK	70
>MAYFAIR, ST JAMES'S, WESTMINSTER & PIMLICO	78
>KNIGHTSBRIDGE, SOUTH KENSINGTON & CHELSEA	94
>HOLBORN, CLERKENWELL & THE CITY	108
>HOXTON, SHOREDITCH & SPITALFIELDS	120
>SOUTH BANK	136
>GREENWICH	150
>KING'S CROSS, EUSTON & ISLINGTON	158
>CAMDEN, HAMPSTEAD & PRIMROSE HILL	166
>NOTTING HILL	176
SNAPSHOTS	**184**
BACKGROUND	**203**
DIRECTORY	**214**
INDEX	**230**

THIS IS LONDON

London, as writer Henry James observed, might not be agreeable or easy, but it's certainly magnificent. This global juggernaut moves at a relentless pace that's even intimidating at times. Yet you just can't help being swept along on its vibrancy and dynamism. As a force of nature – which it is – London is irresistible.

The most culturally diverse city on earth, speaking 300 languages, is also a swirling mass of contradictions. It's stately Big Ben and working-class Bow Bells. It's the medieval Tower in front of the futuristic Gherkin, implacable St Paul's Cathedral opposite awe-inspiring Tate Modern. It's First World; it's Third World. It's cutting-edge and traditional.

In the run-up to the 2012 Olympics, the English capital already holds out more than clichéd images of royalty, tea at the Ritz, black cabs and red buses. It's a leading destination for its excellent and varied shopping, fantastic free museums and football teams like 'Chelski' (Chelsea). At any time of year, 24-hour party people will be immersing themselves in its many pubs and clubs.

Admittedly, only from the lofty heights of the London Eye could anyone fail to notice how grubby the place often is. Away from the tourist headlines, it's bursting at the housing seams and blighted by creaking public transportation. Yet none of this seems to matter to the many newcomers – most recently, eastern Europeans – who head to the city in droves to live and, in doing so, top up its youthful energy.

London's turbo-charged economy, verve and cultural breadth mean it's the only major European capital still expanding, and that's the bottom line about this compelling city. It doesn't need to be agreeable or easy at all for people to keep falling in love with it.

Left Burger stall in front of the Houses of Parliament (p82)

>HIGHLIGHTS

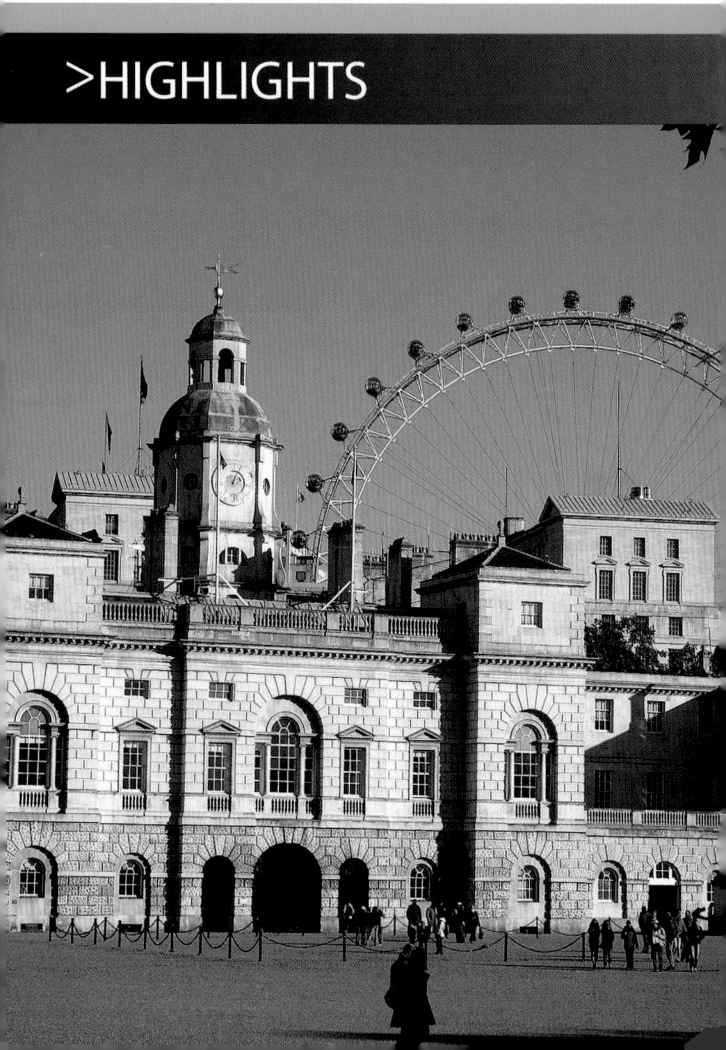

>1 Survey the city from the heights of the
London Eye and along the south bank 10

>2 Revel in contemporary art and stunning
architecture at Tate Modern 12

>3 Grab a snap of Westminster's inspiring silhouette 14

>4 Lose yourself in the Royal Parks' green splendour 15

>5 Check out old masters and famous faces at
the National and National Portrait Galleries 16

>6 Delve into antiquity at the British Museum 17

>7 Journey in body and spirit to the top of St Paul's 18

>8 Relive the Tower of London's gory history 19

>9 Take your pick from art, history and science
at the Kensington museums 20

>10 Watch London glide by from the comfort
of a River Thames cruise 22

>11 Have a fine time in the quaint 'village' of Greenwich 23

>12 Head for a picnic with a view on Hampstead Heath 24

>13 Feel London's retail heart beat at its most
popular markets 25

>14 Dine out with a celebrity chef 26

>15 Go for a curry, a time-honoured London experience 27

>16 Take your seats for the world's best theatre 28

>17 Dig the Hoxton and Shoreditch clubbing scene 30

Tate Modern (p142) and the London Eye (p140)

>1 LONDON EYE & SOUTH BANK

SURVEY THE CITY FROM THE HEIGHTS OF THE LONDON EYE AND ALONG THE SOUTH BANK

Given the notoriously unreliable British weather, it was a brave decision to erect the world's largest observation wheel in London in the year 2000. Yet its creators' faith in the London Eye has been repaid beyond their wildest dreams.

Meant to have been scrap by now, this elegant 'temporary' structure has become one of the city's most recognisable symbols, as well as part of British culture. With an extended lease until 2028, it's made appearances in TV series such as *Dr Who*. Writer Will Self has dubbed it 'God's bicycle wheel'.

Of course, the success of the 135m-tall Eye is down to its sweeping views of this great city. On a good day, you can see 40km in each direction – west to Windsor and east nearly to the mouth of the Thames River.

See p140 for further details about the Eye.

Visiting the Eye is the perfect entrée to another top London experience – walking along the Thames' south bank. Even locals repeatedly come to marvel at the skyline here. Head for the nearby South Bank Centre and continue to the Oxo Tower, Tate Modern and beyond.

In an even greater hurry? Stand on Waterloo Bridge for the best city view, particularly at night.

>2 TATE MODERN

REVEL IN CONTEMPORARY ART AND STUNNING ARCHITECTURE AT TATE MODERN

During its first six years the Tate Modern gallery was like a gorgeous airhead, becoming wildly successful because of its breathtaking appearance. Swiss architects Herzog & de Meuron won the prestigious Pritzker Architecture Prize for their millennial transformation of Bankside Power Station, with refurbished Turbine Hall as the dramatic entrance space. Millions of visitors were too mesmerised by the Thames views to heed newspaper criticisms about the disjointed way this 'supermarket of art' displayed its collection.

Now the world's most popular contemporary art gallery is getting serious about the works within its famous walls. The permanent

collection has been rehung in a more chronological and educational manner, masterpieces in storage have been resurrected and a timeline of 20th-century art movements added.

However, while there are more works displayed, must-sees – including the Mark Rothko room, the Alberto Giacometti stick sculptures, Roy Lichtenstein's *Whaam!* and Jackson Pollock's *Summertime* – are still fairly limited, and the large surrealism section is pretty heavy going.

Ironically given the rethink, none of this matters. The Tate boasts great temporary exhibitions, plus some local gems, like sculptor Anish Kapoor's *Ishi's Light* and photographer Martin Parr's *Common Sense*. And the Tate could almost hang toilet paper on its walls and remain a captivating experience.

See also p142.

>3 WESTMINSTER

GRAB A SNAP OF WESTMINSTER'S INSPIRING SILHOUETTE

The historic seat of British power is suitably impressive and awe-inspiring, with the mother of all parliaments and the father of all Anglican cathedrals nestled side by side. The parliament building, the Palace of Westminster, is the newer – a Victorian, neo-Gothic confection, designed by Charles Barry and Augustus Pugin in 1840 after its predecessor burnt down. By contrast, parts of Westminster Abbey date back to the 13th century.

Visitors inevitably want an exterior snap of parliament's Clock Tower, usually just called Big Ben after the giant bell it contains.

However, the magnificent Abbey is such a serving of gilt, pomp, royalty and history that you really want to step inside. Highlights include Elizabeth I's tomb and funeral effigy, the Chapel of Henry VII, with its fan-vaulted ceiling and wooden knights' stalls, and the oak Coronation Chair. Every monarch since 1301, including Elizabeth II, has been crowned in the chair – which hilariously is covered in carved initials!

The High Altar and Quire are wonderfully ornate, the College Garden is restful and, ahem, dedicated *Da Vinci Code* fans will find Sir Isaac Newton's Memorial in the nave.

Coming for an atmospheric evensong is the way to get in free, but you'll need to respectfully sit through the service first.

See also p82 and p86.

>4 THE ROYAL PARKS

LOSE YOURSELF IN THE ROYAL PARKS' GREEN SPLENDOUR

While royalists race to see the garish innards of Buckingham Palace during its brief summer season, even republicans will relish the Royal Parks (www.royalparks.gov.uk). These eight verdant patches, now publicly owned, are often called London's 'lungs'; they help make it (surprisingly) Europe's greenest city. The list includes Bushy, Green, Greenwich, Regent's and Richmond Parks, but the most convenient and compelling are St James's Park and the joined-at-the-hip Hyde Park and Kensington Gardens.

Bordering Whitehall, St James's Park (p84) features rose gardens, pelicans, ducks, geese and great views of Buckingham Palace over its lakes. The place has garnered attention for its new restaurant pavilion, Inn the Park (p91).

Hyde Park (p98) is better yet. This 140-hectare metropolitan oasis is famous for concerts, political demonstrations, deck-chair rental and Speaker's Corner, but two of its most enjoyable attractions are quite new: the strangely mesmerising Diana, Princess of Wales Memorial Fountain (p95) and the solar ferry that glides across the Serpentine Lake (p101).

In neighbouring Kensington Gardens (p98) you'll encounter the brilliant Serpentine Gallery (p100) and the gleaming, kitsch Albert Memorial (p95) nearby. Further north, the Italian Gardens is another particularly pleasant spot.

>5 NATIONAL GALLERY & NPG

CHECK OUT OLD MASTERS AND FAMOUS FACES AT THE NATIONAL AND NATIONAL PORTRAIT GALLERIES

When coming to the National Gallery don't overlook the separate National Portrait Gallery (NPG) around the corner.

Of course, no-one would impugn the artistic credentials of the National Gallery (p47). It houses more old masters than you can shake a loaded paintbrush at, including works by Caravaggio, Constable, Da Vinci, Monet, Rembrandt, Titian, Van Gogh, Velázquez and Vermeer. But it's a formal affair with a faintly 'eat-your-greens' tone. Grab a free floor plan and decide on a handful of works you want to see.

The NPG (p47) is more of a guilty pleasure. The subjects take precedence over the art, and range from the likes of William Shakespeare to suffragette Emmeline Pankhurst to footballer David Beckham. The 2nd floor has striking portraits of Shakespeare, Henry VII, Elizabeth I and other royals, plus some marvellous miniatures. Near the exit, the ground floor focuses on contemporary stars and latest acquisitions.

There's an IT archive on the mezzanine to ensure you miss nothing in this constantly rotating collection.

*and let thy feet
millenniums hence
be set in midst of knowledge*

>6 BRITISH MUSEUM

DELVE INTO ANTIQUITY AT THE BRITISH MUSEUM

Marx, mummies and marbles are the headliners at Britain's largest – and possibly most crowded! – museum. Parts of its superb antiquities collection are frequently arranged into spectacular special exhibitions. However, several historical highlights are always in the free permanent collection.

Free floor plans are available, but if you see only one thing, make it the Great Court just inside the porticoed main entrance. Renovated by Sir Norman Foster in 2000, this light-filled inner courtyard is covered with a spectacular glass-and-steel roof spanning out from the old British Library's circular Reading Room. Inside this hallowed, book-lined hall, Karl Marx wrote *Das Kapital (Capital)* and Mahatma Gandhi came to study.

The museum also contains the greatest Egyptian collection outside Egypt, including mummies (room 62) and the Rosetta Stone (room 4), the written tablet that helped unlock Ancient Egypt's secrets. Neighbouring galleries venture into Ancient Greece and the museum's most controversial possession. Pretty well ever since the Parthenon Sculptures (aka the Parthenon Marbles; room 18) were shipped to England by British ambassador Lord Elgin in 1806, Greek governments have wanted them back.

If stone statues with missing limbs, African carvings, prehistoric pots, carved jade animals and gleaming mosaics do it for you, you'll love this museum.

See also p64.

>7 ST PAUL'S CATHEDRAL

JOURNEY IN BODY AND SPIRIT TO THE TOP OF ST PAUL'S

There's a special exhilaration in being atop St Paul's. The 360-degree view is brilliant and you feel you've really earned it, having clambered up 530 sometimes precarious steps to the summit's Golden Gallery. The route starts sedately as you ascend to the Whispering Gallery, circling the bottom of architect Christopher Wren's huge dome, but progressively becomes more of an adventure. If you don't have a head for heights, the Stone Gallery (378 steps) offers reasonable views.

Built after the 1666 Great Fire of London and inaugurated in 1697, the cathedral survived the London Blitz of WWII to become a much-loved symbol of British grit. It's also seen Winston Churchill's funeral, the wedding of Charles and Lady Di and major 9/11 memorials.

With interior renovations completed in 2005, the interior – from the black-and-white flagstone flooring to the ceiling mosaics – gleams. Inside is an effigy of John Donne, author of the immortal line 'No man is an island' and one-time dean of St Paul's, and the American Chapel, a memorial to 28,000 American expats killed in WWII.

Wren himself is buried in the crypt, alongside Admiral Nelson, but the floor below the dome bears an epitaph conveying the architect's true feelings: *Lector, si monumentum requiris, circumspice* (Reader, if you seek his monument, look around you).

See also p114.

>8 TOWER OF LONDON

RELIVE THE TOWER OF LONDON'S GORY HISTORY

'Uneasy lies the head that wears the crown': that Shakespeare quote comes quickly to mind at the Tower of London. A uniquely well-preserved medieval castle with a gory past, it's where King Henry VIII's wife Anne Boleyn, among others, was beheaded. It also houses the sparkling British Crown Jewels.

The complex was begun in 1078 under William the Conqueror, with the central White Tower (look for the flag). The surrounding walls, towers, palace and riverside wharf of Traitors' Gate came later. Originally a royal residence, the tower was increasingly used as a prison from the 16th century. Sir Thomas More, Princess (later Queen) Elizabeth and later Nazi Rudolf Hess were held captive here.

Yeoman Warders (Beefeaters) lead free tours half-hourly between 9.30am (10am on Sundays) and 3.30pm; the best strategy is to drift in and out of these groups. Listen out for highlights: the myth of the ravens (see the boxed text, p115); the scaffold site where people faced execution; and the Bloody Tower, where young Edward V and his brother were allegedly murdered, possibly by their uncle Richard III.

Such random eavesdropping is easier after noon, when crowds are thinner. If you buy your entry ticket from a London Underground station you needn't queue, either.

See also p114.

HIGHLIGHTS

>9 THE KENSINGTON MUSEUMS

TAKE YOUR PICK FROM ART, HISTORY AND SCIENCE AT THE KENSINGTON MUSEUMS

Thank the Victorians for kick-starting this handy cluster. They launched the Natural History Museum and the Victoria & Albert Museum, while the Science Museum followed in the 1920s. Now visitors can choose between three very different neighbouring collections.

The Victoria & Albert Museum (p101) focuses on arts, crafts and design exhibits, and a few years ago its four million exhibits were frankly rather jumbled and unfocused. However, it's been having a very efficient tidy-up, especially on the lower floors. The masterpiece is the spectacular Jameel Gallery of Islamic Art, centred on the intricate Ardabil Carpet, but the sculpture collection has also been rearranged, near the re-landscaped garden. There's a tempting, well-lit shop and a new café in the historic Morris and Gamble Rooms.

Coming up is a new education centre in late 2007, a made-over jewellery section in 2008, and revamped medieval and Renaissance collections in 2009. In the meantime, the Fashion Gallery and blockbuster temporary exhibitions are always fantastically engaging.

The Natural History Museum (p99) across the road is a big hit with children. The ornate neo-Gothic main building, by architect Alfred Waterhouse, does feature some state-of-the-art animatronic dinosaurs. Yet ultimately this part of the collection still evokes the musty moth-eaten era of the 19th-century gentleman scientist, with its *Diplodocus* dinosaur skeleton, taxidermic birds, fossils, creepy-crawlies, life-size blue whale model and zoological specimens. Gems

FRIDAY LATES & SCIENCE NIGHT SLEEPOVERS

Even before the Victoria & Albert Museum started sorting out its rambling collection, it was lauded for its educational and community schemes. Now it's gaining a reputation for its social evenings. The last weekend of every month, craft (knitting, pottery, Islamic design etc) meets clubbing at its special Friday Late evenings.

Now the Natural History Museum is following suit, while the Science Museum has a similar social hit, albeit for families. Check the website or ring for details of its occasional Science Night Sleepovers.

and minerals are found in the more modern and opulent, but less unusual, Earth Galleries.

Finally, the superb Science Museum (p100) enthrals kids small and large. Parents are particularly taken with the genuine historical arte-facts, such as the *Apollo 10* command module, Stephenson's Rocket steam-engine train and planes including Amy Johnson's *Gypsy Moth*. Meanwhile, there's an IMAX cinema and plenty of simulator rides to thrill their progeny.

The hi-tech Wellcome Wing at the back of the building and the outstanding Energy Gallery & Ring on the 2nd floor of the main hall both have stimulating hands-on displays, covering a vast range of subjects from identity to future energy sources.

>10 THAMES CRUISE

WATCH LONDON GLIDE BY FROM THE COMFORT OF A RIVER THAMES CRUISE

Its skyline drastically transformed in the past decade with new build-ings, London has never looked so good from a river cruise. Today your journey is not only marked by classic icons like the Houses of Parliament, St Paul's Cathedral and the Tower of London and Tower Bridge, you also sail past 21st-century riverfront symbols like the London Eye, Tate Modern, the Millennium Bridge, City Hall and the 'Gherkin'.

The main sights handily lie between Westminster and the Tower of London piers, but trips downriver to Greenwich (see right) or the Thames Flood Barrier (see the boxed text, p85) are also interesting. Travelling upriver is a relaxing way to reach Kew Gardens (p84) or Hampton Court Palace (p84), but there's less to see in this direction.

Dinner cruises aside, booking is rarely necessary. Operators are listed on p223, but it's simpler just to pop down to the nearest pier. For something a bit newer and more exciting, try a fast RIB London Voyage (see the boxed text, p141).

>11 GREENWICH

HAVE A FINE TIME IN THE QUAINT 'VILLAGE' OF GREENWICH

Leafy Greenwich is home to the Prime Meridian of longitude. It's at zero hour and zero degrees, and thus the global point dictating how all clocks are set. So it's strange how easy it is to lose track of time exploring this beautifully landscaped district.

The most common reason people come is to stand with one foot in the world's western hemisphere and the other in the east at the Royal Observatory. But there are museums, a hillside park, shops and pubs to enjoy too. Greenwich's charm is that it's still a bit like a village.

The Royal Naval College, by Renaissance architect Sir Christopher Wren, is just as essential as the hilltop observatory. Closer to the riverfront, it features two separate wings, considerably leaving unobscured river views from earlier designer Inigo Jones's Queen's House behind it. The University of Greenwich and Trinity College of Music now inhabit Wren's buildings, with just two public rooms: the ornate Chapel and astounding Painted Room.

The nearby National Maritime Museum boasts a beautifully laid-out collection, from a gilded barge to the bullet-torn coat worn by Admiral Nelson at the Battle of Trafalgar. Afterwards, there's still the chance to walk across the River Thames via the underwater Greenwich Foot Tunnel or the opportunity to view the Millennium Dome over a pint in the Trafalgar Tavern.

See also p150.

>12 HAMPSTEAD HEATH
HEAD FOR A PICNIC WITH A VIEW ON HAMPSTEAD HEATH

A slice of quintessential English countryside in the big city, Hampstead Heath is less manicured and more natural feeling than London's parks, and larger than any of its leafy commons. It comprises 320 hectares of meadows, woods, lakes, sculptures, cafés, tennis courts and walking trails, and is a great retreat from the stresses of the city.

A high point is Parliament Hill, Londoners' favourite kite-flying spot and a top place to watch the sun rise, particularly after an all-nighter. It offers expansive views, from the well-heeled surrounding districts to St Paul's Cathedral and the London Eye in the distance.

The heath's renowned bathing ponds are dotted around, with the women's and men's ponds on the eastern border and the mixed pond further west. The neoclassical mansion Kenwood House houses a small painting collection and has appeared in several period films. Its lawn, like the rest of the heath, is perfect for picnics. On summer evenings, pull up a chair for the open-air classical concerts.

The West Heath is such a well-established gay cruising area that the police come to protect the men who spend their nights here.

Actually on the heath, the popular Spaniard's Inn attracts a broad crowd of drinkers, gay and straight.

See also p168.

> 13 SPITALFIELDS & BOROUGH

FEEL LONDON'S RETAIL HEART BEAT AT ITS MOST POPULAR MARKETS

Although it's become more corporate, with a shiny retail and restaurant complex encroaching on its territory in the past few years, Spitalfields Market still does a roaring trade on Sundays. Local hipsters, creative types, yummy mummies and the odd foreign TV crew all rub shoulders among the stalls. The plethora of nearby shops and pubs also keeps it one of London's essential shopping experiences.

Unique clothes and accessories from independent young designers dominate the market's tightly packed core. You'll also find new and vintage homewares, secondhand books, vinyl records, CDs, old turntables and musical instruments.

For more about Spitalfields see p120.

Meanwhile across town, Londoners themselves are flocking to Borough Market (p142), particularly on Saturdays. If you're a short-term visitor, the city's best food market might offer fewer sturdy souvenirs than Spitalfields, but it's also an enjoyable way to get a feel for the contemporary city.

If you're a real market junkie looking for something a bit different, skip Camden (p169) and Portobello (p178) and make a beeline for Broadway Market (see the boxed text, p131) or Columbia Road Flower Market (p127) instead.

>14 GOURMET RESTAURANTS

DINE OUT WITH A CELEBRITY CHEF

In 2005 when US foodie magazine *Gourmet* declared London 'the best place in the world to eat' the snorts of derision could be heard all the way from San Francisco and Sydney. (Well, at least from such a distance these doubters were safe from the f***ing wrath of London's straight-talking mega-chef Gordon Ramsay.) British food has been historically famed for its awfulness, and the past decade's gastronomic renaissance has met with some scepticism, thanks to steep bills and occasionally overenthusiastic reviews.

Yet London restaurants have unquestionably made huge advances. Rising to the demands of an increasingly well-travelled and discerning public, kitchens have proved their mettle with real skill and creativity. Home to some of the best-known, most lauded and ambitious chefs right now, London at least boasts an incredibly exciting dining scene.

It's not all Gordon Ramsay or Jamie Oliver, either, where you'll need to book months ahead. Many others have won Michelin stars and praise from hard-nosed critics. Tom Aikens (p106), Fergus Henderson (p117), Giorgio Locatelli (p77), Marcus Wareing (p106) and Alan Yau (p57 and p66) have all also made a notable impression.

Celebrity haunts (see the boxed text, p90) add glamour, while the emphasis on fresh produce and imaginative preparation has trickled down to cheaper restaurants, if sometimes unevenly.

>15 ...AND CURRY HOUSES

GO FOR A CURRY, A TIME-HONOURED LONDON EXPERIENCE

Even in the dim, dark days when unappetising English food was still scraping the bottom of the barrel – an action, it must be said, consumers then rarely mimicked – one variant was always a world-beater. Thanks to historic ties with the Indian subcontinent, London has long boasted excellent curry houses. Although the 'Indian' dishes served are often post-colonial hybrids, they've certainly won a loyal following.

In London, 'going for a curry' became a mainstream pursuit in the 1980s. With the newly liberalised economy running rampant, macho stockbrokers began charging down restaurant-lined Brick Lane in search of the spiciest vindaloo.

Today Brick Lane endures, but restaurant touts now hassle for business and the street is considered past its prime. However, carnivores will still be wowed by the curry houses of Whitechapel (such as New Tayyab, p130), vegetarians will enjoy the South Indian outlets along Drummond St (such as Chutney's, p162) and adventurous connoisseurs of either persuasion might consider visiting Tooting (see the boxed text, p128).

This being London, the humble curry house is matched by many upmarket restaurants. Venues such as Amaya (p104), Café Spice Namaste (p115), the Cinnamon Club (p90) and the Painted Heron (p106) give Indian cuisine a sophisticated modern twist.

> 16 HIGH DRAMA

TAKE YOUR SEATS FOR THE WORLD'S BEST THEATRE

Depth, breadth, Hollywood names in lights and bums on seats – all are measures of the rude good health London's theatreland currently still finds itself in. Whether you want unforgettable drama, experimental comedy or mainstream musicals, the chance to see a play here is one of life's great pleasures.

London has always enjoyed a sterling reputation on stage, but in the late 1990s it entered a halcyon period. A lot of attention focuses on movie stars treading the boards. But talented acting, by both film stars and experienced stage performers, is only part of the story. Great playwrights and directors are also pivotal.

Nicholas Hytner has been a leading light in this regard, injecting new life into the flagship National Theatre. Under his artistic director-ship, it's been commissioning innovative works from established and new playwrights, adapting classics and creating sometimes unexpected hits. The theatre has also created a new generation of theatre fans, selling thousands of cheap seats as part of its summer-time Travelex season.

Shakespeare's recreated Globe Theatre (pictured above), the Royal Shakespeare Company and Royal Court are other major draws. Meanwhile, smaller theatres and companies like the Almeida, BAC Donmar Warehouse and Young Vic play an excellent support role.

See also p201.

>17 SHOREDITCH NIGHTLIFE
DIG THE HOXTON AND SHOREDITCH CLUBBING SCENE

While New York has the Meat-Packing District, and Berlin boasts Pren-zlauer Berg, London has Shoreditch. This is the archetypal neglected and forgotten neighbourhood that's now been reborn as a creative magnet and nightlife hub. And having first burst on the scene more than a decade ago, the enclave around Hoxton, Shoreditch and Spi-talfields has demonstrated remarkable stamina and longevity.

A formerly uninspiring urban wasteland – following the collapse of its fabric and other industries – Shoreditch first began attracting poverty-stricken artists in the early to mid-1990s, with its cheap warehouse spaces to rent. Today it's one of the planet's hottest 'hoods and continues to hang on to precious street cred by expand-ing into even edgier districts.

Cutting-edge clubs and both super-slick and artfully dishevelled bars now dot the Shoreditch landscape, interspersed with fashion-able restaurants, hip hotels, streetwear boutiques, delis, photo labs and new media start-ups. While new venues spring up regularly, some of the capital's nightlife stalwarts – Cargo, Loungelover, the Vibe Bar, 93 Feet East and 333 to name just a few – are found here. Really, however, the choices are huge.

See also p120.

>LONDON DIARY

London isn't Rio; it doesn't have the weather and it's not a natural festival city. That said, centuries of royal pomp and other ceremonial traditions have taught London how to put on a damn good show when it wants to. Meanwhile, it's starting to let its hair down with an increasing number of summer music festivals. For more details, check www.visitlondon.com, www.bbc.co.uk/london or www.whatsonwhen.com.

The annual village fête at the Victoria & Albert Museum (p101)

JANUARY/FEBRUARY

London Parade, New Year's Day

After the fireworks on New Year's Eve, Westminster's Lord Mayor leads a parade of 10,000 musicians and street performers from Parliament Sq to Berkeley Sq.

Chinese New Year

www.chinatown-online.co.uk

In late January/early February, Chinatown fizzes, crackles and pops in this colourful street festival, which includes a Golden Dragon parade.

MARCH/APRIL

Oxford & Cambridge Boat Race

www.theboatrace.org

Crowds line the Thames from Putney to Mortlake to watch the country's two most prestigious universities go oar-to-oar and hope they don't sink (again).

London Marathon

www.london-marathon.co.uk

Some 35,000 masochists join the world's biggest road race (pictured below), running 26 miles (42km) from Greenwich Park to the Mall.

MAY

Chelsea Flower Show
www.rhs.org.uk
Not just for grannies, the world's most renowned horticultural show brings celebrity gardeners and expensive displays to the Royal Hospital Chelsea.

FA Cup Final
www.thefa.com/TheFACup
The domestic football season climaxes in this match – hopefully held at London's new Wembley Stadium from 2007 (although it was moved to Cardiff in 2006).

JUNE

Trooping the Colour
The Queen's official birthday (she was actually born in April) is celebrated at Horse Guards Parade, Whitehall, with much flag-waving, parades, pageantry and noisy flyovers.

Wimbledon Lawn Tennis Championships
www.wimbledon.com
Two glorious weeks of tennis (pictured above), strawberries and cream, Sue Barker and John McEnroe, female screams (on and off court), intermittent rain and hopefully not Cliff Richard.

OUTDOOR SUMMER MUSIC

London has plenty of rivals to festivals such as Glastonbury:

> Wireless (www.o2wirelessfestival.co.uk) – indie Rock à la The Strokes; Hyde Park, June.
> Kenwood Picnic Concerts (www.picnicconcerts.com) – two months of classical and easy-listening events for middle-youth concertgoers; Hampstead Heath, June.
> Rise (www.london.gov.uk/rise/festival) – anti-racism festival, with urban, African, Asian and Middle Eastern music, comedians and other performers; Finsbury Park, June.
> Somerset House Summer Series (www.somersethousesummer.org.uk) – grown-up pop and soul in the wonderful setting of the building's courtyard; Somerset House, July.
> Lovebox Weekender (www.volvicloveboxweekender.com) – Groove Armada's magnificent weekend extravaganza; Victoria Park, Hackney, July.
> Fruitstock (www.fruitstock.com) – broad, family-friendly entertainment from the likes of Norman Jay to steel bands; Regent's Park, August.
> Loaded in the Park (www.getloadedinthepark.com) – Manchester baggy meets indie rock (Lily Allen meet Pete Doherty, for example); Clapham Common, August.

JULY

Pride

www.pridelondon.org

The gay community paints the town pink in this annual extravaganza, with a march culminating in Trafalgar Sq, an afternoon party and a ticketed evening event.

Proms (BBC Promenade Concerts)

www.bbc.co.uk/proms

Two months of classical concerts lead up to patriotic singing on the Last Night of the Proms at Kensington's Royal Albert Hall (pictured left; now watched on a screen from Hyde Park, too).

AUGUST

Notting Hill Carnival

www.thecarnival.tv

One of Europe's biggest outdoor carnivals (pictured below) celebrates Afro-Caribbean London. There's music, dancing, costumes, floats and, er, a little street crime over the August Bank Holiday weekend.

Caribbean Showcase

www.london.gov.uk

First, Mayor Ken Livingstone wanted to move the Notting Hill Carnival to Hyde Park. Now he hosts this small but controversial alternative in the park on the Carnival's main day, Monday.

SEPTEMBER

Thames Festival

www.thamesfestival.org

Increasingly popular, this cosmopolitan weekend festival celebrates the river with fairs, street theatre, music, fireworks, river races and a spectacular Sunday-night lantern procession.

London Open House

www.londonopenhouse.org

As one of London's biggest treats, the public is invited to peep inside more than 500 normally off-limits buildings for one weekend in late September.

OCTOBER

Dance Umbrella

www.danceumbrella.co.uk

Contemporary dance performances are staged by British and international companies across the city over five weeks.

London Film Festival

www.lff.org.uk

Stars and directors mill around the National Film Theatre and other London cinemas, giving the public a sneak preview of their latest films over two weeks.

NOVEMBER

Guy Fawkes Night (Bonfire Night)

Commemorate Guy Fawkes' foiled attempt to blow up Parliament in 1605 with bonfires, burning effigies of Fawkes, fireworks and general merriment on 5 November.

Lord Mayor's Show

www.lordmayorsshow.org

The new Lord Mayor of the City of London travels in a colourful state procession from Mansion House to the Royal Courts of Justice to seek legal approval.

DECEMBER

Carols in Trafalgar Sq

www.london.gov.uk

The festive lights lining Oxford, Regent and Bonds streets are now switched on by some soap star or boy band as early as November (creating controversy about carbon emissions). Later, a huge spruce is erected in Trafalgar Sq, and carolling under it starts as Christmas grows nearer.

ITINERARIES

You could spend years in London and still not see all the capital has to offer. Fortunately, most of the major sights are clustered together, either in Westminster, on the South Bank, in the West End, in Bloomsbury or in the City of London. If time is tight, consider the following as a broad guide. See also Organised Tours, p222.

ONE DAY

Take a peek at Trafalgar Sq (p51), before heading way down Whitehall to Westminster. Visit the Abbey (p86), view Big Ben and the Houses of Parliament (p82) and then cross Westminster Bridge to the London Eye (p140). Take a spin on the Eye (p10) to admire the views. Afterwards, stroll along the South Bank to Tate Modern (p142). If it's a Thursday, Friday or Saturday, pop south to Borough Market (p142). Otherwise, head across the Millennium Bridge to St Paul's Cathedral (p114). In the evening, head to somewhere like Cargo (p135), the Foundry (p133), Hawksmoor (p134), Loungelover (p134) or the Princess (p130) in Hoxton and Shoreditch.

TWO DAYS

Follow the one-day itinerary. The next day return to Trafalgar Sq to visit the National Gallery (p47) and National Portrait Gallery (p47). Head into Covent Garden (p51) for some retail therapy, then visit the Photographers' Gallery (p47) or maybe even the British Museum (p64). You can continue your shopping around Spitalfields (p120) and Brick Lane – especially if it's a Sunday – or perhaps try TopShop (p66) and Selfridges (p76). Round off the day by sampling a top restaurant like J Sheekey (p56) or Petrus (p106).

THREE DAYS

After your first two action-packed days, relax by catching a boat down the river to Greenwich (p150) and exploring its major attractions and shops. Stop at the Tower of London (p114) on the way back in the afternoon. Alternatively, head north to Hampstead Heath (p24), for a similar 'village'

Top left Speciality butcher, the City Bottom left Hyde Park (p98) Previous Page Big Ben (p82) from the London Eye (p10)

experience. In the evening catch a play at the National Theatre (p149) or a dance performance at Sadler's Wells (p119) – or perhaps you'd prefer somewhere like Camden's Koko (p175) for live music or cabaret?

FOUR DAYS

On your fourth day, head to Knightsbridge and Kensington. Browse through Harrods (p102) first, possibly stopping for cake in Ladurée (see the boxed text, p104). Afterwards, visit the Victoria & Albert (p101), Natural History (p100) or Science (p99) Museums. Following this, walk up Exhibition Rd to Hyde Park (p98), where you'll find the Serpentine Gallery (p100), the Diana, Princess of Wales Memorial Fountain (p95) and plenty of grass to lounge on. Exit at Hyde Park Corner and walk along Constitution Hill to take in the view of Buckingham Palace (p79). On your final evening sample the bit of London nightlife you haven't yet got around to.

FORWARD PLANNING

The trick in London is either to book very early, or to try at the last minute and hope you get lucky.

Three to six months before you go For big-name restaurants, such as the Ivy (p56) and Gordon Ramsay (p105), you need to get organised six months ahead (see also the boxed text, p57). Saturday-night performances of big West End shows (eg *Billy Elliot*, *Spamalot*) sell out three to six months ahead.

Two to three months before you go Check out sites like www.ticketmaster.co.uk and www.seetickets.com, and think about bigger rock-music gigs (eg Babyshambles, Kasabian and Snow Patrol). Also read www.guardian.co.uk/reviews, www.whatsonstage.com or www.timeout.com before booking good Saturday-night tickets for serious theatre (eg Kevin Spacey performing at the Old Vic, p149).

Three to four weeks before you go Check for any Chelsea Football Club (p107) tickets that are to become available to the general public; they'll go on sale five days before a match.

Two weeks before you go Sign up for an email newsletter, such as *Urban Junkies* at www.urbanjunkies.com, and double-check review sites. Two weeks is also usually ample time to get into trendy, interesting restaurants such as Les Trois Garçons (p130).

A few days before you go The latest blockbuster exhibition at the Royal Academy of Arts (p84), Tate Britain (p85) or the Victoria & Albert Museum (p101) can usually be booked a few days beforehand; actually, we've gained entry to the best with just a few hours' wait.

Musicians on Brick Lane (p121)

RAINY DAYS
Rain used to be London's default weather position, so it's well equipped for this contingency. This is when to 'do' the city's many galleries and museums. Alternatively, sneak off for a matinee performance in the West End (see the boxed text, p61), head to the Electric Cinema (p182) in Notting Hill for an unparalleled moviegoing experience, or linger over a gourmet meal (p26).

LONDON FOR FREE
Although it's one of the most world's most expensive cities, London has plenty that doesn't cost a bean. The permanent collections of most major museums and galleries are free of charge, plus you can enjoy the likes Westminster Abbey (p86) for nothing if you go for evensong. Alternatively, wandering along the South Bank (p136), admiring buildings new and old, lounging in wonderful parks and window shopping all are wonderful free experiences. Keep an eye out in newspaper and magazine listings for free concerts in churches and in summer in parks, too.

>1	Soho & Covent Garden	46
>2	Bloomsbury & Fitzrovia	62
>3	Marylebone & Regent's Park	70
>4	Mayfair, St James's, Westminster & Pimlico	78
>5	Knightsbridge, South Kensington & Chelsea	94
>6	Holborn, Clerkenwell & the City	108
>7	Hoxton, Shoreditch & Spitalfields	120
>8	South Bank	136
>9	Greenwich	150
>10	King's Cross, Euston & Islington	158
>11	Camden, Hampstead & Primrose Hill	166
>12	Notting Hill	176

Flower seller, Columbia Road Flower Market (p126)

NEIGHBOURHOODS

London can seem the densest and most impenetrable of cities – a vast, sprawling jigsaw of myriad neighbourhoods that lacks any real focus.

There's a reason for this. London's history is one of different districts merging: the Roman-founded, commercially minded City fusing with the later political base of Westminster via Fleet St, Holborn and Whitehall, or the royal district of St James tapering off into noble Knightsbridge. On the outskirts, once-separate villages, including Hampstead and Greenwich, slowly became sucked into the vortex of the capital's middle.

As a consequence, the only sensible way to approach this city is to break it down into manageable chunks. Once you do, London's apparent diffuseness starts to become a strength rather than a weakness. Each neighbourhood reveals its own distinctive flavour and character, underlining London's versatility and diversity. It allows it to be that rare beast – all things to all people.

Even on a short stay, though, it's always important to remember that London is more than its central districts. Buzzing, restless and vibrant they might be, but Soho, Covent Garden and the rest of the ill-defined 'West End', with their dirty, overcrowded streets and 'take-no-prisoners' attitude, often typify what's worst about the place. So give yourself an easier ride in a city that's not always kind. Take the time to traverse the wider avenues of the South Bank, or explore the less central neighbourhoods where Londoners tend to live.

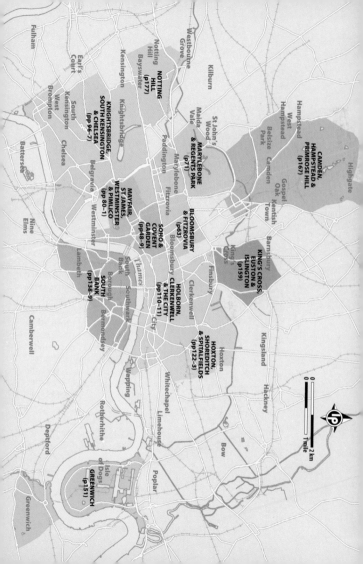

Fulham

Notting Hill

Westbourne Grove

Kilburn

West Hampstead

Hampstead

Highgate

Earl's Court

Kensington

Bayswater

NOTTING HILL (p177)

Maida Vale

St John's Wood

Belsize Park

Camden Town

Gospel Oak

Kentish Town

West Brompton

South Kensington

Knightsbridge

KNIGHTSBRIDGE, SOUTH KENSINGTON & CHELSEA (pp 96-7)

Paddington

MARYLEBONE & REGENTS PARK (p71)

Marylebone

Fitzrovia

CAMDEN, HAMPSTEAD & PRIMROSE HILL (p167)

Battersea

Chelsea

Belgravia

MAYFAIR, ST JAMES, WESTMINSTER, & PIMLICO (pp 80-1)

SOHO & COVENT GARDEN (pp48-9)

BLOOMSBURY & FITZROVIA (p63)

Bloomsbury

Barnsbury

KING'S CROSS, EUSTON & ISLINGTON (p159)

King's Cross

Nine Elms

Westminster

Lambeth

South Bank

Thames

Southwark

City

Finsbury

Clerkenwell

HOLBORN, CLERKENWELL & THE CITY (pp110-11)

Kingsland

Hackney

SOUTH BANK (pp138-9)

Borough

Bermondsey

HOXTON, SHOREDITCH & SPITALFIELDS (pp122-3)

Camberwell

Wapping

Whitechapel

Limehouse

Bow

Deptford

Rotherhithe

Poplar

Isle of Dogs

GREENWICH (p151)

Greenwich

0   1 mile

0   2 km

>SOHO & COVENT GARDEN

Culturally, socially and physically, this is London's heartland. Sure, the 'West End' – of which this is the core – often exemplifies what's worst about the city. It's dirty, crowded and noisy. But it also embodies London's vibrancy and unflagging stamina.

Allegedly taking its name from a medieval hunting call, Soho today is a distinctly bohemian district. To mainline the Soho atmosphere, head to gay-friendly Old Compton St; the surrounding thoroughfares are also packed with restaurants, shops, bars and clubs.

North of Old Compton St lies hanky-sized Soho Sq, jammed with sunbathers in summer. South lie the bright lights and exotic smells of Chinatown and jam-packed Leicester Sq. Through this you'll emerge into revamped Trafalgar Sq.

SOHO & COVENT GARDEN

◉ SEE
National Gallery	1	E6
National Portrait Gallery	2	E5
Photographer's Gallery	3	E4
Somerset House	4	G4
Trafalgar Square	5	E6

⌂ SHOP
Blackout II	6	E3
Coco de Mer	7	E3
Crazy Pig	8	E3
Cyber Candy	9	E4
Fopp	10	D3
Forbidden Planet	11	E2
Habitat	12	A4
Hamleys	13	A4
Liberty	14	A3
Paul Smith	15	F4
Poste Mistress	16	E3
Reckless Records	17	C3
Reckless Records	18	B3
Saco	19	E4

Space NK	20	E3
Tatty Devine	21	C4

⍞ EAT
Andrew Edmunds	22	B3
Arbutus	23	C3
Busaba Eathai	24	C3
Café Mode	(see 6)	
Food for Thought	25	E3
Fresh & Wild	26	B4
Ivy	27	E4
J Sheekey	28	E4
Lindsay House	29	D4
L'Atelier de Joël Robuchon	30	D3
Maison Bertaux	31	D3
Mildred's	32	B4
Patisserie Valerie	33	D3
Yauatcha	34	C3

⍭ DRINK
Bar Italia	35	D3
Coffee, Cake & Kink	36	E3

Floridita	37	C3
LAB	38	D3
Lamb & Flag	39	E4
Monmouth Coffee Company	40	E3
Salisbury	41	E4

★ PLAY
Astoria	42	D2
Comedy Store	43	C5
Curzon Soho	44	D4
Donmar Warehouse	45	E3
End	46	E2
English National Opera	47	E5
Ghetto	48	D2
Heaven	49	F6
Madame Jo Jo's	50	C4
Ronnie Scott's	51	D3
Royal Opera House	52	F3
Tkts Booth	53	D5

Please see over for map

Originally designed by Renaissance architect Inigo Jones, the Covent Garden piazza has become something of a tourist trap. But the remainder of Covent Garden retains its retail allure. Don't forget to explore the smaller streets such as Floral St.

SEE

NATIONAL GALLERY

☎ 7747 2885; www.nationalgallery.org.uk; Trafalgar Sq WC2; admission free, prices vary for exhibitions; ⏱ 10am-6pm Thu-Tue, 10am-9pm Wed, tours 11.30am & 2.30pm Sun-Fri, plus 6.30pm Wed, 12.30pm & 3.30pm Sat; ⊖ Charing Cross
This impressive gallery is one of the world's largest, with masterpieces including Constable's *Hay Wain*, Holbein's *Ambassadors*, Seurat's *Bathers at Asnières*, Van Gogh's *Sunflowers* and Van Eyck's *Arnolfini Portrait*. Among these heavy hitters, *Hoogstraten's Peepshow*, which creates a 3-D illusion, provides a bit of fun. Grab a free gallery plan or join a free introductory tour. See also p16.

NATIONAL PORTRAIT GALLERY

NPG; ☎ 7306 0055; www.npg.org.uk; St Martin's Pl WC2; admission free, prices vary for exhibitions; ⏱ 10am-6pm, to 9pm Thu & Fri; ⊖ Charing Cross or Leicester Sq
The National Portrait Gallery is a fantastic institution that has been putting faces to British names over the last five centuries. Although more about history

than art, it's a modern place with an exciting and playful approach to its potentially fusty remit. See also p16.

PHOTOGRAPHERS' GALLERY

☎ 7831 1772; www.photonet.org.uk; 5 & 8 Great Newport St WC2; admission free; ⏱ 11am-6pm Mon-Sat, noon-6pm Sun; ⊖ Leicester Sq
So small that it uses the walls of its neighbouring café as additional exhibition space, this cutting-edge gallery punches

CULTURAL DINING

While too many museum restaurants offer poor quality and food, the National Gallery and National Portrait Gallery are both bucking the trend.

> Portrait (NPG) – people rave about the views over Trafalgar Sq, but really they're of Nelson's backside! Fresh ingredients underpin the tasty modern British cuisine; there's also good afternoon tea.

> National Dining Rooms (National Gallery) – it's back to the future with Oliver Peyton's modern take on British staples, found in the gallery's Sainsbury wing.

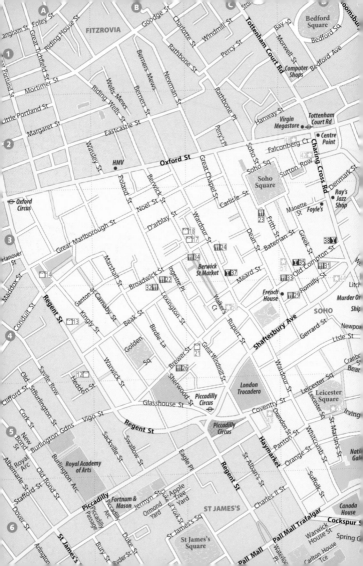

well above its weight in influence. Past winners of its prestigious Deutsche Börse (formerly Citigroup) Photography Prize (held January to March every year) include big names like Richard Billingham, Andreas Gursky, Boris Mikhailov and Juergen Teller. There's always something thought-provoking here.

☞ SOMERSET HOUSE

☎ 7845 4600; www.somerset-house .org.uk; The Strand; ☼ Great Court 7.30-11pm; ⊖ Temple or Covent Garden
As well as its museums (right), this splendid Palladian mas-

THE FOURTH PLINTH

One corner features a statue of King George IV; another two commemorate establishment figures. Yet Trafalgar Sq's fourth corner plinth was vacant for 150 years.

That changed in 2005 when, endorsed by Mayor Ken Livingstone, *Alison Lapper Pregnant* – Marc Quinn's statue of a friend born without arms and with shortened legs – went up.

For 18 months from April 2007, Thomas Schütte's *Hotel for the Birds* will be on the pedestal. This multicoloured Perspex sculpture is an interesting choice, given Livingstone's £225,000-plus campaign – including the hiring of a hawk – to shoo off the square's pigeons.

---

terpiece is much loved for its courtyard and lovely sunny terrace – with café – overlooking the river embankment. The courtyard has 55 dancing fountains. When they're switched off, it becomes a concert stage. In winter it's an ice rink – the first of London's current spate (see www.somersethouse icerink.org and the boxed text, p168).

☞ SOMERSET HOUSE MUSEUMS

☎ 7845 4600; www.somerset-house .org.uk; The Strand; UK students free, adult/concession 1 museum £5/4, 2 museums £8/7, 3 museums £12/11; ☼ 10am-6pm; ⊖ Temple or Covent Garden
Somerset Houses contains three museums, of which the **Courtauld Institute of Art** (☎ 7848 2526; www .courtauld.ac.uk) is the best. Although it has several old masters, its speciality is impressionism and post-impressionism, with works by Cézanne, Degas, Gauguin, Monet, Matisse, Renoir and Van Gogh. The **Hermitage Rooms** (☎ 7845 4630; www.hermitagerooms .com) are an outpost of St Petersburg's State Hermitage Museum and are only as good as their current exhibition. The **Gilbert Collection of Decorative Arts** (☎ 7420 9400; www.gilbert-collection.org.uk) is generally less appealing, unless you like cabinets lined with

Skaters in the courtyard of Somerset House

European silver, gold snuffboxes, Italian mosaics and miniature portraits.

TRAFALGAR SQARE
⊖ Charing Cross

Newcomers might not immediately realise it, but this renowned public space is looking better than it has for many years, with fewer pigeons (except in the northwest corner!), a new pedestrian plaza and contemporary artworks on the once-empty fourth plinth. The church of St Martin-in-the-Fields on the corner (you can skip its brass-rubbing sessions, right?) has been having a facelift, as has the 150-year-old Nelson's Column. On his 52m pedestal, the greatest British sailor now has a cleaner face, while visitors continue to clamber over the lions at his feet.

 SHOP

☐ FOPP

☎ 7379 0883; www.fopp.co.uk; 1 Earlham St; ☒ 10am-10pm Mon-Sat, noon-6pm Sun; ⊖ Leicester Sq

This branch of the popular music store offers the same competitive prices as its larger sister in Tottenham Court Rd (p65).

NEIGHBOURHOODS

SOHO & COVENT GARDEN

HABITAT

☎ 7237 6525; www.habitat.net; 121-123 Regent St W1; ⏰ 10am-6pm Mon-Wed, to 8pm Thu, to 6.30pm Fri, 9.30am-6.30pm Sat, noon-6pm Sun; ⊖ Oxford Circus

Terence Conran's trendy but affordable homewares store has only got better since it started commissioning more young designers. This is one of the chain's best-looking stores, having retained the moulded ceiling from the original Art Deco building. There's also a branch in Tottenham Court Rd (p65).

HAMLEYS

☎ 0870 333 2455, 7494 2000; www .hamleys.com; 188-196 Regent St W1; ⏰ 10am-8pm Mon-Sat, noon-6pm Sun; ⊖ Oxford Circus

The largest toy store in the world is buzzing with childlike excitement at the layer upon layer of different toys, from computer games to Lego.

LIBERTY

☎ 7734 1234; www.liberty.co.uk; 210-220 Regent St W1; ⏰ 10am-7pm Mon-Sat, to 8pm Thu, noon-6pm Sun; ⊖ Oxford Circus

This old-fashioned, mock-Tudor department store is traditionally known for its printed fabrics, but has recently added a 1st-floor lingerie section, and now boasts

SHOPPING TIPS

The best shops for:
> Bags – Mulberry (p89)
> Cakes – Ladurée (see the boxed text, p104), Konditor & Cook (p143), Patisserie Valerie (p57)
> Cosmetics – Liberty (below left), Space NK (p54), Selfridges (p76)
> High St fashion – Topshop (p66)
> Shoes – Poste (p90) for men, Poste Mistress (below) for women
> Young designers' fashion – Laden Showrooms (p127), Spitalfields Market (p128)

one of London's best cosmetics selections on the ground level.

PAUL SMITH

☎ 7379 7133; www.paulsmith.co.uk; 40-44 Floral St WC2; ⏰ 10am-6.30pm Mon-Sat, to 7pm Thu, noon-5pm Sun; ⊖ Covent Garden

Paul Smith represents the best of British classic with innovative twists in both his menswear and womenswear. For bargains, try the sale shop (p90).

POSTE MISTRESS

☎ 7379 4040; 61-63 Monmouth St; ⏰ 10am-7pm Mon-Sat, noon-6pm Sun; ⊖ Covent Garden or Leicester Sq

It's always worth buying something at this boudoir-like shoe store just to get your mitts on one of its delicately floral pale-pink bags. But

specialities

Ane Haugli,
Hair stylist at Saco

Best things about working in Covent Garden It's always bustling, so you really know you're in the heart of London. There's a real mix of people, plus lots of side streets and hidden history. At **Saco** (☎ 7240 7897; 71 Monmouth St), we even think we have a friendly ghost! **Favourite local shops** A lovely boudoir packed with really nicely kept vintage clothes is **Blackout II** (51 Endell St). Poste Mistress (left) is good for shoes, and **Pout** (32 Shelton St) sells makeup that smells nice, tastes nice and plumps up your lips. **Quirkiest stores** The **Crazy Pig** (38 Shorts Gardens) sells jewellery to rock stars like Ozzy Osbourne, while there's nothing else like sci-fi film, toy and bookshop **Forbidden Planet** (179 Shaftesbury Ave). My favourite is **Cyber Candy** (3 Garrick St), which sells limited-edition sweets from around the world. **Secret tip for lunch** Fantastic Italian is found at **Café Mode** (☎ 0871 3327159; 57 Endell St). You have to try their calamari and their ham-and-rocket pizza. **Other lunch spots** Sitting out in the courtyard at Neal's Yard is great, or pop to Soho for a salad from **Fresh & Wild** (69-75 Brewer St). Vegetarian restaurant **Food for Thought** (31 Neal St) has been there for ages but it's healthy and comforting.

stuffed with pastel wellies, plastic Crocs or shoes from Emma Hope, Vivienne Westwood, Miu Miu or Eley Kishimoto, that bag feels even more like Christmas.

🎦 RECKLESS RECORDS
☎ 7437 4271; www.reckless.co.uk; 26 & 30 Berwick St W1; ⊖ Oxford Circus
The new or secondhand records and CDs at these two great stores run the gamut from punk to soul, dance, independent and mainstream.

🎦 SPACE NK
☎ 7379 7030; www.spacenk.co.uk; Thomas Neal Centre, 37 Earlham St WC2; ⏱ 10am-7pm Mon-Wed, Fri & Sat, to 7.30pm Thu, noon-5pm Sun; ⊖ Covent Garden
An antidote to cosmetic surgery, the UK's leading cult cosmetics chain not only stocks hair, skin

CENTRAL SHOPPING SPOTS
Shopping is one of the main reasons to visit Covent Garden and Soho by day, and there are more stores than any book could reasonably list. So to help you plan your retail-therapy tour, here's what to expect in the squares and streets of this neighbourhood.
> Berwick St (B3) – lined with record shops, plus a fruit and veg market
> Carnaby St (B4) – a former shadow of its 1960s heyday, this now features very commercial streetwear outlets
> Charing Cross Rd (D2) – the road with bookstores, including Borders, Foyle's (with the famous Ray's Jazz Shop), Murder One (for thrillers) and Shipley (for art books)
> Covent Garden Piazza (F4) – overflowing with gimmicky shops, crowds, jugglers, mime artists and other performers
> Floral St (E4) – this tucked-away street boasts a few cool fashion shops, like Paul Smith (p52) and Ted Baker
> Long Acre (E4) – full of affordable High St chains, including Warehouse, Reiss and Zara. Also superlative travel bookshop Stanfords
> Monmouth St (E3) – lots of floaty women's fashion and accessories are found in fun, cool boutiques, including Orla Kiely and Koh Samui
> Neal St (E3) – more street fashion, including Urban Outfitters and Diesels. Birkenstock, the Natural Shoe Store and even a Rough Trade record outlet (in the basement of No 16) are also here. Thomas Neal Centre is packed with urban/skate/surf fashions
> Oxford St (B2) – London's sclerotic shopping artery should be avoided as much as possible, although it does house HMV and the Virgin Megastore (the latter on the corner with Tottenham Court Rd)
> Shorts Gardens (E3) – more of the same as Neal St around the corner, plus menswear-meisters Duffer of St George and Neal's Yard Dairy

Shopping arcade, Covent Garden

and make-up products from Dr Hauschka, Eve Lom, Kiehl's and Phyto but also anti-ageing ranges like 24/7 and Dr Sebagh. There are branches across the city.

TATTY DEVINE
☎ 7434 2257; www.tattydevine.com; 57b Brewer St W1; ☼ noon-7pm Mon-Sat; ⊖ Oxford Circus

There's more room to move here than in the Brick Lane store (p128), so the cheeky quirky jewellery on sale is also laid out in tempting displays. Turn down the little arcade, and the store is at the back.

🍴 EAT

🍴 ANDREW EDMUNDS
Modern European   ££-£££
☎ 7437 5708; 46 Lexington St W1; ☼ lunch & dinner Mon-Fri, lunch Sat & Sun; ⊖ Oxford Circus

With two floors of cramped, wood-panelled bohemia and a menu of French and European country cooking, this tiny place is just the sort of restaurant that you should be able to find easily in Soho, but rarely do. It's best to book ahead.

🍴 ARBUTUS
Modern European   ££-£££
☎ 7734 4545; www.arbutusrestaurant
.co.uk; 63-64 Frith St W1; ⊖ Tottenham
Court Rd
Minimalist-looking Arbutus burst onto the scene in 2006, winning three awards in quick succession, so here's hoping that doesn't go to its head. The changing menu is mouthwatering, with dishes like beef bavette tartare, saddle of rabbit, bouillabaisse and even braised pig's head. Wine handily comes in carafes.

🍴 BUSABA EATHAI
Thai   ££
☎ 7255 8686; 106-110 Wardour St;
🕐 noon-11pm Mon-Thu, to 11.30pm Fri & Sat, to 10.30pm Sun; ⊖ Piccadilly Circus
It's harder to get a seat at this, the original branch of this popular Thai chain, than at its Store St (p66) equivalent. Still it's busy and full of life.

🍴 IVY *Modern British*   ££££
☎ 7836 4751; www.caprice-holdings
.co.uk; 1 West St WC2; 🕐 lunch & dinner Mon-Sat, lunch Sun; ⊖ Leicester Sq
The renowned favourite of the great and good, the Ivy has liveried doormen and paparazzi permanently on its doorstep. As a fellow diner though, you might only see celeb customers passing by, so you'll have to make do with enjoy-

ing the updated British food – including shepherd's pie and steak tartare.

🍴 J SHEEKEY
Seafood   £££-££££
☎ 7240 2565; www.caprice-holdings
.co.uk; 28-32 St Martin's Ct WC2;
🕐 lunch & dinner; ⊖ Leicester Sq
Many Londoners prefer this smart, historic institution to its sister, the Ivy. While you might spot a famous face, it's less impressed by the celebrity circus. The signature dish is a scrumptious fish pie, which by a handy coincidence is the cheapest thing on the menu.

🍴 LINDSAY HOUSE
Irish   £££-££££
☎ 7439 0450; www.lindsayhouse.co.uk;
21 Romilly St W1; 🕐 lunch & dinner Mon-Fri, dinner Sat; ⊖ Leicester Sq
Richard Corrigan is the chef behind this superb restaurant, where you'll be won over to 'new Irish cuisine'. Dishes are simple and hearty but exquisitely executed and there's a residential air – you have to ring the bell to get in.

🍴 L'ATELIER DE JOËL ROBUCHON
French   ££-££££
☎ 7010 8600; 13-15 West St W1;
⊖ Leicester Sq
The multiple Michelin star–holding French chef who taught

HOW LONG FOR A TABLE?

> Ivy (p56) – nearly six months for weekend dinners, four to five weeks for midweek lunches
> Locanda Locatelli (p77) – only takes bookings up to one calendar month ahead; doesn't need credit-card details to secure your booking
> Gordon Ramsay (p105) – tables must be booked beforehand exactly two months to the day. Lines open at 9am and the restaurant is often booked out by the time you get through, so you'll need to persevere!

Gordon Ramsay and other top London chefs is taking them on, with this sister to his Parisian restaurant on a historically unlucky site near the Ivy. Robuchon's food has won plaudits, but the original no-booking policy for the informal, open-plan dining room downstairs was abandoned quickly for lunch-time – and by now might also have been for dinner.

🍴 MAISON BERTAUX
Café £

☎ 7437 6007; 28 Greek St W1; 🕑 8.30am-8pm; ⊖ Leicester Sq or Tottenham Court Rd

Maison Bertaux has exquisite confections, unhurried service, a French bohemian vibe and 130 years of history on this spot.

🍴 MILDRED'S
Vegetarian ££

☎ 7494 1634; www.mildreds.co.uk; 45 Lexington St W1; 🕑 noon-11pm Mon-Sat; ⊖ Piccadilly Circus

Central London's most famous veg-gie restaurant now has light, airy modern premises, but its food still fits into the old-fashioned 'whole-some' description, with salads, stir-fries, bean burgers, burritos and a memorable ale pie. Despite some surly service, it does a roaring trade.

🍴 PATISSERIE VALERIE
Café £

☎ 7437 3466; www.patisserie-valerie .co.uk; 44 Old Compton St W1; 🕑 7.30am-9pm Mon-Fri, from 8.30am Sat, 9.30am-7pm Sun; ⊖ Tottenham Court Rd or Leicester Sq

Although there's a growing number of Patisseries Valerie across London, this sweet Soho outlet was the original, established in 1926. Delicious, delicate pas-tries, stylish sandwiches and filled croissants are joined by – bliss! – a no-mobile-phone policy.

🍴 YAUATCHA
Chinese ££-££££

☎ 7494 8888; 15 Broadwick St W1; 🕑 9am-11pm Mon-Sat, to 10.30pm Sun; ⊖ Oxford Circus

This glamorous dim-sum restau-rant and teahouse (another Alan Yau special) is a feast for the eyes and the stomach. In the blue light of the upstairs tearoom, you can enjoy the sight of the hypnotisingly beautiful cakes, before eating them. The downstairs dining space has a smarter feel with constellations of light-bulb stars in the ceiling, plus an exquisite menu.

DRINK

BAR ITALIA

☎ 7437 4520; www.baritaliasoho.co.uk; 22 Frith St W1; 24hr; ⊖ Leicester Sq

Soho's original red-eye special still conjures up Italy c 1950, with black-and-white photos, bunting, panettone, coffee machines and even football photos moving on the hoarding next door. A favourite at any time of day or night – or in any state.

FLORIDITA

☎ 7314 4000; www.floriditalondon.com; 100 Wardour St W1; 4pm-midnight Mon-Sat, 4pm-12.30am Sun; ⊖ Tottenham Court Rd or Leicester Sq

This glamorous, mirrored basement bar-restaurant should echo the Havana original, but it's more Terence Conran (the restaurateur backer) than Cuban and we're not sure Hemingway would have approved. Still, plenty of others do, arriving for the Latin bands (always good), food (good, but not great value) and cocktails (variable). There's often a £6 cover charge.

LAB

☎ 7437 7820; www.lab-townhouse.com; 12 Old Compton St W1; 4pm-midnight Mon-Sat, 4pm-12.30am Sun; ⊖ Tottenham Court Rd or Leicester Sq

With other cocktail bars such as Floridita grabbing the headlines now, the London Academy of Bartending is not as fashionable as it was. But, damn it, it's still somewhere to come if you like your drinks seriously well mixed.

LAMB & FLAG

☎ 7497 9504; 33 Rose St WC2; ⊖ Leicester Sq or Covent Garden

Everyone's 'find' in Covent Garden, this loft-like 17th-century place is always jammed. It's reached through a small alley and has bags of history.

MONMOUTH COFFEE COMPANY

☎ 7836 5272; www.monmouthcoffee.co.uk; 27 Monmouth St WC2; ⊖ Tottenham Court Rd or Leicester Sq

A little bit more about buying and tasting ground coffee beans than its equivalent in Borough (p147), this nevertheless has a little space where you can sup a delicious brew.

SALISBURY

☎ 7836 5863; 90 St Martin's Lane WC2; ⊖ Leicester Sq

Pop in quickly to see the beautifully etched and engraved Victorian windows and ornate Art Nouveau light fittings of this attractively refurbished 1898 pub. Don't plan to stay though; everyone else is passing through.

 # PLAY

ASTORIA
☎ 7434 9592, 7434 6963; 157 Charing Cross Rd WC2; ⊖ Tottenham Court Rd
People love this large, dark, sweaty venue despite all its faults, and when possible redevelopment plans came to light, punters were outraged. The place hosts many regular gay nights, especially on Saturday, as well as indie gigs.

COMEDY STORE
☎ Ticketmaster 0870 060 2340; www .thecomedystore.biz; Haymarket House, 1a Oxendon St SW1; ⏲ Tue-Sun; ⊖ Piccadilly Circus
One of the first (and still one of the best) comedy clubs in London pulls in the big names. Wednesday features the famous improv outfit, the Comedy Store Players (often with the superb Paul Merton from *Have I Got News For You*).

CURZON SOHO
☎ information 7439 4805, bookings 7734 2255; www.curzoncinemas.com; 93-107 Shaftesbury Ave W1; ⊖ Leicester Sq
A great central cinema, and not just because of its good taste and art-

SEX ON THE BRAIN
Londoners certainly seem to have their mind on erotic matters lately. There's even a sex museum planned for the **Trocadero** (www.troc.co.uk)! Meanwhile, the following venues fit perfectly with the cabaret boom:
Coffee, Cake & Kink (☎ 7419 2996; www.coffeecakeandkink.co.uk; 61 Endell St W1; ⊖ Covent Garden) Enjoy coffee and cake seated among an interesting display of sex implements.
Coco de Mer (☎ 7836 8882; www .coco-de-mer.co.uk; 23 Monmouth St WC2; ⊖ Covent Garden) A very classy, almost French take on silky lingerie and ticklers, spankers etc.

house leanings in the programming department. Upstairs is a Konditor & Cook café (see p143), while downstairs there's a convivial bar.

DONMAR WAREHOUSE
☎ 7369 1732; www.donmar-warehouse .com; 41 Earlham St WC2; ⊖ Covent Garden
This tiny theatre carries a lot of baggage; it was here Nicole Kidman administered 'theatrical Viagra' by stripping in Sam Mendes' *Blue Room* in the 1990s. However, current artistic director Michael Grandage is also writing a wonderful new chapter, with excellent productions by David Mamet and Patrick Marber, plus heavyweight

hits like *Frost/Nixon*. It's a wonderfully intimate little space.

⭐ END

☎ 7419 9199; 18 West Central St WC1; 🕙 10pm-3am Mon & Wed, 10pm-4am Thu, 10pm-5am Fri, 10.30pm-7am Sat; ⊖ Holborn

A mainstream West End club you might actually bother with! Despite big-name DJs like Laurent Garnier, Layo & Bushwacka! and LTJ Bukem, the music is frequently innovative in this industrial/futuristic space. Monday's Trash night – a mix of disco/glam/punk/'80s electronica – is one of London's coolest. Sister bar AKA is next door.

⭐ ENGLISH NATIONAL OPERA

ENO; ☎ 7632 8300; www.eno.org; Coliseum, St Martin's Lane WC1; ⊖ Leicester Sq or Charing Cross

The English National Opera (ENO) successfully renovated its home, the Coliseum, a few years back and has returned to the business of making opera modern and relevant, with recent productions even stretching to an opera based on Libya's Colonel Gadaffi! Some £10 tickets are available weekdays.

⭐ GHETTO

☎ 7287 3726; www.ghetto-london.co.uk; 5-6 Falconberg Ct W1; 🕙 10pm-3am Mon-Wed, 10pm-4am Thu & Fri, 10pm-5am Sat; ⊖ Tottenham Court Rd

Ronnie Scott's nightclub

In a very sweaty basement, this leading gay club has nevertheless established itself as one of Soho's hippest, with its 1950s American milk bar–style white seats and red walls. The leading regular is Wednesday's Nag, Nag, Nag.

⭐ HEAVEN

☎ 7930 2020; www.heaven-london
.com; Under the Arches, Villiers St WC2;
🕑 10.30pm-3am Mon & Wed, 10.30pm-
6am Fri, 10pm-6am Sat; ⊖ Charing
Cross or Embankment

The commercial house music
makes Saturday the most popular
night at Heaven, London's best-
known gay club, but it pulls in
nearly as many punters with
Monday's cheap-and-cheerful,
student-oriented Popcorn and
Wednesday's cheeky midweeker
Fruit Machine.

⭐ MADAME JO JO'S

☎ 7734 2473; www.madamejojos.com;
8 Brewer St W1; 🕑 8pm-3am Tue, from
10.30pm Wed-Fri, from 9pm Thu, cabaret
7pm-10pm Sat, club 10pm-3am Sat;
⊖ Piccadilly Circus

Keb Darge's Deep Funk night on Fri-
days is legendary, but Madame Jo
Jo's was first and foremost a cabaret
bar, and with the rise of the genre
across London, it's also returning to
its kitsch and sleazy roots.

⭐ RONNIE SCOTT'S

☎ 7439 0747; www.ronniescotts.co.uk;
47 Frith St W1; ⊖ Leicester Sq

Ronnie Scott died in 1996, but his
50-year-old club continues to be
the hub of Britain's jazz scene. In
new hands now, it's had a major
refit. The basic look – terraced
seating and dim table lighting –

WEST END THEATRE

There are some 50 theatres in London's
West End, so you'll need a listings
guide like www.timeout.com or www
.whatsonstage.com for the latest productions. For tickets, including to music
gigs, comedy shows etc, try Ticketmaster (☎ 0870 060 2340; www
.ticketmaster.co.uk); a booking fee is
charged. For last-minute booking, turn
to the tkts booth (🕑 10am-7pm
Mon-Sat, noon-3pm Sun; ⊖ Leicester Sq) in Leicester Sq, which sells half-
price, same-day tickets for a reasonable
commission.

---

hasn't changed, but the place
seems more elegant, has better (if
not world-beating) food and has
banned smoking. Most importantly, it still attracts top performers and has great acoustics.

⭐ ROYAL OPERA HOUSE

☎ 7304 4000; www.royaloperahouse
.org; Royal Opera House, Bow St WC2;
⊖ Covent Garden

Once starchy, 'Covent Garden' (as
it's nicknamed) has been attracting a younger, wealthy audience
since its £210-million redevelopment at the turn of the century.
More adventurous programming
includes operas such as Shosta-
kovich's Lady Macbeth of Mtsensk.
The Royal Ballet (www.royalballet.co.uk)
also performs here.

>BLOOMSBURY & FITZROVIA

Bloomsbury and Fitzrovia create a small neighbourhood with a self-contained character and history. Leafy Bloomsbury is traditionally known as London's liberal intellectual hub. When the so-called Bloomsbury Group of artists and intellectuals, including Virginia Woolf and EM Forster, moved here in the early 20th century, they were following in the footsteps of Charles Dickens, Charles Darwin, Anthony Trollope and William Butler Yeats. Today, the area continues to have academic overtones, dominated by its university faculties. Of late it has become the epicentre of one of London's quirkier trends – ten-pin bowling.

Fitzrovia, although slightly more bohemian, was also populated by writers, with George Orwell perhaps the most famous to frequent its many pubs, including the Fitzroy Tavern.

Today, the area is dotted with media production companies, plus the restaurants and bars that provide them with lunch and after-work drinks. Because it feels in many ways like a Soho overspill, some people call the area 'Noho' – to the annoyance of other Londoners.

BLOOMSBURY & FITSROVIA

📷 SEE
British Museum 1 C5
Pollock's Toy
Museum 2 B5

🏠 SHOP
Fopp 3 B5
Habitat 4 B5

Heal's............................ 5 B5
Topshop & Topman 6 A6

🍴 EAT
Busaba Eathai 7 B5
Fino 8 B5
Hakkasan...................... 9 B6
Salt Yard 10 B5

🍸 DRINK
Annexe 3 .... 11 A6
Bradley's Spanish Bar.. 12 B6
Lamb 13 D4
Princess Louise........... 14 D6

⭐ PLAY
All Star Lanes 15 D5
Bloomsbury Bowling .. 16 C4

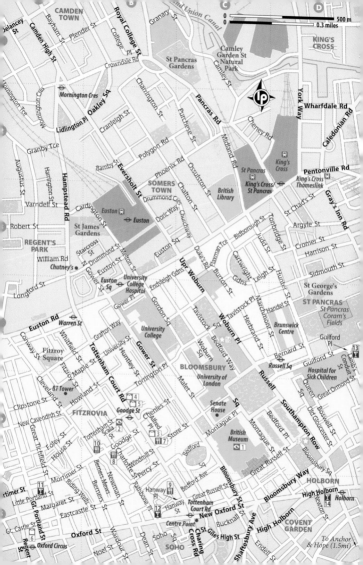

SEE

BRITISH MUSEUM

☎ 7323 8000, tours 7323 8181; www
.thebritishmuseum.ac.uk; Great Russell
St WC1; admission free, £3 donation sug-
gested; ⏰ galleries 10am-5.30pm Sat-
Wed, 10am-8.30pm Thu & Fri, Great Court
9am-6pm Sun-Wed, 9am-11pm Thu-Sat;
⊖ Tottenham Court Rd or Russell Sq

Sir Hans Sloane bequeathed his
humble 'cabinet of curiosities' to
the nation in 1753, and it formed
the basis for the British Museum.
The museum has been augmented
over the years through judicious
acquisition and, ahem, the controversial plundering of empire, until it
now comprises some seven million
items. It's a huge undertaking, so

Great Court, British Museum

LOVE-OR-HATE LONDON BUILDINGS

> Barbican (p119) – this once-loathed labyrinthine 1970s housing and entertainment complex is now a des res, while public areas are being redeveloped.
> BT Tower (A5) – the former Post Office tower had a rotating restaurant on the 34th floor; it closed after a 1971 IRA bomb. The tower featured in the *Goodies*' 'Kitten Kong' episode.
> Centre Point (C6) – concrete tower block from the 1960s, Heritage-listed in 1995 and bizarrely loved by *Wallpaper*. Best seen from Falconberg Ct at night.
> Senate House (C5) – the University of London's 63m, Art Deco HQ is tagged 'fascist' by left-wingers, 'Stalinist' by right-wingers and loved by others still. Screen appearances include *1984* (starring John Hurt).

consider taking one of the frequent tours (£8), or grab an audioguide (£3.50). See p17 for must-sees.

POLLOCK'S TOY MUSEUM

☎ 7639 3452; www.pollocksweb .co.uk; 1 Scala St W1; adult/child £3/1.50; 🕑 10am-5pm Mon-Sat; ⊖ Goodge St

Ignore what it says on the website; this absolutely delightful toy museum and shop is still open and well worth a detour if you're in the neighbourhood. It's a quirky and eccentric blast from the past.

SHOP

🛍 FOPP

☎ 7580 6935; www.fopp.co.uk; 220-224 Tottenham Court Rd W1; 🕑 10am-6pm Mon-Wed, to 8pm Thu, to 6.30pm Fri, 9.30am-7pm Sat, noon-6pm Sun; ⊖ Goodge St

Fopp has always beaten record chains like Virgin and HMV with its reasonable prices, but with this new flagship store it's even start-

ing to take the big boys on in terms of range. There's a smaller branch at Earlham St (p51).

🛍 HABITAT

☎ 7631 3880; www.habitat.net; 196-199 Tottenham Court Rd W1; 🕑 10am-6pm Mon-Wed, to 8pm Thu, to 6.30pm Fri, 9.30am-6.30pm Sat, noon-6pm Sun; ⊖ Goodge St

This upbeat and affordable homewares store doesn't have the stunning ceiling of the Regent St branch (p52), but its in-store displays are equally artistic and it's handily located next door to Heal's for a furniture-shopping binge.

🛍 HEAL'S

☎ 7636 1666; www.heals.co.uk; 196 Tottenham Court Rd W1; 🕑 10am-6pm Mon-Wed, to 8pm Thu, to 6.30pm Fri, 9.30am-6.30pm Sat, noon-6pm Sun; ⊖ Goodge St

Having 'just had the builders in', this long-standing institution looks better than ever, with a tempting array of good-quality homewares in the latest 'maximalist' style.

TOPSHOP & TOPMAN
☎ 7636 7700; www.topshop.co.uk; 36-38 Great Castle St W1; ⏱ 9am-8pm Mon-Sat, to 9pm Thu, noon-6pm Sun; ⊖ Oxford Circus

The flagship stores of these two allied national chains have encapsulated London's supreme skill at bringing catwalk fashion to the youth market affordably and quickly. Topshop's work with design talent has even resulted in a Kate Moss range, although some doubt has been cast over its future by the recent loss of key brand director Jane Shepherdson.

🍴 EAT

🍴 BUSABA EATHAI
Thai   ££
☎ 7299 7900; 22 Store St WC1; ⏱ noon-11pm Mon-Thu, to 11.30pm Fri & Sat, to 10.30pm Sun; ⊖ Goodge St

From the Alan Yau stable that created Wagamama, this upmarket version (sort of) is a relaxed, convenient and cheap way to sample the cuisine of one of London's best restaurateurs. Lined with dark wood, this restaurant has square communal tables, ceiling fans and golden Buddhas, while creamy and spicy Thai curries head up a very reliable

menu. There's another branch at Wardour St (p56).

🍴 FINO *Spanish*   £££
☎ 7813 8010; www.finorestaurant.com; 33 Charlotte St; ⏱ lunch & dinner Mon-Sat; ⊖ Tottenham Court Rd

A glamorous and quality basement tapas bar, decorated with original artworks, Fino is popular with the media types who work in and around Charlotte St and are relentlessly fussy about their food. Come here for innovative and delightful Spanish cooking. The entrance is on Rathbone St.

🍴 HAKKASAN *Chinese*   ££££
☎ 7907 1888; 8 Hanway Pl W1; ⏱ lunch & dinner Mon-Sat, lunch Sun; ⊖ Tottenham Court Rd

Alan Yau's flagship establishment is still something special, several years on from becoming the first Chinese restaurant to win a Michelin star. Hidden down an alley like all fashionable haunts should be, this basement hideaway has lots of black lacquer, ultraviolet light and a long, glinty cocktail bar. The often flamboyantly presented food tastes every bit as good as it looks.

🍴 SALT YARD *Spanish*   ££
☎ 7637 0657; www.saltyard.co.uk; 54 Goodge St W1; ⏱ noon-11pm Mon-Fri, 5-11pm Sat; ⊖ Goodge St

While Salt Yard is less swanky than Fino (left), many say they prefer its tapas, which displays distinct Italian influences and is cheaper too. The place itself is all understated elegance, with an upstairs bar-café and a basement main dining room.

DRINK

☢ ANNEXE 3
☎ 7631 0700; 6 Little Portland St W1; ☽ noon-3pm & 6.30-11pm Mon-Sat, noon-3pm Sun; ⊖ Oxford Circus

This is Loungelover-lite (see p134) from the same overdecorated stable. It looks opulently fantastic, with gold banquettes, quirky paintings, a mishmash of wallpapers and an antique mini-funfair ride. But without its sister venue's scruffy surroundings it does feel less of a find, and the overall atmosphere is slightly more corporate. Still, it's convenient.

☢ BRADLEY'S SPANISH BAR
☎ 7636 0359; 42-44 Hanway St W1; ⊖ Tottenham Court Rd

Low ceilings, cramped quarters, vaguely Spanish décor, a vintage vinyl jukebox and a convivial atmosphere are the features of this tiny hostelry, which is one of the most ordinary boozers in the West End and therefore among the best. Treat yourself to the Cruzcampo beer.

☢ LAMB
☎ 7405 0713; 94 Lamb's Conduit St WC1; ☽ closed Sun; ⊖ Russell Sq

The venerable and atmospheric Lamb has a central mahogany

The Lamb public house

bar with beautiful Victorian dividers and good food. It's wildly popular though, so come early to bag a booth.

▼ PRINCESS LOUISE
☎ 7405 8816; 208 High Holborn WC1; 🕓 closed Sun; 🚇 Holborn

One of the two prettiest pubs in the West End (the other is the Salisbury, p58). This heritage-listed pub has some ornate Art Deco features, with engraved mirrors and a moulded ceiling. The atmosphere here isn't really very inspiring, but it's worth having a quick gander.

Princess Louise public house

⭐ PLAY

⭐ ALL STAR LANES

☎ 7025 2676; www.allstarlanes.co.uk; Victoria House, Bloomsbury Pl; 🕙 5pm-midnight Mon-Thu, from noon Fri-Sun; ⊖ Holborn or Russell Sq

Leading the way in bringing skittles back in fashion (harking back to cult 1990s film *The Big Lebowski*) this 'boutique' bowling alley devotes as much attention to its bar cocktails and diner booths as it does to its four bowling alleys. It is ridiculously busy though, so book early if you're interested.

⭐ BLOOMSBURY BOWLING

☎ 7691 2610; www.bloomsbury bowling.com; Tavistock Hotel, Bedford Way; 🕙 noon-1am Sun-Thu, to 3am Fri & Sat; ⊖ Russell Sq

The former car park of the Tavistock Hotel has been turned into a kitsch, retro, ten-pin bowling alley, with karaoke booths and a cinema, lanes and a horseshoe-

shaped bar flown in from the States. It's not as luxurious as All Star Lanes, but it's easier to get a lane here.

QUIRKY LONDON TRENDS

Yes, we know. As soon as a *guidebook* lists something, it must be well on its way out of fashion; but here are just some of the pastimes popular in London in, well, at least the past few years.

> Cabaret and burlesque – see p194
> Ice-skating (pictured above) – see the boxed text, p168
> Ten-pin bowling – see above
> Raves – look for flyers in record stores

>MARYLEBONE & REGENT'S PARK

Marylebone today is as interesting to visit as it is to pronounce. (That's *mar*lee-bone to the uninitiated.) Until the 18th century, this was a largely rural community known after its parish church beside the River Tyburn. But 'St Mary's by the Bourne' gradually morphed into one of London's most desirable residential neighbourhoods, with the sophistication and buzz of the West End but without the latter's dirt, crowds and chaos.

Home to Madame Tussauds, Sherlock Holmes, Regent's Park and Marylebone Cricket Club at Lords, this area has long been on the tourist radar. In the past few years it's also emerged as one of London's most exciting foodie and shopping destinations, following a 10-year programme to upgrade Marylebone High St.

Add to this the nearby greenery of the park, and the neglected delights of the superb Wallace Collection, and this is one corner of 21st-century London that you don't want to miss.

MARYLEBONE & REGENT'S PARK

◉ SEE
London Zoo
(Entrance) 1 C1
Lord's Cricket Ground...... 2 A2
Madame Tussauds........... 3 C4
Regent's Park 4 C2
Wallace Collection 5 C5

🛍 SHOP
Alfie's Antiques
Market............................ 6 A4
Daunt Books.................... 7 C4
Rococo 8 C4
Selfridges 9 C5
Tracey Neuls 10 C5

🍽 EAT
Eat & Two Veg 11 C4
Golden Hind 12 C5
Le Pain Quotidien......... 13 C4
Locanda Locatelli 14 C5
Ozer 15 D5
Providores & Tapa Room. 16 C5

⊙ SEE

⊙ LONDON ZOO

☎ **7722 3333; www.zsl.org/london-zoo; Regent's Park NW1; adult/child/concession £14/10.75/12; ⏱ 10am-5.30pm Mar-Oct, 10am-4pm Nov-Jan, 10am-4.30pm Feb; ⊖ Baker St or Camden Town**
This zoo enjoys a wonderful location in Regent's Park, but it's not an unqualified success. It's small and costly, and in past years has featured many empty and rundown enclosures. A long-term modernisation plan includes a walk-through monkey house and, from Easter 2007, a new gorilla house and small-animals enclosure. But the modernisation may need to go much further to silence critics.

⊙ LORD'S CRICKET GROUND

☎ **tours office 7616 8595, switchboard 7616 8500; www.lords.org; St John's Wood Rd NW8; tours adult/child/concession/family £7/4.50/5.50/20; ⏱ tours when there's no play 10am, noon & 2pm Apr-Sep, noon & 2pm Oct-Mar; ⊖ St John's Wood**
Cricket fans – and there are more since 2005's nail-biting Ashes series – will be the first in line for the MCC (Marylebone Cricket Club aka Lords). However, architecture groupies will also enjoy part of the 90-minute tour. Passing through the Long Room, where members watch the games surrounded by

TICKET TO RIDE

For a few days in London it might seem too troublesome to buy a smart-card travel ticket, but it's worth it, really. Fares are much cheaper with London's Oyster Card and it cuts down enormously on hassle, especially buying bus tickets in central London, where you must feed your money into a machine *before* boarding. See p218 for more information.

portraits of cricketing greats, and stopping by the Ashes urn, the tour then heads to the striking, spaceship-shaped media centre.

Steven Spielberg in wax, Madame Tussauds

Regent's Park

◉ MADAME TUSSAUDS

☎ 0870 400 3000; www.madame
-tussauds.com; Marylebone Rd NW1;
adult/under 16 yr incl planetarium £20/16;
🕑 9.30am-5.30pm Mon-Fri, 9am-6pm Sat
& Sun, planetarium 12.30-5.30pm Mon-
Fri, 10.30am-6pm Sat & Sun; ⊖ Baker St

Madame Tussauds is a disheart-
ening proposition, when you
consider it's peddling a centuries-
old art, the popularity of which
should have declined with the
advent of photography. Perhaps
humankind hasn't advanced
much since the eponymous model maker started making death
masks of those killed during the

French Revolution? It's beyond us
to explain why people still come
here; the waxworks aren't even
that life-like. However, the place
does stay on top of the game
with models of the latest stars
and interactive gimmicks like the
chance to 'Enter the Big Brother
Diary Room' etc, etc.

◉ REGENT'S PARK

☎ 7486 7905; 🕑 5am-dusk; ⊖ Baker
St or Regent's Park

The most elaborate and ordered
of London's parks, Regent's
was created around 1820 by
architect John Nash. His plan for

an aristocratic estate never quite
came off, but you can see what
was intended along Cumberland
Tce and the Outer Circle. Apart
from London Zoo (p72), there's an
open-air theatre where Shakespeare is performed in summer,
as well as ponds, rose gardens,
football pitches and softball
diamonds.

WALLACE COLLECTION
☎ 7563 9500; www.wallacecollection
.org; Hertford House, Manchester Sq
W1; admission free; ⏰ 10am-5pm;
⊖ Bond St
Clothes designer Vivienne
Westwood is a fan of this sumptu-
ously restored Italianate mansion,
which seems wholly appropriate.
Shamefully overlooked, even by
Londoners themselves, it offers
an enthralling glimpse into
18th-century aristocratic life, with
its treasure-trove of porcelain,
armour, artefacts, furniture and
17th- and 18th-century paintings
including works by Rembrandt,
Hals, Delacroix, Titian, Rubens,
Poussin, Van Dyck, Velázquez,
Reynolds and Gainsborough.

🛍 SHOP
Marylebone High St is now one of
London's most interesting retail
strips. So when coming to visit the
following small selection of stores,
leave plenty of time to investigate

A GREAT TOURISTY SOUVENIR
Forget those models of black cabs
and red buses, Beefeater teddy bears,
Underground-logo T-shirts and other
tacky tat. We reckon one of London's
best 'touristy' souvenirs is a picture
book by a Czech animator. And no,
we're not on commission, because
four-year-olds and trendy graphic
designers alike seem to swoon over
Miroslav Sasek's charming and witty
This is London (Universe Publish-
ing). Produced in 1959 in an almost
Ronald Searle–esque style, the book
has asterisks leading to 21st-century
updates, but it's amazing how much
of it is still current. You can usually
check it out for yourself in Daunt
Books (right).

others along that road, including
the Conran Shop (No 55), Calmia
(No 52), Cath Kidston (No 51) and
Shoon (No 94).

ALFIE'S ANTIQUES MARKET
☎ 7723 6066; www.alfiesantiques.com;
13-25 Church St NW8; ⏰ 10am-6pm Tue-
Sat; ⊖ Edgeware Rd or Marylebone
Its higgledy-piggledy maze of
exclusive vintage fashion and
retro homewares (from lighting
to posters) makes this complex
a wonderful window-shopping
experience, even if you find the
prices too high. For female shoppers, an undoubted highlight is

the **Girl Can't Help It** (www.thegirl
canthelpit.com).

📷 DAUNT BOOKS
☎ 7224 2295; 83-84 Marylebone High
St W1; ⏰ 9am-7.30pm Mon-Sat, 11am-
6pm Sun; ⊖ Baker St
Don't just look in and leave think-
ing this is any old bookshop. Walk
up the back, on the right-hand
side, and you'll come to a long,
wood-panelled room with a
skylight. It feels more like a library
in here.

📷 ROCOCO
☎ 7935 7780; www.rococochocolates
.com; 45 Marylebone High St W1;
⏰ 9.30am-6pm Mon-Fri, 9.30am-5pm
Sat; ⊖ Baker St
The main branch of London's most
tempting chocolate shop is along
King's Rd (p102), but here you
don't have to travel so far to get
your hit of inventively flavoured,
organic, sugar-free or interestingly
shaped cocoa delights. Broken
slabs packaged into bags are the
best bargain.

Marylebone antique-shop window

☐ SELFRIDGES

☎ 7629 1234; www.selfridges.com; 400 Oxford St W1; ☿ 10am-8pm Mon-Fri, 9.30am-8pm Sat, noon-6pm Sun; ⊖ Bond St

Behind the inventive window displays and impressive Art Deco façade lies the funkiest and most vital of London's department stores. Fashion runs the gamut from street to formal, the food hall is fantastic and the ground-floor cosmetics hall is the largest in Europe.

☐ TRACEY NEULS

☎ 7935 0039; www.tn29.com; 29 Marylebone Lane W1; ☿ 11am-6.30pm Mon-Fri, to 8.30pm Thu, noon-5pm Sat; ⊖ Bond St

This great-looking shoe shop – with bookshelves full of knick-knacks, and boots, shoes and sandals hanging from the ceiling – is the place to come for unique footwear. Canadian designer Neuls doesn't really follow the latest fashions, and yet her output is somehow perfectly timely.

EAT

❙❙ EAT & TWO VEG

Vegetarian   ££

☎ 7258 8595; www.eatandtwoveg.com; 50 Marylebone High St W1; ⊖ Baker St

Perfect for when carnivores and vegetarians get together, this American diner-style restaurant specialises in fake meat, with veggie sausages, soya protein burgers and even ersatz chicken wings. It's not a gourmet experience, but for veggies missing a

Selfridges

good Sunday roast, it sure delivers comfort food.

⅋ GOLDEN HIND
Fish & Chips ££

☎ 7486 3644; 73 Marylebone Lane W1; ⏱ noon-3pm & 6-10pm Mon-Fri, 6-10pm Sat; ⊖ Bond St

This 90-year-old chippy has a classic Art Deco interior, chunky wooden tables and contractors sitting alongside pinstriped business types. From the vintage fryer come quite possibly the best cod and chips in London.

⅋ LE PAIN QUOTIDIEN
French £-££

☎ 7486 6154; www.lepainquotidien .com; 72-75 Marylebone High St W1; ⏱ 7am-7pm Mon-Fri, 8am-6pm Sat & Sun; ⊖ Baker St

The attractively simple, stripped-down wooden interior of the dining room here makes a lovely spot for lunch or dinner. 'Daily bread' has a bakery section, which also sells jams, among other things. The food is a delicious selection of *tartines* complemented by salads and soups, but the service can be quite indifferent.

⅋ LOCANDA LOCATELLI
Italian ££££

☎ 7935 9088; www.locandalocatelli .com; 8 Seymour St W1; ⏱ lunch & dinner; ⊖ Marble Arch

The 'non-celebrity' celebrity chef Giorgio Locatelli eschews TV appearances to concentrate on producing London's most sublime Italian cuisine. But despite, or perhaps because of, his famed egalitarianism, A-list stars love this discreetly luxurious restaurant. See what happens when you play hard to get, Giorgio! Book ahead.

⅋ OZER *Turkish*
£-££

☎ 7323 0505; 5 Langham Pl W1; ⏱ lunch & dinner Mon-Sat; ⊖ Oxford Circus

This is a great spot for a meal during or after a shopping spree on nearby Oxford St; the delicious Turkish food is lighter than the norm (in both content and portion size) and won't weigh you down.

⅋ PROVIDORES & TAPA ROOM
Fusion ££-£££

☎ 7935 6175; www.theprovidores .co.uk; 109 Marylebone High St W1; ⏱ breakfast in the Tapa Room, lunch & dinner; ⊖ Baker St or Bond St

New Zealanders in particular will be drawn to this two-floored restaurant, where Kiwis Peter Gordon and Anna Hansen have teamed up to produce Spanish-tinged cuisine. While not as groundbreaking as Gordon's Pacific-fusion 'Sugar Club' days, it's still an incredibly memorable experience, and the wines are excellent. Downstairs is more casual with breakfast and tempting tapas.

>MAYFAIR, ST JAMES'S, WESTMINSTER & PIMLICO

Home to Queen and Parliament, this broad sweep of neighbourhood is London's historical power base. While royalists will enjoy Buckingham Palace, practically everyone will be impressed by the neo-Gothic 'people's palace' – the Palace of Westminster, or parliament building.

Edward the Confessor first anointed Westminster, relocating the 11th-century royal court here, to keep an eye on the builders working on Westminster Abbey. (Although its completion ultimately took longer than the ill-fated new Wembley Stadium…)

Six centuries later, after a Civil War and royal beheading, King Charles II fled Westminster for St James's, creating a new royal district. As its great Georgian squares were built in the 18th century, St James's began to spill over into Mayfair. Meanwhile, Westminster was spilling over into Pimlico.

Today, this entire area is not only essential London sightseeing. There are also upmarket shops, gourmet restaurants and leading galleries, such as the Royal Academy, Tate Britain and White Cube.

MAYFAIR, ST JAMES'S, WESTMINSTER & PIMLICO

◉ SEE
Buckingham Palace.........1 C5
Cabinet War Rooms..... (see 2)
Churchill Museum 2 F5
Horse Guards Parade......3 F4
Houses of Parliament.....4 G6
Institute of
Contemporary Arts 5 F3
No 10 Downing Street....6 G4
St James's Park.............7 E5
Wellington Arch............8 A5
Westminster Abbey 9 G6
White Cube Gallery 10 D3

🏠 SHOP
Burberry 11 C1
Burlington Arcade........12 D2

Dover Street Market.....13 C2
Fortnum & Mason 14 D3
Kilgour.......................15 D2
Matthew Williamson(see 20)
Mulberry....................16 B1
Ozwald Boateng.........17 D2
Paul Smith Sale Shop...18 B1
Poste.........................19 B1
Stella McCartney 20 B2
Waterstone's 21 D2

🍴 EAT
Cinnamon Club............22 F6
Galvin @ Windows 23 A4
Gordon Ramsay
at Claridges 24 B1

Inn the Park................25 F4
Mango Tree 26 B6
Maze.........................27 A1
Nobu.........................28 A4
Sketch.......................29 C1
Wolseley....................30 C3

🍷 DRINK
Nobu Berkeley.............31 C3

⭐ PLAY
Pigalle 32 E2

Please see over for map

SEE

BUCKINGHAM PALACE

☎ 7766 7300; www.the-royal
-collection.com; Buckingham Palace
Rd SW1; adult/child/concession
£13.50/7/11.50; ☺ 9.30am-4.30pm early
Aug-Sep; ✪ St James's Park, Victoria or
Green Park

Buck House, as it's popularly
nicknamed, is only worth visiting
if you *know* you'll like it – if your
admiration for royalty won't be
dented by the reality of, say,
kitschy his-and-her pink chairs
initialled 'ER' and 'P' in the Throne
Room. Temporary exhibits, including one of the Queen's dresses,
have been thrown in to try to sex
things up in recent years, but the
best of the 19 public rooms is still
the Picture Gallery. Entry tickets
can be bought from a kiosk in
Green Park; there is a timed entry
system in place with admission
every 15 minutes.

CABINET WAR ROOMS &
CHURCHILL MUSEUM

☎ 7930 6961; www.iwm.org.uk; Clive
Steps, King Charles St SW1; adult/under
16 yr/senior/student/unemployed £10/
free/8/8/5; ☺ 9.30am-6pm, last entry
5pm; ✪ Charing Cross

You might be surprised how engaging you find the bunker where
Prime Minister Winston Churchill
met his cabinet and generals dur-

CHANGING OF THE
GUARD

This is a London 'must see', although
the *idea* is more fun than the experience. The old guard (Foot Guards of the
Household Regiment) comes off duty
to be replaced by the new guard on the
forecourt of Buckingham Palace, and
tourists get to gape – from sometimes
as many as 10 people behind – at the
bright-red uniforms and bearskin hats
of shouting and marching soldiers for
just over half an hour. The official name
for the ceremony is Guard Mounting,
which, we dare say, sounds more interesting. It takes places at 11.30am April
to May and alternate days, weather
permitting, August to March.

---

ing WWII, especially now it's been
joined by a whiz-bang exhibition
devoted to 'the greatest Briton'. The
Cabinet War Rooms, especially the
bedrooms, evoke a period of dep-
rivation and duty. Then comes: 'We
will fight them on the beaches' and
more in the Churchill Museum. Winston's replayed speeches still send
shivers down the spine, although
the official centrepiece is the huge,
tabletop interactive lifeline.

HORSE GUARDS PARADE

☎ 0906 866 3344; ☺ Changing of
the Guard 11am Mon-Sat, 10am Sun;
✪ Westminster

Another traditional tourist magnet, this parade is where poor

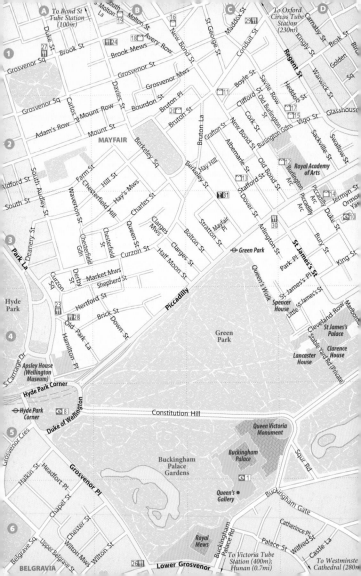

A

To Bond St
Tube Station
(100m)

Duke St

Grosvenor Sq

Brook St

27

South Molton La

Molton St

19

18 Avery Row

B

New Bond St

16

Brook Mews

24

Davies St

Grosvenor Mws

Grosvenor St

Carlos St

Mount Row

Bourdon St

Bruton Pl

20

Bruton St

Adam's Row

Mount St

Berkeley Sq

MAYFAIR

C

Maddox St

29

St George St

Conduit St

Boyle St

Clifford St

Grafton St

New Bond St

Albemarle St

11

D

To Oxford
Circus Tube
Station
(230m)

Barnaby St

Beak St

Kingly St

Regent St

Warwick St

Golden
Sq

Savile Row

Old Burlington St

Heddon St

17

15

Vigo St

Glasshouse

Swallow St

Sackville St

Heddon St

Cork St

Old Bond St

Burlington Gdns

12 **Royal Academy
of Arts**

Farm St

Hill St

Chesterfield Hill

Hay's Mws

Waverton St

South Audley St

Aldford St

South St

Chesterfield Gdn

Chesterfield St

Queen St

Charles St

Clarges Mws

Berkeley St

Hay Hill

13

Stafford St

Dover St

Burlington Arc

Piccadilly Arc

14

Jermyn St

10

Ormond
Yard

Park La

Deanery St

Curzon St

Curzon Sq

Derby St

Market Mws

Shepherd St

Hertford St

Half Moon St

Stratton St

Bolton St

Clarges St

Mayfair Pl

Arlington St

Green Park

31

30

Bury St

Piccadilly Arc

Duke St

King St

St James's St

**Hyde
Park**

Brick St

Down St

Old Park La

Hamilton Pl

23

28

4

Park Pl

Queen's Walk

St James's Pl

Little St-James's St

**Spencer
House**

Cleveland Row

St James's
Palace

Stable Yard Rd (Private)

Marlborough

**Apsley House
(Wellington
Museum)**

S Carriage Dr

Hyde Park Corner

Hyde Park
Corner

8

Duke of Wellington

Piccadilly

**Green
Park**

Constitution Hill

**Lancaster
House**

**Clarence
House**

5

Grosvenor Cres

Halkin St

Headfort Pl

Grosvenor Pl

Chapel St

Chester St

**Queen Victoria
Monument**

**Buckingham
Palace
Gardens**

**Buckingham
Palace**

1

Squ Rd

Queen's Gallery

Buckingham Gate

6

Belgrave Sq

Upper Belgrave St

Wilton Mws

Wilton St

BELGRAVIA

26

**Royal
Mews**

Buckingham Palace Rd

Lower Grosvenor

Palace St

Catherine Pl

Wilfred St

Castle La

To Victoria Tube
Station (400m);
Hunan (0.7mi)

To Westminster
Cathedral (280m)

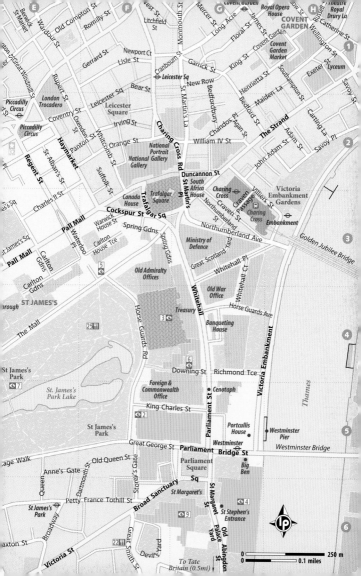

NEIGHBOURHOODS

MAYFAIR, ST JAMES'S, WESTMINSTER & PIMLICO

guardsmen sweat impassively beneath their towering bearskin hats while little boys pull faces at them before sidling up for a photo. On the Queen's official birthday in June, the Trooping of the Colour is staged in the parade ground. During the London 2012 Olympics the beach volleyball will be held here.

☉ HOUSES OF PARLIAMENT

☎ tours 0870 906 3773, individual visits 7219 4272; www.parliament.uk; St Stephen's Entrance, St Margaret St; admission free, tours adult/concession £7/5; ☯ during Parliamentary sessions 2.30-10.30pm Mon, 11.30am-7pm Tue & Wed, 11.30am-6.30pm Thu, 9.30am-3pm Fri; ⊖ Westminster

Many visitors will be happy enough with a glimpse of the Big Ben clock tower of this impressive building. Otherwise, the most usual route to gaining a glimpse inside the Houses of Parliament is via a 75-minute tour during summer (or Easter or Christmas) when parliament isn't sitting. The tour covers the Houses of Commons and Lords, as well as the newly refurbished Westminster Hall (hopefully finished by summer 2007) and more. Check the website for bag restrictions. Watching the politicians debate during parliamentary sessions is going to be dull

Big Ben

unless you come during Prime Minister's Question Time, and tickets for this event are harder to come by than for a last-minute Madonna gig.

☉ INSTITUTE OF CONTEMPORARY ARTS

ICA; ☎ 7930 3647; www.ica.org.uk; The Mall SW1; day membership during exhibitions adult/concession Mon-Fri £1.50/1, Sat & Sun £2.50/1.50; ☽ noon-10.30pm Mon, noon-1am Tue-Sat, noon-11pm Sun; ⊖ Charing Cross or Piccadilly Circus

Kind of like a style magazine come to life, and currently run by a former journalist from that background, the ICA focuses on all that is experimental, progressive, radical, street, obscure and, above all, cool. A couple of arthouse cinemas, some good gigs and club nights and a top bookshop add to the allure. Its convivial café-bar is a good bolthole from St James's Park…if you don't mind paying the day membership.

☉ NO 10 DOWNING STREET

www.number10.gov.uk; 10 Downing St SW1; ⊖ Westminster

Despite the iconic door at No 10, the British Prime Minister's residence is actually one of the most humble official state residences on the planet. It's still worth a

LONDON STEREOTYPES

Neither is particularly flattering or nice, but it might help you to know the following terms.

> Chav – anyone of the working class who has the 'audacity' to spend lots of money on designer labels or imitations, including young men with earrings, gold chains, white trainers and Burberry caps; teenage Vicky Pollard in TV series *Little Britain*; and Colleen McLoughlin, footballer Wayne Rooney's girlfriend.

> Nathan Barley – irritating Hoxton/Shoreditch creative with a silly haircut, who signals his approval by saying 'well weapon'. Prone to jumping on flash-in-the-pan trends, they run pointless websites, or, as the TV character on which they're based would describe it, are 'self-facilitating media nodes'.

quick glance – that's all you can get, in fact, as you peer through an iron gate that's cordoned off the street. In 1997 PM Tony Blair and his larger family swapped their official abode with the chancellor Gordon Brown in No 11 – which became a source of soap opera when the two families later became embroiled in arguments over betrayal, lies and curtains.

◉ ROYAL ACADEMY OF ARTS
☎ 7300 8000; www.royalacademy.org
.uk; Burlington House, Piccadilly W1;
admission varies; ⏱ 10am-6pm, to
10pm Fri; ⊖ Green Park

There isn't a permanent exhibition to speak of at the much-
respected Royal Academy, Britain's first art school. But even if
the latest in its rolling programme
of high-profile temporary shows
(check listings) doesn't appeal,
it's worth briefly sticking your
head into its courtyard for a free
sculpture fix. The annual Summer

Exhibition displaying art by the
general public is as dreadful as it
sounds.

◉ ST JAMES'S PARK
☎ 7930 1793; www.royalparks.gov.uk;
The Mall SW1; ⊖ St James's Park

The view of Buckingham Palace
from the footbridge spanning
St James's Park Lake is stunning.
The large lake, with its swans and
other waterfowl, acts as a focal
point, while the flowerbeds are
a blaze of summer colour. At the
merest hint of sunshine, it's not

ALONG THE RIVER

Three sights outside central London are located along the River Thames: the Hampton Court
Palace, Kew Gardens and Thames Flood Barrier. For a different experience the river can be
used to visit them.

Hampton Court Palace (☎ 0870 751 5175; www.fhrp.org.uk; East Molesy; all-
inclusive ticket adult/5-15 yr/senior/student/family £12.30/8/10/10/36.40, maze only
adult/child £3.50/2.50; ⏱ 10am-6pm Apr-Oct, 10am-4pm Nov-Mar; 🚢 Hampton Ct
from Waterloo, or via Wimbledon tube station) is a magnificent Tudor palace dating from
1514 and inextricably associated with the owner, King Henry VIII. It is a schlep from central
London, but you won't ever find anything quite like it, with state apartments, the country's
best hammer-beam ceiling, the ghost of a beheaded wife, Tudor kitchens, tennis courts and
that famous 800m-long maze.

The 12-hectare **Kew Gardens** (☎ 8332 5000, 8940 1171; www.rbgkew.org.uk; Kew
Rd; adult/under 16 yr/senior, student or over 16 yr £10/free/7; ⏱ gardens 9.30am-
6.30pm Mon-Fri, to 7.30pm Sat & Sun late Mar-Aug, 9.30am-6pm Sep-Oct, 9.30am-
4.15pm Nov-Feb, glasshouses 9.30am-5.30pm late Mar-Oct, 9.30am-3.45pm Nov-Feb;
⊖ Kew Gardens) truly deserve their World Heritage Site status, with fabulous Victorian
greenhouses, the evil-smelling 'corpse flower' Titan Arum and the 200-million year old Wollemi
pine from Australia. There's also the newly reopened Kew Palace and the chance to climb the
pagoda in season. The **Kew Explorer minitrain** (adult/child £3.50/1.50) covers the site in 40
minutes, but any visit needs at least half a day, especially when you include travel time.

just the flowers that come out, but hordes of pallid sunbathers who drape themselves across the grass, the benches and the rentable deck chairs.

☉ TATE BRITAIN
☎ 7887 8000 or 7887 8888; www.tate .org.uk; Millbank SW1; admission free, prices vary for temporary exhibitions, audio tours adult/concession £3/2.50; ⏲ 10am-5.50pm; ⊖ Pimlico
Tate Britain shattered box-office records in 2005 when it devised a barnstorming exhibition of Thames paintings by Turner, Whistler and Monet. Now it – and every other darn gallery in London – seems obsessed with the money-spinning, headline-grabbing 'spectacular'. Check online for the latest. The permanent collection of British art from the 16th to the late-20th centuries runs the gamut from Constable, Gainsborough and Turner to Hockney, Bacon and even Tracey Emin and Anthony Gormley.

The sci-fi looking **Thames Flood Barrier** (☎ 8305 4188; www.environment-agency .gov.uk; 1 Unity Way SE18; barrier free, downstairs information centre adult/child/senior £1.50/0.75/£1; ⏲ 11am-3.30pm Oct-Mar, 10.30am-4.30pm Apr-Sep; 🚉 Charlton from Charing Cross, 🚌 177 or 180 from Greenwich) has been preventing London's river from bursting its banks for more than 25 years now, but if you're going to visit there are two things to know: by far the best way to see it is to simply take a boat cruise around it, and it's only really worth visiting when its tall, silver Sydney-Opera-House-style sails are raised. To check which dates the barrier is raised, call the Thames Barrier Visitor Centre or check the website. Otherwise, there's a small exhibition at the visitor centre, reachable by road.

All three of these sights can be reached by river between April and October. Because the journey upriver to Hampton Court takes three hours each way, **Thames River Boats** (formerly Westminster Passenger Services Association; ☎ 7930 2062; www.wpsa .co.uk; adult/child one way £13.50/6.75, return £19.50/9.75) only operates one service a day from Westminster Pier, usually at 11am. The same company also operates four daily services to Kew (adult/child one way £10.50/5.25, return £16.50/8.25, 10am to 2pm, 1½ hours) between April and August, with fewer services in September.

Thames River Services (☎ 7930 4097; www.westminsterpier.co.uk; adult/child one way £11/5.50) operates three-hour round trip services to the Thames Barrier from Westminster Pier (on the hour from 11am to 3pm, leaving Greenwich an hour later, with an extra 4pm service in July and August).

NEIGHBOURHOODS

MAYFAIR, ST JAMES'S, WESTMINSTER & PIMLICO

◉ WELLINGTON ARCH
☎ 7930 2726; www.english-heritage
.org.uk; Hyde Park Corner W2; adult/
student or child/senior £3/1.50/2.30;
⏰ 10am-5pm Wed-Sun; ⊖ Hyde Park
Corner

England's answer to the Arc
de Triomphe commemorates
a French defeat (specifically,
Napoleon's at the hands of
Wellington). Erected in 1826, it's
now topped by Britain's biggest
bronze sculpture, *Peace Descend-
ing on the Quadriga of War*. It's
enough to look at the outside,
without entering the museum.
The pale-green granite sweep
behind it is the Australian War
Memorial.

◉ WESTMINSTER ABBEY
☎ 7222 5152; www.westminster-abbey
.org; Dean's Yard SW1; adult/child/con-
cession £10/free/6; ⏰ 9.30am-3.45pm
Mon-Fri, to 6pm or 7pm Wed, 9.30am-
1.45pm Sat, last entry 1hr before closing;
⊖ Westminster

Although guided tours and audio
guides are offered, the free pam-
phlets (in several languages) are
really enough to steer you through
the many riches of this, the greatest of all Anglican churches. The
abbey lives up to expectations and
the relatively hefty entrance fee
will be long forgotten on leaving.
For a slightly fuller description of
the interior, see p14.

◉ WESTMINSTER CATHEDRAL
☎ 7798 9055; www.westminster
cathedral.org.uk; Victoria St SW1;
cathedral free, tower adult/concession
£3/1.50, audioguides £2.50; ⏰ cathedral 7am-7pm, tower 9am-5pm Apr-Nov,
9am-5pm Thu-Sun Dec-Mar; ⊖ Victoria

The unfinished state of its British
headquarters – the money ran
out – underlines the Roman
Catholic Church's secondary
status here. But inside this candy-
striped cathedral is quite a fascinating contrast of rich mosaics
and bare brick, plus there's a lift
up the bell tower. London's paler
version of Barcelona's La Sagrada
Familia.

TAILOR-MADE
London's Savile Row is still renowned for
its customised suits. It's not a budget option, but the following tailors are among
the most interesting:
Kilgour (☎ 7734 6905; 8 Savile Row
W1; ⊖ Green Park) Conventional
with a modern twist, Kilgour sells a
ready-to-wear range, as well as tailor-
made suits from £1400.
Ozwald Boateng (☎ 7437 0620;
www.ozwaldboateng.com; 12a
Savile Row W1; ⊖ Green Park)
His flamboyance makes Boateng
more a couturier than a tailor, with
striking colours and fabrics in his £3000
bespoke suits.

WHITE CUBE GALLERY

☎ 7930 5373; www.whitecube.com; 25-26 Mason's Yard SW1; admission varies; ⏰ 10am-6pm Tue-Sat; ⊖ Green Park or Piccadilly Circus

Spiffy man-about-town and husband to artist Sam Taylor-Wood, the White Cube's owner Jay Jopling was second only to adman Charles Saatchi in promoting the 1990s 'Britart' movement. This new, impressive White Cube, cosily tucked away in a mews-like 'yard', means you don't need to trek to Hoxton Sq (see p125) to see his latest cutting-edge exhibition.

 # SHOP

With prices extremely high in this well-heeled part of London, many visitors come purely to window shop. But, given the stores' opulence, this alone generally proves a more-than-satisfying experience.

BURBERRY

☎ 7839 5222; www.burberry.com; 21-23 New Bond St SW1; ⏰ 10am-7pm Mon-Sat, noon-6pm Sun; ⊖ Bond St or Green Park

Desperate to distance itself from 'chavs' wearing baseball caps in its

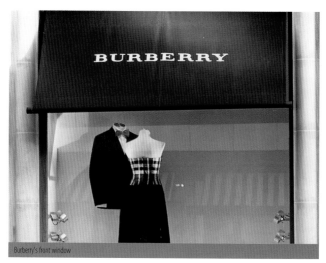
Burberry's front window

trademark yellow tartan, the first trad-Brit brand to go trendy is now concentrating on its sleek and frequently monochrome Prorsum range. See the boxed text on p131 for its factory shop.

🏛 BURLINGTON ARCADE
**www.burlington-arcade.co.uk;
51 Piccadilly W1; ⊖ Green Park**
The most famous of London's olde-worlde shopping arcades remains an echo of a bygone era, with elaborate 19th-century storefronts. It even has its own security guards, the Burlington Berties, who patrol the area keeping an eye out for punishable offences such as running, chewing gum and whistling.

ROUTEMASTER ROUTES
The Routemaster is dead, long live the Routemaster! When London's mayor took the old-fashioned red double-decker bus out of service in the 2005, he must have known it couldn't last long. Such was Londoners' love for the old 1950s models, with conductor and open back doors, the outcry was enormous. Now the bus is back (sort of), working two 'heritage' routes, so you can at least sample the experience. Route 9 goes from the Royal Albert Hall to the Strand and loops back to Piccadilly Circus. Route 15 runs from Trafalgar Sq past St Paul's Cathedral to Tower Hill. Normal tickets are valid; for more details see www.tfl.gov.uk/buses.

A LIGHT READ
Need a little time to put up your feet and find yourself along Piccadilly? Pop into **Waterstone's** (☎ 7851 2400; www.waterstones.co.uk; 203-206 Piccadilly W1; ⊖ Piccadilly Circus). Not only is this, the chain's flagship, the biggest bookstore in Europe, it boasts a top-floor café where you can pull up a chair and book, and enjoy the great backdoor views across London's rooftops.

🏛 DOVER STREET MARKET
☎ 7518 0680; www.doverstreetmarket.com; 17-18 Dover St W1; ⏱ 11am-6pm Mon-Sat, to 7pm Thu; ⊖ Green Park
Name-checked by every fashionista worth their Jimmy Choos, this small, six-floor shopping arcade showcases clothes and accessories by Comme des Garçons and tenants. It's modishly spartan, with concrete floors, corrugated-iron market-style 'stalls' and some interesting art dotted around, but prices are of the order of £80 for a T-shirt and £300 for a cushion.

🏛 FORTNUM & MASON
☎ 7734 8040; www.fortnumandmason.co.uk; 181 Piccadilly W1; ⏱ 10am-6.30pm Mon-Sat, noon-6pm Sun; ⊖ Piccadilly Circus or Green Park
Celebrating its 300th birthday in 2007, this venerable store is treating itself to a makeover, introducing an

atrium, revamping the famous food hall and adding a wine bar.

🏠 MATTHEW WILLIAMSON

☎ 7629 6200; www.matthewwilliamson .com; 28 Bruton St W1; ⏱ 10am-6pm Mon-Sat; ⊖ Green Park

Williamson is couturier to stars such as Sienna Miller, Keira Knightley, Kate Hudson and Joely Richardson; and even if you can't afford the £800 dresses, his 'boho deluxe' style is worth appreciating up close.

🏠 MULBERRY

☎ 7491 3900; www.mulberry.com; 41-42 New Bond St W1; ⏱ 10am-6pm Mon-Wed, Fri & Sat, to 7pm Thu; ⊖ Bond St

The leather bags – with personalised names like Tyler and

Burlington Arcade

NEIGHBOURHOODS

MAYFAIR, ST JAMES'S, WESTMINSTER & PIMLICO

NEIGHBOURHOODS

MAYFAIR, ST JAMES'S, WESTMINSTER & PIMLICO

CELEBRITY HAUNTS
> Ivy (p56)
> Nobu (p92)
> J Sheekey (p56)
> Sketch (p92)
> Wolseley (p92)

Roxanne – are the biggest hit at this revamped Brit brand. Both men's and women's clothes are fairly restrained.

🛍 PAUL SMITH SALE SHOP
☎ 7493 1287; 23 Avery Row W1; ⏱ 10am-6pm Mon-Sat, to 7pm Thu, 1-5pm Sun; ⊖ Bond St
Discounted items from the classic British designer (see also p52).

🛍 POSTE
☎ 7499 8002; 10 South Molton St; ⏱ 10am-7pm Mon-Sat, noon-6pm Sun; ⊖ Bond St
This very cool shop is aimed at boys and men who like good shoes, and stocks everything from vintage street labels to razor-sharp Italian imports.

🛍 STELLA MCCARTNEY
☎ 7518 3100; www.stellamccartney .co.uk; 30 Bruton St W1; ⏱ 10am-6pm Mon-Sat, to 7pm Thu; ⊖ Green Park
Impeccably tailored trouser suits that flatter, sweater dresses, bags, perfumes and sunglasses are showcased in this three-storey terraced Victorian home, which still retains its domestic atmosphere.

 # EAT

🍴 CINNAMON CLUB
Indian   £££
☎ 7222 2555; www.cinnamonclub.com; Old Westminster Library, 30 Great Smith St W1; ⏱ lunch & dinner Mon-Fri, dinner Sat; ⊖ St James's Park
With domed skylights, high ceilings, parquet flooring and a book-lined mezzanine harking back to the former library on this spot, this is one of London's older posh Indian restaurants. It's still doing the business with refined, slightly fusion dishes; it will suit those who prefer a very formal environment.

🍴 GALVIN @ WINDOWS
French   ££££
☎ 7208 4021; London Hilton on Park Lane, 22 Park Lane W1; ⏱ breakfast, lunch & dinner Mon-Fri, breakfast & dinner Sat, breakfast & lunch Sun; ⊖ Hyde Park Corner
Galvin's is a potent combination. Here a raised central platform makes the best of views from the 28th floor – including a peep into the Queen's back garden – and excellent French cuisine based on fresh British ingredients, like Angus beef tournedos and Scottish

langoustines. While pricey and a bit sterile, Galvin's is nevertheless miles ahead of London's other 'great view' restaurants.

GORDON RAMSAY AT CLARIDGES
Modern British   ££££
☎ 7499 0099; www.gordonramsay.com; 53 Brook St W1; ✆ lunch & dinner; ⊖ Bond St

The coming together of London's most celebrated chef and its grandest hotel was probably a match made in heaven and sent down to earth as His way to apologise for the historic awfulness of British food. All is forgiven. A meal in this gorgeous Art Deco dining room is a special occasion indeed, with good to superlative food as well as impeccable service – if you can manage to get a table in the first place, that is.

HUNAN
Chinese   ££–££££
☎ 7730 5712; 51 Pimlico Rd SW1; ✆ lunch & dinner Mon-Sat; ⊖ Sloane Sq

The service and food here are quirky and unique. Mr Peng presides and initially seems brusque, but if you let him select your dishes (telling him about dietary limitations), two things happen: he warms up and you get the best, informed choices. Dishes like chilli crab, de-boned steamed

fish and frog's legs are different from the norm too.

INN THE PARK *Café*   ££
☎ 7451 9999; www.innthepark.co.uk; St James's Park SW1; ✆ breakfast, lunch & dinner, snacks 8am-10pm Mon-Fri, 9am-10pm Sat & Sun; ⊖ St James's Park

Although it's a definite step up from most park cafés, we're not such unqualified fans as many others. Yes, it's a nice-looking building and the British-influenced food is good. However, it's not super value, the service is variable and the loos are typical park loos. Still, if you want to eat surrounded by London greenery, you could do much worse.

MANGO TREE *Thai*   £££
☎ 7823 1888; www.mangotree.co.uk; 46 Grosvenor Pl SW1; ✆ lunch & dinner Sun-Fri, dinner Sat; ⊖ Hyde Park Corner

There's been a huge buzz about this Thai restaurant, which gains

ALTERNATIVE AFTERNOON TEAS

Give the grand London hotels and their overpriced silver platters a miss and try the following:

> Coffee, Cake & Kink (see the boxed text, p59)
> Ladurée (see the boxed text, p104)
> Wolseley (p92)
> Yauatcha (p57)

plaudits for its delicious, authentic cuisine. The décor is streamlined and modern, although the large room can be slightly problematic – unless it's full it lacks atmosphere and when it's full it's very noisy.

🍴 MAZE
Modern International ££££

☎ 7107 0000; www.gordonramsay.com; 10-13 Grosvenor Sq W1; ⏰ lunch & dinner; ⊖ Bond St

If you're the sort who likes to sample a bit of everything, Maze is the Gordon Ramsay restaurant for you. Chef Jason Atherton's small, tapas-sized courses (most people order about seven or eight) keep customers, including lots of businessmen, very pleased. Here BLT (bacon and onion cream, chilled lettuce velouté, tomato gelée) joins honey-and-soy roasted quail, pâté de foie gras and risotto of carnaroli, and there's even a peanut butter and jam sandwich dessert.

🍴 NOBU *Japanese* ££££

☎ 7447 4747; Metropolitan Hotel, 19 Old Park Lane W1; ⏰ lunch & dinner; ⊖ Hyde Park Corner

While the cocktail-drinking glitterati have switched allegiance to flash-looking sister restaurant-bar Nobu Berkeley (p93), this arguably still holds the food crown. Black cod and the chocolate bento box (a cake shell packed with gooey chocolate) remain favourites, while the comfortably minimalist décor and anonymously efficient service make the whole thing seem effortless.

🍴 SKETCH
International £££-££££

☎ 0870 777 4488; www.sketch.uk.com; 9 Conduit St W1; ⏰ Mon-Sat; ⊖ Oxford Circus

Not as cool or essential as a few years ago, flamboyant, over-the-top Sketch is nevertheless worth seeing for its shimmering white, vibrant pinks, video art projections and egg-shaped loos. Ground-floor Gallery and Glade do Modern European and French food respectively; the upstairs Lecture Room has *haute cuisine* at very *haute* prices.

🍴 WOLSELEY
Modern European ££-££££

☎ 7499 699; www.thewolseley.com; 160 Piccadilly; ⏰ 7am-midnight Mon-Fri, 9am-midnight Sat, 9am-11pm Sun; ⊖ Green Park

A former Bentley car showroom has been transformed into this opulent Viennese-style brasserie – all golden chandeliers and black-and-white tiles. Add flexible service and great sleb (celeb) spotting opportunities, and you

NEIGHBOURHOODS

MAYFAIR, ST JAMES'S, WESTMINSTER & PIMLICO

St James's Park (p84)

have one of the best spots in London for morning or afternoon tea. (Meals, trickier to book anyway, can be slightly disappointing.)

DRINK

NOBU BERKELEY

☎ 7290 9222; 15 Berkeley St W1;
6pm-1am Mon-Sat; Green Park

Drinking in Mayfair is a seriously well-heeled business, but if you're intrigued to see the city's beautiful young things (allegedly) at play, dress up and pop your head into this amazing James Bond–style set of metal, wood and twinkling tree sculptures. There's an equally glamorous restaurant upstairs.

⭐ PLAY

PIGALLE

☎ bookings 0845 345 6053, information 7734 8142; www.thepigalleclub.com; 215 Piccadilly W1; Piccadilly Circus

Re-creating the kind of 1940–50s supper club Frank Sinatra patronised in *Rat Pack Confidential*, you'd usually feel safe bringing your dad, as well as your friends to this great 'cabaret' venue. Performers have included top burlesque performer Immodesty Blaize, but tend more towards the likes of Boy George, Jools Holland and Bryan Ferry. There are £30 dinner packages; if you just want to sit at the bar, entrance before 10pm is usually free.

>KNIGHTSBRIDGE, SOUTH KENSINGTON & CHELSEA

The area comprising Knightsbridge, South Kensington and Chelsea boasts many royal as well as other sights.

Kensington Palace was not only home to the late Princess Diana, but also the birthplace of Queen Victoria. That 19th-century matriarch left several legacies: Victoria & Albert Museum, Albert Hall and the Albert Memorial. Hyde Park and Kensington Gardens jointly create the biggest expanse of Royal Park in central London, where there's the superb Serpentine Gallery. The V&A combines with the neo-Gothic Natural History Museum and early 20th-century, Science Museum to create a cluster of leading exhibitions.

Yet despite all these cultural touchstones, the area's indisputable draw is the retail mile of Knightsbridge. This neighbourhood makes for better shopping and seeing than it does for everyday drinking, and after sunset, you can treat yourself to a meal at a gourmet restaurant.

KNIGHTSBRIDGE, SOUTH KENSINGTON & CHELSEA

SEE
Albert Memorial	1	B2
Chelsea Physic Garden	2	D5
Diana, Princess of Wales Memorial Fountain	3	C2
Kensington Palace	4	A2
Natural History Museum	5	B3
Royal Geographical Society	6	C3
Royal Hospital Chelsea	7	D5
Saatchi Gallery	8	H2
Science Museum	9	C3
Serpentine Gallery	10	C2
Victoria & Albert Museum	11	C3

SHOP
After Noah	12	C5
Harrods	13	D3
Harvey Nichols	14	D3
Joanna Booth	(see 12)	
Rococo	15	C5
Shop @ Bluebird	16	C5
Steinberg & Tolkien	17	C5

EAT
Amaya	18	D3
Bibendum	19	C4
Boxwood Café	20	D2
Daquise	21	C4
Gordon Ramsay	22	D5
La Bouchée	23	B4
La Poule au Pot	24	E4
Ladurée	(see 13)	
Montparnasse Cafe	25	A3
Painted Heron	26	C6
Petrus	(see 20)	
Racine	27	C3
Tom's Kitchen	28	C4
Zuma	29	D3

DRINK
Blue Bar	(see 20)	
Bosuns	30	D4
Elephant & Castle	31	A2
Troubadour	32	A5

PLAY
Chelsea Football Club	33	A6
Royal Albert Hall	34	B3
Royal Court Theatre	35	D4

Please see over for map

SEE

ALBERT MEMORIAL

☎ 7495 0916; www.aptg.org.uk;
Kensington Gardens, Kensington Gore
W8; 45min guided tours adult/concession
£4.50/4; ⏰ tours 2pm & 3pm 1st Sun of
the month; ⊖ Knightsbridge or South
Kensington

Gaudy, glitzy and kitsch it might
be, but the 52.5m memorial to
Queen Victoria's German husband
Albert (1819–61) takes on a whole
other dimension when you learn
the humble prince wanted no
such thing. 'If it became an artistic
monstrosity, it would upset my
equanimity to be permanently
ridiculed and laughed at in effigy,'
he said. Poor Albert. Don't laugh.
Architect George Gilbert Scott did
the dirty deed.

CHELSEA PHYSIC GARDEN

☎ 7352 5646; www.chelseaphysic
garden.co.uk; 66 Royal Hospital Rd SW3;
adult/concession £5/3; ⏰ noon-5pm Wed,
2-6pm Sun Apr-Oct, noon-5pm during the
Chelsea Flower Show; ⊖ Sloane Sq

The surprise of finding a tucked-
away garden here delights even
jaded Londoners. Founded
in 1673 for students studying
medicinal plants and healing, it's a
tidy line-up of plants used in tribal
and Western medicine, perfume
and aromatherapy, including rare
and exotic species.

DIANA, PRINCESS OF WALES MEMORIAL FOUNTAIN

Kensington Gardens W8; ⊖ Knightsbridge or South Kensington

You needn't have even liked
the woman to find this fountain

The Islamic Room, Victoria & Albert Museum (p101)

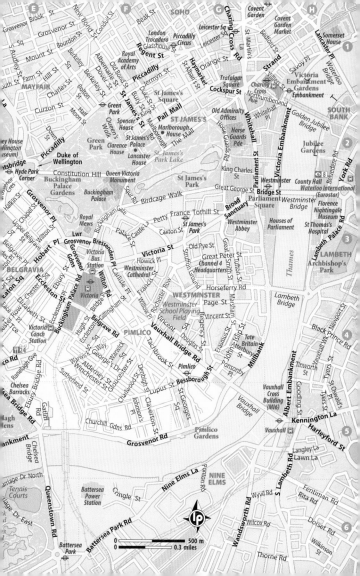

incredibly alluring. A 'moat without a castle' draped 'like a necklace', it's a circular stream on a small incline, with water rushing both clockwise and anticlockwise from the summit, and being whirled into patterns by irregularities in the concrete base. Add people lounging on the lip of Kathryn Gustafson's creation, dipping their feet on a sunny day, and it's a life-affirming scene. Teething troubles are long forgiven.

HYDE PARK & KENSINGTON GARDENS
www.royalparks.gov.uk; Hyde Park Corner, Marble Arch, Knightsbridge, Queensway, High St Kensington or Lancaster Gate

These are officially two separate parks, but visitors rarely notice or care as they wander from one to the other without crossing appreciable boundaries. Hyde Park is the eastern 145 hectares; it offers open-

LONDON'S UPSIDE-DOWN TABLE
Looking across from the northern end of Chelsea Embankment, you can't miss the monolithic Battersea Power Station (Map pp96–7, F5) – with four corner smokestacks making it look like an upside-down table. A much-loved landmark that's appeared in art and film, it stopped generating power in 1983. But this 38-acre building is, hopefully, being redeveloped as an entertainment and accommodation complex, with a possible thrill ride in one of its (replaced) smokestacks. In 2006 part of the complex was publicly reopened with a temporary Serpentine Gallery exhibition. Further plans are still afoot; visit www.thepowerstation.co.uk for the latest.

air concerts and is a great spot to relax. Kensington Gardens technically belongs to Kensington Palace and starts west of the Serpentine Lake. See p15 for more details.

THE NEW SPEAKER'S CORNER?
Who would have thought the fusty old Royal Geographical Society – the one-time stamping ground of explorers such as David Livingstone – could ever be sexy? But while Speaker's Corner in northeastern Hyde Park has been hit by the Internet chatroom phenomenon, the RGS (☎ 7591 3000; www.rgs.org; 1 Kensington Gore SW7), with entrance on Exhibition Rd, is thriving on its highbrow credentials. Its Intelligence Squared debates (www.intelligencesquared.com) attract the world's most desirable talking heads; Bernard-Henri Levy v Christopher Hitchens provoked some interesting declarations of lust from the audience! Discussion range from Iraq, Europe and global warming to cocaine, Tesco and working-class 'chavs', and seats are booked out a phenomenal three months ahead.

⊙ KENSINGTON PALACE

☎ 0870 751 5170; www.hrp.org.uk; Kensington Gardens W8; adult/5-15 yr/concession/family £11.50/7.50/9/34; ⏰ 10am-4.30pm; ⊖ Queensway, Notting Hill Gate or High St Kensington.

Still best remembered as the residence of the late Diana, Princess of Wales after her divorce from Prince Charles, Kensington Palace gives royal fans the chance to see inside a London palace even in Buckingham Palace's off-season. It's a tad more tasteful and less standoffish, too, with highlights including the Cupola Room, the Sunken Garden and nearby Orangery, where you can have afternoon tea.

⊙ NATURAL HISTORY MUSEUM

☎ 7938 9123; www.nhm.ac.uk; Cromwell Rd SW7; admission free, highlights tours £3, half-hourly tours of 'wet' zoological exhibits in the Darwin Centre free; ⏰ 10am-5.50pm Mon-Sat, 11am-5.50pm Sun; ⊖ South Kensington

The main action, such as the dinosaur skeletons and robots, plus thousands of other exhibits, is in the main Gothic Revival building, created by architect Alfred Woodhouse in 1880. The Earth Galleries section around the corner feels like walking into a swanky Italian nightclub but is curiously less absorbing. See p20 for further details.

Hyde Park

SUMMER AT THE SERPENTINE

Summer is best for visiting the Serpentine Gallery, and not just because of the weather. Each year it invites leading world architects to build a temporary, but always striking, pavilion. Past structures include a sweeping tent-like design by the creator of Brasilia, Oscar Niemeyer, and a luminous domed folly by Dutch star Rem Koolhaas. The Serpentine's summer party attracts the glitterati, while the public flocks to open-air events and films here.

ROYAL HOSPITAL CHELSEA
☎ 7881 5200; www.chelsea-pensioners.co.uk; Royal Hospital Rd SW3; admission free; 🕙 10am-noon & 2-4pm Mon-Sat, 2-4pm Sun May-Sep, 10am-noon & 2-4pm Mon-Sat Oct-Apr; ⊖ Sloane Sq

For most people, this Christopher Wren building is only of interest during May, when the Chelsea Flower Show (p33) takes place in its grounds. However, it's possible to view a few rooms here too. War veterans, known as Chelsea Pensioners, live on the premises – or will do again when renovations are complete – and are renowned for their striking ceremonial outfits (scarlet in summer, navy blue in winter).

SAATCHI GALLERY
www.saatchi-gallery.co.uk; Duke of York's HQ, Sloane Sq SW3; ⊖ Sloane Sq

After a run of bad luck in its South Bank location, the Saatchi is due to reopen here in sleek modern style in 2007. Collector, adman and 'Mr Nigella Lawson', Charles Saatchi still owns some seminal Britart sculptures from the 1990s, but now seems fonder of showing paintings by US artists. Check the website for visiting information.

SCIENCE MUSEUM
☎ 0870 870 4868; www.sciencemuseum.org.uk; Exhibition Rd SW7; admission free, separate charges for IMAX cinema & rides; 🕙 10am-6pm; ⊖ South Kensington

One of the most progressive and accessible museums of its kind, this does a terrific job of bringing to lustrous life a subject that is often dull and impenetrable for kids and adults alike. With five floors of interactive and educational exhibits – from an original steam engine to an Apollo space capsule to the latest energy-saving technology – it's informative and entertaining for all. See also p20.

SERPENTINE GALLERY
☎ 7402 6075; www.serpentinegallery.org; Kensington Gardens W8; admission free; 🕙 10am-6pm; ⊖ Knightsbridge

There's no such thing as a disappointing show at this 1930s

former tea pavilion. Director Julia Peyton-Jones and colleagues seem to have the Midas touch when it comes to filling the small space with contemporary art and installations from the likes of Andreas Gursky, Louise Bourgeois, Tomoko Takahashi and Thomas Demand. But if the current exhibition somehow isn't to your taste, there's always the fantastic parkland setting, plus from May to September the summer pavilion (see the boxed text, opposite).

SERPENTINE LAKE
Kensington Gardens W8; ⊖ Knightsbridge or South Kensington
Hyde Park is separated from Kensington Gardens by the squiggly L-shaped Serpentine lake, which was created when the West-

bourne River was dammed in the 1730s. At Christmas, it's the site of a brass-balls swimming race, and in summer people like to rent pedalos. The latest attraction is a solar ferry (adult/child £2.50/1.50), going veeerry slowly from the boathouse to the Lido Café. It's in operation year-round, they assure us, although we presume it must depend on the weather.

VICTORIA & ALBERT MUSEUM
☎ 7942 2000; www.vam.ac.uk; Cromwell Rd SW7; admission free, donation of £3 requested, prices vary for temporary exhibitions; ⏱ 10am-5.45pm, to 10pm Wed & last Fri of month; ⊖ South Kensington
This once disorganised and slightly overwhelming museum

Science Museum

of decorative art and design has been putting its house in order, literally, and it's made a huge difference. Crowds are particularly drawn to the fashion and Islamic galleries. Recent blockbuster shows, from Modernism to Leonardo Da Vinci, have also breathed fresh life into the joint. For more details, see p20.

 # SHOP

Knightsbridge and the King's Rd are the two retail hubs here. The former boasts London's most famous store, Harrods. The latter became synonymous with the Swinging London of the '60s and '70s. Since the '80s it's been more 'Sloaney' (after the posh set associated with starting point Sloane Sq). Today it's an amalgam of High St chains, expensive designer boutiques and the odd reminder of the hippy and punk eras.

☐ HARRODS
☎ 7730 1234; www.harrods.com; 87 Brompton Rd SW1; ☀ 10am-8pm Mon-Sat, noon-6pm Sun; ⊖ Knightsbridge
This unique store is like a theme park for fans of the British establishment and is crowded with slow tourists, but the famous food hall will make you drool. The memorial fountain to Princess Diana and Dodi Fayed (son of Harrods owner Mohammed) is extremely kitsch.

☐ HARVEY NICHOLS
☎ 7235 5000; www.harveynichols .com; 109-125 Knightsbridge SW1; ☀ 10am-8pm Mon-Sat, noon-6pm Sun; ⊖ Knightsbridge
In London's temple of high fashion, you'll find all the names that matter in local and international high couture. There's a great food hall and café on the 5th floor (with late opening, depending on demand), a softly lit lingerie department, an extravagant perfume department and exquisite jewellery.

☐ ROCOCO
☎ 7352 5857; www.rococochocolates .com; 321 King's Rd SW3; ☀ 9am-7pm Mon-Sat, noon-6pm Sun; ⊖ Sloane Sq, then bus 11,19 or 22
Undoubtedly one of London's best chocolate shops, this is a feast for the eyes as well as the stomach, with all sorts of shaped sweets. There's also a branch in Marylebone (p75).

☐ SHOP AT BLUEBIRD
☎ 7351 3873; 350 King's Rd SW3; ☀ 10am-7pm Mon-Sat, from 9am Wed & Thu, noon-6pm Sun; ⊖ Sloane Sq, then bus 11, 19 or 22
Putting excitement back into the increasingly bourgeois King's Rd is this stunning Terence Conran–owned emporium of young designer fashion, accessories, furniture and books. Set in a 1930s

 Alex Allen,
Sales Assistant, Shop at Bluebird

Best down-to-earth place to go out I tend to drink more near Kensington High St – in tucked-away pubs in residential areas such as the **Elephant & Castle** (40 Holland St), not far from Kensington Palace, or the **Scarsdale** (23a Edwardes Sq) further west. Closer to Chelsea, **Bosuns** (138a King's Rd) is popular; it's a club beneath the West Cornwall Pasty shop that has open-mic nights. Also, the **Troubadour** (263-267 Old Brompton Rd) in Earl's Court; they have live poetry readings. **Particular boutiques** Vintage fashion store **Steinberg & Tolkien** (193 King's Rd) is legendary. There are also antiques stores such as **After Noah** (261 King's Rd) and **Joanna Booth** (247 King's Rd). **Favourite local corner** Thackeray St south of Kensington High St. It's full of character and has the sort of coffee shops you'd hope to find in London, places such as French café **Montparnasse Cafe** (22 Thackeray St). Finally, speaking of French food, **La Bouchée** (☎ 7589 1929; 56 Old Brompton St) is my favourite restaurant. It does the best potato dauphinoise in London.

NEIGHBOURHOODS

KNIGHTSBRIDGE, SOUTH KENSINGTON & CHELSEA

Gordon Ramsay

Art Deco building, it's not just about product on shelves – although some of that is not only covetable but surprisingly affordable. There are also plenty of mesmerising displays to hold a browser's attention.

TREAT YOURSELF

A little bit of Paris has recently come to London, with the French tearoom **Ladurée** (☎ 3155 0111; Harrods, 87 Brompton Rd SW1; ☆ 8am-9pm Mon-Sat, noon-6pm Sun; ⊖ Knightsbridge) opening its first concession inside Harrods (Hans Rd entrance). So there's no need to cross La Manche for a little bit of Marie Antoinette opulence. Even by Harrods' *de trop* standards, the café is amazingly ornate and the cakes look fantastic. Don't forget to sample the signature macaroons.

EAT

AMAYA

Indian £££-££££

☎ 7823 1166; Halkin Arcade, 19 Motcomb St SW1; ⊖ Knightsbridge

Although most people associate Indian food with curry, this chic restaurant is best for its grills – Tandoori chicken, lamb shanks etc. That said, the menu has a special section for vegetarians, while the modern, bejewelled interior takes some of the edge off the admittedly high bill.

🍴 BIBENDUM
French   ££-££££
☎ 7581 5817; www.bibendum.co.uk;
81 Fulham Rd SW3; ⏰ lunch & dinner;
⊖ South Kensington

The Art Deco dining room, with wonderful stained-glass windows, is the key attraction at this long-standing venture in Michelin House (1911). But the wide choice of reliable and enjoyable food doesn't let the side down either, plus there's an oyster bar downstairs.

🍴 BOXWOOD CAFÉ
Modern European   £££-££££
☎ 7235 1010; www.gordonramsay.com;
Berkeley Hotel, Wilton Pl SW1; ⏰ lunch & dinner; ⊖ Knightsbridge

Gordon Ramsay's most 'relaxed' restaurant is summed up by its pâté de foie gras and veal burger – it might not vaguely approach the formal excellence of his signature restaurant, but it's posh enough still. Food is generally first-rate, especially the perennial fried oysters with fennel and lemon *confit*.

🍴 DAQUISE *Polish*   £-££
☎ 7589 6117; 20 Thurloe St SW7;
⊖ South Kensington

Rebuilt after a recent fire, this lowly gem isn't as wonderfully shabby as it once was; it needs to wear in a bit. But there's still an old-fashioned atmosphere in the service and the menu of *pierogi*

(dumplings), *bortsch*, cabbage rolls, pork etc. Such proudly stodgy fare works best in winter.

🍴 GORDON RAMSAY
Modern European   ££££
☎ 7352 4441; www.gordonramsay.com;
68-69 Royal Hospital Rd SW3; set lunch/dinner/degustation £35/65/80; ⏰ lunch & dinner Mon-Fri; ⊖ Sloane Sq

London's most famous gastronomic temple – the only restaurant with three Michelin stars. This is one of the city's most elusive tickets, and booking must be planned with clinical efficiency (see the boxed text, p57). While it had an interior makeover in 2006 (all cream and muted tones) and a slight tweak of the menu, old favourites like lobster, langoustine and salmon ravioli are still in existence.

CHEZ BRUCE

Sometimes it seems London's best gourmet dining happens in Knightsbridge and Chelsea, but that's not necessarily true. One of the most consistently excellent restaurants is in the relative wilds of Wandsworth. **Chez Bruce** (☎ 8672 0114; 2 Bellevue Rd SW17; ⏰ lunch & dinner; 🚉 Wandsworth Common) has won awards and a Michelin star for chef Bruce Poole's French cuisine. Yet it's served in a relaxed, friendly and unpretentious environment – a combination that makes it well worth the trip.

⅋ LA POULE AU POT
French £££

☎ 7730 7763; 231 Ebury St SW1; lunch & dinner; ⊖ Sloane Sq

Crammed with country-kitchen collectibles, candlelit and full of little private nooks, the 'Chicken in the Pot' is considered one of London's most romantic restaurants... at least by all of the media couples who are continually spotted here!

⅋ PAINTED HERON
Indian £££

☎ 7351 5232; www.thepaintedheron .com; 112 Cheyne Walk SW10; lunch Mon-Fri, dinner Sat; 🚌 11, 19, 22 or 319

This starchy white restaurant with minimalist interior isn't exactly central and it's not cheap, but that's all atoned for by the utterly fantastic food. It's an East-West mix in a league of its own, with dishes like rabbit tikka, crab *dhosa*, stir-fried cod and okra and Tandoori roasted rack of lamb.

⅋ PETRUS
Modern European £££-££££

☎ 7235 1200; www.gordonramsay .com; Berkeley Hotel, Wilton Pl SW1; lunch & dinner Mon-Fri, dinner Sat; ⊖ Knightsbridge

Gordon Ramsay protégé Marcus Wareing has zipped right past the boss here in running a celebrity gourmet restaurant that – astoundingly – seems to attract

almost no negative reports. It's all about indulgence, from the elaborate claret interior to the Norfolk suckling pig that's been cooked for 24 hours.

⅋ RACINE *French* £££

☎ 7584 4477; 239 Brompton Rd SW3; lunch & dinner; ⊖ South Kensington or Knightsbridge

The key to the success of this splendid creation is that it limits its ambitions and then achieves them with panache. Regional French cooking is the vehicle and dedicated service to the customer the destination (although the latter comes with a 15% charge that some diners do gripe about!).

⅋ TOM'S KITCHEN
Modern European ££-£££

☎ 7349 0202; www.tomskitchen.co.uk; 27 Cale Street SW3; 7.30am-midnight Mon-Fri, 8am-midnight Sat & Sun; ⊖ South Kensington

There's never been any question about chef Tom Aikens' technical skill, but his cooking has sometimes been criticised as overly fussy. In this new brasserie-style 'diffusion' restaurant, however, this Michelin-starred genius is not only bringing good, more affordable food to the mass market, he's sticking to uncomplicated fare such as soups, casseroles and pies, plus classic fish, meat and poultry dishes.

NEIGHBOURHOODS

KNIGHTSBRIDGE, SOUTH KENSINGTON & CHELSEA

THE BERKELEY'S BLUE BAR

As if housing the Boxwood Café and Petrus restaurant wasn't enough, the Berkeley Hotel has another gem. If you're coming to either restaurant, or you just fancy a cocktail, champagne or whisky in gorgeous duck-egg-blue luxury, pop into the hotel's **Blue Bar** (☎ 7235 6000; ⏱ 4pm-1am Mon-Sat, 3pm-midnight Sun); make sure you're dressed to impress.

ZUMA

Japanese   £££

☎ 7584 1010; www.zumarestaurant
.com; 5 Raphael St SW7; ⏱ lunch & dinner Mon-Sat; ⊖ Knightsbridge
With locals having (ever so slightly) turned their backs on this swish Japanese restaurant, now's the time for the rest of us to get in and appreciate its extensive menu of delicious food. Lunch is a good bet.

PLAY

🔲 CHELSEA FOOTBALL CLUB

☎ information 0870 603 0005, match tickets 7915 2951; www.chelsea village.com; Fulham Rd SW6; tours adult/child £10/6; ⏱ tours 11am, 1pm & 3pm Mon-Fri, noon & 2pm Sat & Sun; ⏱ souvenir store 10am-6pm Mon-Sat, 11am-4pm Sun; ⊖ Fulham Broadway

There's something corporate and bland about the home of London's richest football club, Chelsea, but supporters who are after a souvenir kit or a tour won't care. They'll be even more over the moon if they snaffle a rare available ticket to a match. There are two interlinked hotels in the building.

🔲 ROYAL ALBERT HALL

☎ 7589 3203; www.royalalberthall
.com; Kensington Gore SW7; ⊖ South
Kensington
Long 'blessed' with terrible acoustics, this former exhibition hall turned over a new leaf in 2004 with a complete aural and aesthetic refit. The ritual Proms (or Promenade Concerts; see p35) here every summer only involve embarrassing, flag-waving patri-otism on the last weekend, while the hall also hosts rock concerts, circus performances and book readings.

🔲 ROYAL COURT THEATRE

☎ 7565 5000; www.royalcourttheatre
.com; Sloane Sq SW1; ⊖ Sloane Sq
The Royal Court Theatre hasn't mellowed. Having launched *Look Back in Anger* in 1956, it still con-centrates exclusively on work by new and challenging playwrights.

>HOLBORN, CLERKENWELL & THE CITY

It's confusing to arrive in London to find a 'City' within a city; the one with the capital letter refers to the 'Square Mile' or the central financial district. While the focus here is relentlessly capitalistic, there are a few interesting things to see, including St Paul's Cathedral, St Bartholomew-the-Great, the Museum of London and the Barbican arts centre.

Just north of the city, Clerkenwell has experienced a mini-boom in the past decade, as young media companies have joined the long-established *Guardian* newspaper here. Clubs, pubs and bars have sprung up near the still-working meat market at Smithfield and beyond.

Heading west out of the City, you'll hit Holborn (*hoe*-burn), the cradle of English law, with the neo-Gothic Royal Courts of Justice on the Strand and the charming Lincoln's Inn. Before crossing over into Covent Garden, pause to take in the eccentric Sir John Soane's Museum.

HOLBORN, CLERKENWELL & THE CITY

◉ SEE
30 St Mary Axe	1	F4
Bank of England & Museum	2	E4
Leadenhall Market	3	E4
Lincoln's Inn	4	B3
Monument	5	E5
Museum of London	6	D3
Sir John Soane's Museum	7	A3
St Bartholomew-the-Great	8	C3
St Paul's Cathedral	9	D4
Tower Bridge	10	F6
Tower of London	11	F5

🛍 SHOP
Lesley Craze Gallery	12	C2

🍴 EAT
Café Spice Namaste	13	G4
Club Gascon	14	C3
Coach & Horses	15	B2
Eagle	16	B2
Medcalf	17	B2
Moro	18	B2
Smiths of Smithfields	19	C3
St John	20	C3

🍸 DRINK
Jerusalem Tavern	21	C3
Vertigo 42	22	E4
Ye Olde Cheshire Cheese	23	C4
Ye Olde Mitre	24	B3

★ PLAY
Barbican	25	D3
Cafe Kick	26	B2
Fabric	27	C3
Sadler's Wells	28	C1
Turnmills	29	C2
Volupté Lounge	30	B4

Please see over for map

SEE

BANK OF ENGLAND & AROUND

☎ 7601 5545; www.bankofengland
.co.uk; Bartholomew Lane EC2; ⊖ Bank

The Bank of England still boasts the
curtain wall left from the Sir John
Soane original and inside there's a
museum (free, audioguides £1; ☺ 10am-
5pm Mon-Fri) where you can feel how
heavy – amazingly heavy – a gold
bar is. The Royal Exchange building
opposite houses shops and a courtyard café.

LEADENHALL MARKET

www.leadenhallmarket.co.uk; Whit-
tington Ave EC1; ☺ 7am-4pm Mon-Fri;
⊖ Bank

Narrow your eyes and make
believe you're stepping back into
Victorian London here. The cob-
blestones and late-19th-century
ironwork of this dimly lit, covered
mall hark back to that period,
and even the modern restaurants
and chain stores copy it, while
catering to modern-day financial
workers. The market is located off
Gracechurch St.

Leadenhall Market

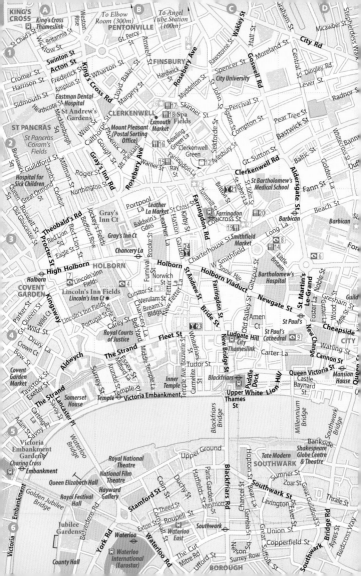

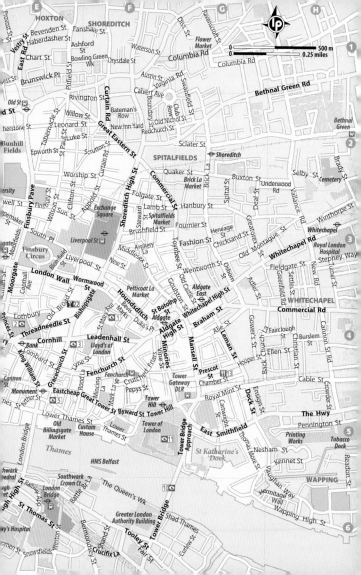

◉ LINCOLN'S INN

☎ 7405 1393; Lincoln's Inn Fields WC2; ⏱ grounds 9am-6pm Mon-Fri, chapel 12.30-2.30pm Mon-Fri; ⊖ Holborn

All London barristers work from one of four so-called Inns of Courts (13th-century trade associations akin to the Freemasons in their intricate protocol). Among these, Lincoln's Inn is the prettiest, with a chapel, pleasant square and picturesque gardens. Come to soak up the dreamy atmosphere; there's even a restaurant, the Terrace, here.

◉ MONUMENT

☎ 7626 2717; Monument St EC3; adult/child 5-15 yr £2/1; ⏱ 9.30am-5pm; ⊖ Monument

Christopher Wren's memorial to the 1666 Great Fire of London remains a major City landmark. However, you need to be keen to ascend its 311 narrow, winding steps. Sure, you get a certificate saying you did it (which makes it best for kids) but the view is better from St Paul's, the London Eye and Tower Bridge.

◉ MUSEUM OF LONDON

☎ 0870 444 3582, 7600 0807; www .museumoflondon.org.uk; Barbican Gate No 7, 150 London Wall EC2; admission free; ⏱ 10am-5.50pm Mon-Sat, noon-5.50pm Sun; ⊖ Barbican

This museum's excellence is all the more appreciated because it's generally unexpected; it doesn't get much publicity outside London. But while the Roman remains, superb new medieval gallery, Cheapside Hoard of 16th- and 17th-century jewellery, London Fire diorama and gilded Lord Mayor's state coach are all individually appealing, the whole helps visitors get under London's skin, from the Ice Age to 1914.

◉ SIR JOHN SOANE'S MUSEUM

☎ 7405 2107; www.soane.org; 13 Lincoln's Inn Fields WC2; admission free, tours £3 ⏱ 10am-5pm Tue-Sat, 6-9pm 1st Tue of month, museum tours 2.30pm Sat; ⊖ Holborn

A satisfyingly unique effort, this is a must for lovers of English eccentricity. The former home of architect and inveterate hoarder Sir John Soane (1753–1837), it's bursting with statuary, *objets d'art* and paintings. Did he ever spring-clean? Notably, there's an Egyptian hieroglyphic sarcophagus and a picture gallery where paintings unfold to reveal others behind. Candlelit Tuesday evenings are particularly atmospheric. Tickets for tours are sold from 2pm.

ST BARTHOLOMEW-THE-GREAT

☎ 7606 5171; www.greatstbarts.com; West Smithfield EC1; ⏱ 8.30am-5pm Tue-Fri, 10.30am-1.30pm Sat, 8am-8pm Sun; ⊖ Barbican or Farringdon

Never mind the more famous Westminster Abbey and St Paul's; St Bartholomew-the-Great is the capital's most atmospheric church. A weathered and blackened Norman construction from 1123, its dark wooden carvings and low lighting lend it an ancient calm. Scenes from the films *Shakespeare in Love* and *Four Weddings and a Funeral* were shot here.

St Paul's Cathedral (p114)

NEIGHBOURHOODS

HOLBORN, CLERKENWELL & THE CITY

INSIDE THE GHERKIN

Visitors to London often look at the so-called 'Gherkin' tower, and lament the lack of public access. Well, we thought you might like to know the top-floor restaurant is yours to hire for £9000 (plus tax). Otherwise try desperately to get in during an open-house weekend (see p36), a scheme in which the building sometimes participates. Despite its sci-fi look, Norman Foster's 2002–3 building for Swiss Re insurers – officially called **30 St Mary Axe** (Gherkin; www.30stmaryaxe .com; 30 St Mary Axe EC3; ⊖ Bank or Aldgate) – is an eco-friendly affair, with internal gardens to reprocess air and multiple energ savings.

⊙ ST PAUL'S CATHEDRAL

☎ 7236 4128; www.stpauls.co.uk; St Paul's Churchyard EC4; adult/child 6-16 yr/senior or student £9/8/3.50; ⏲ 8.30am-4pm (last entry) Mon-Sat; ⊖ St Paul's or Blackfriars

Told he couldn't build a circular dome because it was too 'Catholic', Sir Christopher Wren progressively tweaked his design in secret; and it was too late for his masters by the time they realised what they were getting. Now climbing the dome is a highlight of any cathedral visit; see p18 for more a more detailed description.

⊙ TOWER BRIDGE

☎ exhibition 7940 3985, information on next lifting 7940 3984; www.towerbridge .org.uk; adult/under 5 yr/senior, student or child 5-15 yr £5.50/free/4.25, family £10-20; ⏲ exhibition 10am-6pm Apr-Oct, 10.30am-6pm Nov-Mar; ⊖ Tower Hill

Get your camera finger ready. Even if you're not planning to photograph this world-famous neo-Gothic icon, someone else is bound to ask you to snap them standing on it. The bridge was built in 1894 and its famous drawbridge mechanism still opens a couple of times a week for oncoming ships. The exhibition in the towers above is fairly embarrassing, but offers panoramic views.

⊙ TOWER OF LONDON

☎ tickets 0870 756 7070, recorded information 0870 756 6060; www.hrp.org.uk; Tower Hill EC3; adult/child 5-15 yr/senior or student/family £15/9.50/12/43; ⏲ 9am-6pm Tue-Sat, 10am-6pm Sun & Mon Mar-Oct, 9am-5pm Tue-Sat, 10am-5pm Sun & Mon Nov-Feb, last admission 1hr before closing; ⊖ Tower Hill

This stunningly well-preserved medieval castle should be seen at least once in every lifetime. Close to 10 centuries of royal intrigue, imprisonment, execution, torture and murder, plus the legendary 105-carat Koh-i-Noor (Mountain of Light) diamond, claimed by India and Afghanistan but determinedly remaining in the late Queen Mother's crown, are all here. Guided tours and audioguides available. See p19 for a fuller description.

SHOP

Clerkenwell is the centre of London's gems trade, with other more traditional jewellers lining the major artery of Hatton Garden (B3). For records, more jewellery and quirky gifts, Exmouth Market (B2) is also worth a look.

LESLEY CRAZE GALLERY
☎ 7608 0393; www.lesleycrazegallery .co.uk; 33-35a Clerkenwell Green EC1; ⏲ 10am-5.30pm Tue-Sat; ⊖ Farringdon
One of Europe's leading centres for contemporary jewellery, this has exquisitely understated, and sometimes pricey, metal designs, as well as a small selection of cheaper, mixed-media pieces. Perfect if you're looking for something out of the ordinary.

EAT
CAFÉ SPICE NAMASTE
Indian   £££
☎ 7488 9242; www.cafespice.co.uk; 16 Prescot St E1; ⏲ lunch & dinner, closed Sun & lunch Sat; ⊖ Tower Hill
Fresh and unusual Indian cuisine – it's Parsee/Goan – is served in

RAVEN MAD
For years, English schoolchildren and visiting tourists have been told of a 'centuries-old' superstition that the monarchy would fall should the Tower of London's ravens ever leave. And at least six birds are kept in residence, with wings cropped to prevent them flying the coop.

It's bunkum, of course. In 2004 an official historian discovered that ravens had only definitely been kept here since 1895 and the tale was probably a Victorian invention. Records have also revealed the Tower had no ravens during WWII.

this colourful yet contemporary former magistrates' court. *Dhansaak* (traditionally lamb, but now also vegetable stew with rice, lentils and vegetables) is joined by other divine surprises, such as the *papeta na pattice* (mashed potato cakes, filled with green peas, grated coconut, chopped nuts and spices).

CLUB GASCON
French   ££££
☎ 7796 0600; 57 West Smithfield EC1; ⏲ lunch & dinner, closed lunch Sat & Sun; ⊖ Farringdon or Barbican
The proud owner of a Michelin star, Club Gascon takes a different approach to fine French cuisine, with a selection of tapas-style portions; about five to six constitute

a meal. There's duck, squid, cassoulet and an entire menu section devoted to pâté de foie gras. For economy, there's a cheaper wine bar next door or try the restaurant's tasting menu.

🍴 COACH & HORSES
Modern European   ££

☎ 7278 8990; 26-28 Ray St EC1; ⏱ lunch & dinner Mon-Fri, dinner Sat, lunch Sun; ⊖ Farringdon

The Coach and Horses' sign shows a pumpkin and four mice, and this really is a Cinderella story. Converted into a gastropub a few years ago, its simply, unfussy and streamlined menu soon made it an award winner. It's not quite at the forefront any more, but still holding its own. Lunches are the busy meal; you're more likely to get a seat at dinner, and there's a bar menu in between.

🍴 EAGLE *Mediterranean*   ££

☎ 7837 1353; 159 Farringdon Rd EC1; ⏱ lunch & dinner, closed dinner Sun; ⊖ Farringdon

London's first gastropub is still going strong. Even though the original owners and many chefs have left, the customers still come, at lunch or after work, for its Mediterranean-influenced food. As it's no long part of the 'scene' per se, the atmosphere is nicely relaxed.

DOOR TO THE BARBICAN

Getting into the Barbican has long involved serious orienteering skills. This huge 1980s complex boasts several split levels and cantilevered, multidirectional walkways, and can be accessed from two tube stations via several entrances. With audiences losing their way, the place has often, as the *Guardian* puts it, 'resembled a car park full of bewildered ballet enthusiasts'. This might not change immediately, but the Barbican is trying. For its 25th birthday in 2007, it installed a £14-million front door on Silk St. A front door? What a novel idea!

🍴 MEDCALF *British*   ££

☎ 7833 3533; 40 Exmouth Market EC1; ⏱ noon-3pm & 6-10pm Mon-Thu, noon-3pm Fri, noon-4pm Sat, noon-4pm Sun; ⊖ Farringdon

A beautifully converted butcher shop, Medcalf is both interesting and quirky, while at the same time delivering consistently excellent and affordable food. The changing menu here might include the likes of Welsh rarebit, pork-and-prune meatballs, or smoked salmon and anchovy terrine, but there's also a bar in between kitchen hours, and DJs take over on Friday night.

🍴 MORO
Spanish/North African £££
☎ 7833 8336; 34-36 Exmouth Market EC1; 🕐 12.30-2.30pm & 7-10.30pm Mon-Fri, 12.30-3pm & 7-10.30pm Sat; ⊖ Farringdon

The exulted Moro's reputation precedes it, which is probably why opinions are so mixed. Some are devoted fans, while others complain about small portions, crowding and slipping standards. The only way to find out for yourself is to risk it. On the changing menu, dishes seem to make regular appearances, like crab with *harissa,* and char-grilled lamb with artichokes.

TOP LONDON VIEWS
> Galvin @ Windows (p90) – remarkable view over exclusive neighbourhoods, including into the Queen's back garden
> London Eye (p10) – truly as far as the eye can see
> St Paul's Cathedral (p18) – well-earned and exhilarating views
> Tate Modern (p12) – from the 4th-floor coffee shop and balconies
> Vertigo 42 (p118) – great views from this skyscraper bar; sadly, views looking down on the neighbouring Gherkin are blocked by the loos

🍴 SMITHS OF SMITHFIELDS
British ££-£££
☎ 7252 7950; www.smithsofsmithfield.co.uk; 67-77 Charterhouse St EC1; 🕐 lunch & dinner Sun-Fri, dinner Sat; ⊖ Farringdon

Too much of an institution for us to ignore, Smiths is a huge multi-layered eating and drinking barn. Frankly, the ground-floor bistro-bar is nasty – a meat-market – and the fine-dining restaurant on level four can be unreliable. However, the third-level brasserie usually delivers a decent meal. (There's a cocktail bar on level two.)

🍴 ST JOHN
British ££-££££
☎ 7251 0848; www.stjohnrestaurant.co.uk; 26 St John St EC1; 🕐 lunch & dinner, closed lunch Sat & Sun; ⊖ Farringdon

Pretty well everything you need to know about this excellent restaurant – apart from the rooftop view – is summed up in its signature dish of bone-marrow salad. As author of *Nose to Tail Eating,* chef Fergus Henderson is not afraid to include adventurous meaty specialities, like veal heart and chicken neck, among more familiar fare. Not one for vegetarians.

NEIGHBOURHOODS

HOLBORN, CLERKENWELL & THE CITY

 # DRINK

A series of reasonably trendy bars can also be found lining Charterhouse St (C3) in Clerkenwell.

JERUSALEM TAVERN
☎ 7490 4281; 55 Britton St EC1; ⊖ Farringdon

It's hard to know what to rave about most at the small Jerusalem Tavern – the 18th-century décor where plaster walls are adorned with occasional tile mosaics, or the range of drinks, which includes organic bitters, wheat and fruit beers. Its recent incarnation seeks to pass it off as older than it really is, but despite this faux-tradition it's still a charming place.

'BABY FOOT' & POOL

Bowling (see p69) isn't the only sport that Londoners enjoy with a beer. Table football and pool are also popular accompaniments, and probably no more so than at the following two venues.
Elbow Room (☎ 7278 3244; 89-91 Chapel Market N1; ⊖ Angel) Row upon row of pool tables are found in this friendly, convivial venue.
Cafe Kick (☎ 7837 8077; www .cafekick.co.uk; Exmouth Market EC1; ⊙ noon-11pm; ⊖ Farringdon) A bare-boards bar with a Continental European feel, where the action centres around the handful of 'fussball' tables.

VERTIGO 42
☎ 7877 7842; 25 Old Broad St EC2; ⊙ closed Sat & Sun; ⊖ Bank

Prices aren't cheap in this 42nd-storey bar (the UK's highest), but that's hardly a problem. Once you've enjoyed the fantastic views for an hour (max), you're not exactly inspired to hang around with the city plutocrats up here. So get in and get out quick, preferably at sundown to watch the lights come on across London. For security reasons, you *must* book.

YE OLDE CHESHIRE CHEESE
☎ 7353 6170; Wine Office Court, 145 Fleet St EC4; ⊙ 11am-11pm Mon-Fri, noon-11pm Sat, noon-3pm Sun; ⊖ Blackfriars

A one-time haunt of literary greats like Charles Dickens, Mark Twain and Samuel Johnson, this dimly lit historic pub – lined with lots of black wood – is now a regular on the tourist trail, despite being in the contemporary no-man's land that's Fleet St. The trick is not to just stop in the first few bars you hit, but to continue to explore the cellar bars below and the upstairs rooms.

YE OLDE MITRE
☎ 7405 4751; 1 Ely Ct EC1; ⊙ closed Sat & Sun; ⊖ Chancery Lane or Farringdon

Hidden down a side alley (near 8 Hatton Gardens) this rickety little warren of rooms is one of

London's oldest extant pubs, dating back to the mid-16th century. An atmospheric spot for an old-fashioned pint.

PLAY

BARBICAN
☎ information 7382 7000, bookings 7638 8891; www.barbican.org.uk; Silk St EC2; ⊖ Moorgate or Barbican
A self-contained arts village, the anthill-like Barbican quadruples as a theatre, concert venue (classical, jazz and leftfield pop), dance stage and cinema, with adventurous arthouse programming in a very civilised, comfortable environment.

FABRIC
☎ 7336 8898 or 7490 0444; www.fabriclondon.com; 77a Charterhouse St EC1; ⏱ 9.30pm-5am Fri & Sun, 10pm-7am Sat; ⊖ Farringdon
The first stop on the London scene for many international clubbers, 1500-capacity Fabric is still going strong, with lengthy queues waiting to feel the music through its main 'bodysonic' dance floor. The music – mainly electro, house, drum and bass, and breakbeat – is as good as you'd expect from London's top-rated, like Ali B, James Lavelle and Andrew Weatherall. Live music is a newer addition.

SADLER'S WELLS
☎ 7863 8000; www.sadlers-wells.com; Rosebery Ave EC1; ⊖ Angel
Bolder, more adventurous and generally lighter on its feet than the Royal Ballet, Sadler's Wells is one of London's leading dance venues, where you can expect to see names like Carlos Acosta, Matthew Bourne, Sylvie Guillem and Akram Khan.

TURNMILLS
☎ 7250 3409; 63 Clerkenwell Rd EC1; ⏱ 6pm-midnight Tue, 10.30pm-7.30am Fri, 9pm-5am Sat; ⊖ Farringdon
Famed most of all for its friendly vibe, this cavernous, long-running institution still manages to pull in big-name DJs, including the likes of Judge Jules, Sister Bliss and Roger Sanchez, with its kickin' beats – ranging from house and techno to Latin and trance.

VOLUPTÉ LOUNGE
☎ 7831 1622; www.volupte-lounge.com; 9 Norwich St; ⊖ Chancery Lane
One of the more hardcore London cabaret venues, with burlesque striptease acts playing peekaboo with fans, feathers and nipple tassels, this place still draws a large female crowd to its boudoir-style basement performance room. Regular events include Wednesday night's Cabaret Salon, Friday's 1920s-themed Roar of the Flappers and Afternoon Tease on some Saturdays. It's off Fetter Lane.

>HOXTON, SHOREDITCH & SPITALFIELDS

This is London's leading enclave of cool. The Hoxton phenomenon began in the 1990s, when creative types chased out of the West End by prohibitive rents began buying warehouses in this then urban wasteland. By the late 1990s, the area was seriously cool, having spawned its own indigenous haircut (the Hoxton fin) and even a self-satirising fanzine (the former *Shoreditch Twat*). Bars, clubs, galleries and restaurants opened up to cater to the new media-creative-freelance squad.

Today, the area is still flourishing. On streets where a decade ago there were only poverty-stricken newsagents and the occasional rough pub, you'll now find delis, busy bars and thriving clothes shops. The neighbourhood remains rough enough around the edges to feel like a bit of an adventure, but even the partial redevelopment of Spitalfields Market hasn't stopped it in it tracks, and it remains one of London's best nightlife scenes.

HOXTON, SHOREDITCH & SPITALFIELDS

☉ SEE
Brick Lane........................1 G6
Christ Church
Spitalfields........................2 F5
Dennis Severs' House......3 F5
Geffrye Museum.............4 F2
Sunday Up Market &
Truman Brewery.............5 G5
White Cube Gallery.........6 E3
Whitechapel Art Gallery . 7 G6

⌂ SHOP
A Gold..............................8 F5
Absolute Vintage.............9 F5
Beyond Retro 10 G4
Columbia Road Flower
Market 11 F3

Laden Showrooms 12 G5
Spitalfields Market 13 F5
Start 14 E4
Tatty Devine 15 G4

⑪ EAT
Canteen.........................16 F5
Fifteen...........................17 D3
Giraffe ....(see 16)
Green & Red 18 G4
Les Trois Garçons 19 F4
Princess 20 E4

▼ DRINK
Big Chill Bar..................21 G5
Dragon Bar 22 E4

Dreambagsjaguarshoes..23 F3
Favela Chic....................24 E4
Foundry 25 E4
George & Dragon..........26 F3
Golden Heart.................27 F5
Hawksmoor...................28 F5
Loungelover..................29 F4
Ten Bells 30 F5
Vibe Bar.........................31 G5

★ PLAY
333.................................32 E4
93 Feet East..................33 G5
Bethnal Green Working
Men's Club 34 H3
Cargo 35 F4

Please see over for map

SEE

BRICK LANE
Aldgate East

Brick Lane is the centrepiece of a thriving Bengali community in an area nicknamed Banglatown, and today it's one long procession of curry and balti houses intermingled with sari and fabric shops, Indian cookery stores and, to the north, streetwear boutiques. The street's reputation as a place to eat has declined over the years, and the numerous restaurant touts (or curry pimps) don't help. The 24-hour Brick Lane Beigel Bake (No 159) remains an institution, serving insomniacs, taxi drivers and clubbers. But if you're serious about your curry, you're better off going to New Tayyab in Whitechapel, or making the trek to Tooting (see the boxed text, p128). See also p27.

DENNIS SEVERS' HOUSE
☎ 7247 4013; www.dennissevershouse.co.uk; 18 Folgate St E1; Sun/Monday/Mon evening £8/5/12; noon-2pm 1st & 3rd Sun of the month, noon-2pm Mon following 1st & 3rd Sun of the month, every Mon evening (times vary); Liverpool St

Utterly unique, Dennis Severs' House is worth noting if you're in town on the right weekend or Monday eve. Its 'still-life drama',

MONICA ALI'S BRICK LANE

Just as Brick Lane's cooking today doesn't quite live up to its former reputation, there's a distance itself between Brick Lane and Monica Ali's well-known book of the same name. Although critically acclaimed and defended by some in the local community, the book upset others in the area, who didn't like the picture it painted. In 2006 several public meetings railed against the filming of Ali's book. Eventually, the producers and co-financiers Film Four abandoned plans to shoot scenes along Brick Lane itself.

where you visit the home of a family of 18th century-Huguenot silk weavers, is quite thrilling. Not only are the interiors meticulously restored, but creaking floorboards, rumpled sheets and partially abandoned meals also create the impression the family has just left the room.

GEFFRYE MUSEUM
☎ 7739 9893; www.geffrye-museum.org.uk; 136 Kingsland Rd E2; admission free, donation requested; 10am-5pm Tue-Sat, noon-5pm Sun; Old St or Liverpool St

It's hard not to be charmed by this museum of English interior design, unexpectedly sitting in a sun-dappled green lawn on a distinctly run-down part of Kingsland Rd. Set in

14 ivy-clad almshouses built for the poor, the museum guides you from the 17th to 21st centuries with a line of re-created period rooms.

KINETICA

☎ 7392 9674; www.kinetica-museum .org; Spitalfields Market E1; admission free, prices vary for talks; 🕙 11am-6pm Wed-Sun; ⊖ Liverpool St

There always seems to be something eye-catching going on within the clear glass walls of the UK's first museum dedicated to kinetic, electric and magnetic art. Whether it's a robot playing drums or a giant inflatable figure 'squirming' on the floor, it just seems to draw passers-by in.

The Old Truman Brewery

THE DEVIL'S CHURCH?

While pundits rave about the recent renovation, we're still chuckling at the 'Satanic' myths surrounding 18th-century **Christ Church Spitalfields** (☎ 020 7377 6793; www.christ churchspitalfields.org; Commercial St E1; ⏱ 11am-4pm Tue, 1-4pm Sun, plus if not in use 10am-4pm Mon & Wed-Fri; ⊖ Liverpool St). Designed by Nicholas Hawksmoor, a reputed Dionysian, its small portholes above tall, narrow windows are supposed to replicate pagan fertility symbols, and allegedly a pentacle star can be drawn between this and other Hawksmoor churches. What's beyond doubt is that Christ Church is built on a Roman cemetery and took a direct lightning hit in 1841.

◐ SUNDAY UP MARKET & TRUMAN BREWERY

☎ 7770 6100; www.sundayupmarket .co.uk, www.trumanbrewery.com; Dray Walk E1; ⏱ Up Market 10am-5pm Sun; ⊖ Liverpool St

The Old Truman Brewery was once the capital's largest, but since the early 1990s it has been home to a host of creative businesses. Today you'll find shops, bars and a Sunday barbecue along Dray Walk, bordering the building. Inside is the Up Market, housing many of the stallholders who lost plots in the main Spitalfields Market when the new retail development there moved in. It's more of the same young designer fashion, but with loads more space to breath between the stalls.

◐ WHITE CUBE GALLERY

☎ 7930 5373; www.whitecube.com; 48 Hoxton Sq N1; admission free; ⏱ 10am-6pm Tue-Sat; ⊖ Old St

While the main operations of this cutting-edge private gallery have relocated to Mason's Yard (p87), this tiny, two-floored cube continues with some intriguing exhibitions.

◐ WHITECHAPEL ART GALLERY

☎ 7522 7888; www.whitechapel.org; 80-82 Whitechapel Rd; admission free, charges for a few exhibitions; ⏱ 11am-6pm Tue, Wed & Fri-Sun, 11am-9pm Thu; ⊖ Aldgate East

Along with the ICA (p83), Photographers' Gallery (p47), and Serpentine Gallery (p100), this is much loved by art-college students, their lecturers and the avant-garde cognoscenti. But check its events programme, as well as exhibitions. Friday nights have already seen one local cult in the Wired Women event and the place is due to double in size in 2008.

NEIGHBOURHOODS

HOXTON, SHOREDITCH & SPITALFIELDS

SHOP

A GOLD

☎ 7247 2487; 42 Brushfield St E1;
🕑 11am-8pm Mon-Fri, 11am-6pm Sun;
⊖ Liverpool St

A lovingly restored Georgian building houses this old-fashioned British shop, with damson gin, ginger beer, elderflower cordial, pork pies, Eccles cakes, fudge, jars full of boiled sweets and other nostalgic treats.

ABSOLUTE VINTAGE

☎ 7247 3883; www.absolutevintage
.co.uk; 15 Hanbury St E1; 🕑 noon-7pm
Tue-Sat, 11am-7pm Sun; ⊖ Liverpool St

'Vintage' dressing has been the fashion in London recently. Of

A Gold

course, that's just a posh word for secondhand, as is patently clear in this store full of unusually affordable women's frocks and men's suits. Choice rather than quality is the watchword here.

BEYOND RETRO
☎ 7613 363; www.beyondretro.com; 112 Cheshire St E2; 🕙 10am-6pm Mon-Sat, 11am-7pm Sun; ⊖ Liverpool St
Another huge warehouse, this time stacked full of 10,000 pieces of secondhand American clobber. Beyond Retro is not only worth visiting in its own right, it's also the perfect excuse to explore the growing number of funky outlets lining Cheshire St.

COLUMBIA ROAD FLOWER MARKET
www.columbia-flower-market.freespace .com; Columbia Rd E2; 🕙 8am-2pm Sun; ⊖ Old St or Bethnal Green, 🚌 Cambridge Heath, 🚌 26, 48 or 55
A lovely mix of the urban and natural, this busy, buzzing market lets you mooch between potted plants and blooms – from common to exotic – while popping into the shops and cafés lining the route.

LADEN SHOWROOMS
☎ 7247 2431; www.laden.co.uk; 103 Brick Lane E1; 🕙 noon-6pm Mon-Sat, 10.30am-6pm Sun; ⊖ Liverpool St or Aldgate East

Columbia Road Flower Market

Recently redecorated and repainted, this is a great place to come to get your eye tuned in to what's fashionable on the streets of London. Unlike many other über-cool boutiques, it's stuffed to the gills with a wide variety and quantity of clothes for guys and gals from different young designers.

🏠 SPITALFIELDS MARKET
www.spitalfields.co.uk; Brushfield St E1; ⏰ 10am-4pm Mon-Fri, 9am-5pm Sun, Fine Foods Market 10am-5pm Thu, Fri & Sun; ⊖ Liverpool St
Admittedly, the new corporate retail development taking up half the space means this market doesn't feel quite as cutting-edge cool as it once did. However, it's still pretty damn funky, and there are more things you could pack in your suitcase to take home than at the equally popular but food-orientated Borough Market (p142). See p25 for what's on sale at Spitalfields. Sunday is the main day. The market is located off Brushfield St.

🏠 START
☎ 7739 3636; 42-44 Rivington St; ⏰ 10.30am-6.30pm Mon-Fri, 11am-6pm Sat, 1-5pm Sun; ⊖ Liverpool St
Punk rock meets designer in a womenswear boutique that offers labels like Cacharel, Issa and Junya Watanabe but also prides itself on offering some of London's most flattering jeans.

🏠 TATTY DEVINE
☎ 7739 9009; www.tattydevine.com; 236 Brick Lane E1; ⏰ 10am-6pm Mon-Fri, 11am-7pm Sat & Sun; ⊖ Liverpool St
Although this store has become famous for its baked Perspex name necklaces (get your own for £25), there's much more here. Cheeky, funky jewellery and accessories are created from surprising materials such as crisps, crochet, berries, guitar plectrums and price tags. The latest collections have added a sci-fi space theme. There's also a branch in Soho (p55).

HEAD DOWN TO TOOTING
If you're a true curry junkie and neither Brick Lane nor Whitechapel will do, the capital's contemporary hotspot is in the suburban wilds of SW17 – or Tooting. Near Tooting Broadway and Tooting Bec tube stations, you'll find rows of neighbouring curry houses, from Bangladeshi to Sri Lankan, including the following:
Kastoori (☎ 8767 7027; 188 Upper Tooting Rd SW17) Excellent Gujarati cuisine, by way of Africa, which is obviously lovingly homemade rather than churned out on an assembly line. Like no other Indian food you'll ever eat.
Masaledar (☎ 8767 7676; 121 Upper Tooting Rd SW17) Tandoori house with East African specialities.
Radha Krishna Bhavan (☎ 8767 3462; 86 Tooting High St SW17) Serving superlative Keralan cuisine.

EAT

🍴 CANTEEN

British   ££

☎ 0845 686 1122; www.canteen.co.uk;
2 Crispin Pl E1; 🕙 11am-11pm Mon-Fri,
9am-11pm Sat & Sun; ⊖ Liverpool St

If the Crispin Pl retail development that's taken over half of Spitalfields market has brought some benefits, this is certainly one. It's nice to linger in Canteen's minimalist modern interior, while the British menu is hearty and filling, with roasts, fresh fish and classics like macaroni cheese, pork belly with apples and devilled kidneys.

🍴 GREEN & RED

Mexican   ££

☎ 7749 9670 1122; www.greenred
.co.uk; 51 Bethnal Green Rd E1; 🕙 lunch
& dinner Mon-Fri, noon-10.30pm Sat &
Sun; ⊖ Liverpool St

Good-looking Green & Red is a real boon to the dodgy-looking end of Shoreditch, with its devotion to tequila (it's good as a bar, too) and its authentic Mexican menu. Dishes like *ceviche* with pomegranate, *birria* (lamb shank in beer, cloves and chilli) and *carnitas* (slow-roasted pork belly with chilli and orange salt) are light years away from bog-standard Tex-Mex fare.

MORE EAST END JAPES

Bistrotheque (☎ 8983 7900; www
.bistrotheque.com; 23-27 Wadeson
St E2; 🕙 dinner Mon-Sat, lunch
& dinner Sun; ⊖ Bethnal Green)
made a splash in 2006 by bringing 'guerrilla dining' to London, when it launched a 'pop-up' Christmas-only restaurant in the Truman Brewery. However, this cult venue's reputation for food is rather mixed (even within Lonely Planet). So you're safer coming to this converted East End warehouse for its cocktails and cabaret 'happenings'. Enjoy delicious drinks with quirky names like Camp Harry (based on Campari) and Hard Lemonade, or watch cabaret stars the Puppini Sisters, Tranny Lip-Synching and the occasional bit of gay bingo.

🍴 FIFTEEN

Italian   ££-££££

☎ 0871 330 1515; www.fifteen
restaurant.com; 15 Westland Pl;
🕙 breakfast, lunch & dinner; ⊖ Old St

UK youngsters have been foolishly suspicious of Jamie Oliver's healthy school dinners, but persuading customers to eat has never been a problem in his restaurant, where people battle with a hellish phone system to get a booking. The best solution is to try the more informal, cheaper trattoria, where a proportion of the seating is kept aside for walk-ins. Food ranges from good to superlative.

NEIGHBOURHOODS

HOXTON, SHOREDITCH & SPITALFIELDS

🍴 GIRAFFE
Modern International   ££

☎ 3116 2000; www.giraffe.net; 1 Crispin Pl E1; ⏰ 8am-11pm Mon-Fri, 9am-10.30pm Sat & Sun; ⊖ Liverpool St

Don't baulk at this being a chain outlet; its 'world food' of burgers, coarse-cut chips, falafel, salad wraps, burritos, stir fries and shakes (particularly the Giddy Giraffe) is all fresh and delicious, plus there are more choices for vegetarians than at Canteen (p129), next door. Giraffe's staff sometimes make people queue even when tables are free, but don't baulk at that either.

🍴 LES TROIS GARÇONS
French   £££-££££

☎ 7613 1924; 1 Club Row E1; ⏰ dinner Mon-Sat; ⊖ Liverpool St

Crammed full of stuffed animals in tiaras, hanging handbags

FOR COCKTAIL-LOVERS
In the mood for a mojito? Don't do it! At least, that's the plea from leading London bar staff, who say they're sick of mixing this ubiquitous cocktail of the moment. If on the other hand, you're up for being more adventurous with your mixed drinks, try one of the following:
> Annexe 3 (p67)
> Blue Bar (see the boxed text, p107)
> Hawksmoor (p134)
> LAB (p58)
> Loungelover (p134)

and a standing alligator with a sceptre, this is a piece of theatre as much as it's a restaurant. So, luckily, you're usually too absorbed in your surroundings to care that the overly fussy French cuisine is only passable for the price. It's great for celebrations and sometimes good for star-spotting too.

🍴 NEW TAYYAB
          Indian   £-££

☎ 7247 9543; 83 Fieldgate St E1; ⏰ dinner; ⊖ Whitechapel

One of London's finest, this buzzing Punjabi restaurant specialises in *seekh* kebabs, *masala* fish and other sizzling and delicious hot plates. While it's great for meat-lovers, some vegetarians might find some of the *karahi* wok dishes a little oily. BYO alcohol.

🍴 PRINCESS
Gastropub   ££

☎ 7729 9270; 76 Paul St EC2; ⏰ lunch & dinner Mon-Fri, dinner Sat; ⊖ Old St

This is a great-looking, great-tasting gastropub with an upstairs dining room combining bold, swirly floral wallpaper and Balinese seating. The menu combines Mediterranean and a few Southeast Asian influences, with lovely meringues for dessert. Service tends towards 'relaxed' though, so give yourself plenty of time to enjoy it.

DRINK

BIG CHILL BAR

☎ 7392 9180; www.bigchill.net; Truman Brewery, Dray Walk E1; ⏱ noon-midnight Mon-Thu, to 1am Fri & Sat, 11am-11pm Sun; ⊖ Old St

This DJ bar is also a good venue for a morning-after comedown and aims to recreate the semi-grown-up atmosphere of the Big Chill festival, with food, low sofas, a chandelier and an animal trophy or two.

DRAGON BAR

☎ 7490 7110; 5 Leonard St N1; ⏱ noon-11pm Sun & Mon, to midnight Tue & Wed, to 1am Thu, to 2am Fri & Sat; ⊖ Old St

Super-cool, in that louche, moody (as opposed to overtly posey)

HACKNEY & BETHNAL GREEN

When a TV property show in 2006 named Hackney 'the worst place in the UK to live' it provoked a huge backlash from locals who began churning out 'I love Hackney' badges in revenge. In fact, the area is swiftly gentrifying. Hackney is starting to happen, particularly if the fact that Nike recently purloined the borough's logo – and got its knuckles rapped – is anything to go by. Although it's still a fairly urban and gritty neighbourhood, rising property prices in nearby Shoreditch mean trendy flat-buyers, restaurants, shops and clubs are all moving in here. Not an area everyone visits on a short trip to London, it appeals to those who are a little ahead of the crowd, for, among others, the following reasons:

Broadway Market (www.broadwaymarket.co.uk; Broadway Market E8; ⏱ Sat; ⊖ Bethnal Green, 🚊 London Fields) London's best up-and-coming market, with food stalls selling cheeses, fairy cakes and Indian dishes, plus clothes stalls, with restaurants, pubs, and interesting boutiques lining the street.

Bethnal Green Museum of Childhood (☎ 8980 2415; www.vam.ac.uk/moc; Cambridge Heath & Old Ford Rds E2; ⏱ 10am-5.45pm; ⊖ Bethnal Green) An already brilliant collection of toys throughout that ages, reopened after refurbishment in late 2006.

Burberry Factory Shop (☎ 8985 3344; 29-53 Chatham Pl E9; ⏱ 11am-6pm Mon-Fri, 10am-5pm Sat, 11am-5pm Sun; ⊖ Bethnal Green) For discounts on samples, seconds or last season's collection of this 'no chavs please' Brit brand.

Primark (☎ 8985 2689; www.primark.co.uk; 365-371 Mare St E8; ⏱ 9am-6pm Mon-Sat, 10am-4pm Sun; ⊖ Hackney Central) Turning out a much-wanted spotted summer dress and cheap cashmere cardigans has earned this discount clothes chain the nickname 'Primani'. Check the website for other branches.

Nick Strangeway,
General manager of Hawksmoor and leading mixologist

Cocktails London does best Bars are returning to the classics, rediscovering old recipes and tweaking them to modern tastes. There's not really one 'London' drink, but bar guru Dick Bradsell's wonderful Bramble (gin soured with lime or lemon juice, topped with *crème de mure* and blackberries) is on many bar lists. **Which cocktail to order** As a customer in an untested bar, I would stick to a classic like a martini or Manhattan, specify how I would like it (ie dry or wet with the martini, or dry, perfect or sweet with a Manhattan) and maybe even suggest a brand of spirit. **Londoners as customers** They're becoming more aware of what they're drinking as part of a broader awareness of food and wine. The bar scene is a natural extension to London's new, dynamic and world-class restaurants. **Should good old London pubs be worried?** Hopefully not. I enjoy a good pint as much as anyone, particularly in the Golden Heart (right) in Spitalfields or Soho's **French House** (Map p48, D4; ☎ 7437 2477; 49 Dean St W1). I do worry, though, that the local boozer might be replaced by the ubiquitous wooden-floored gastro-palace serving mediocre midchannel Med cuisine!

Hoxton way, Dragon is all exposed brick, secondhand sofas, Chinese lanterns, velvet curtains and ironic retro touches. Look down for the sign; it's on the stairs. Alternatively, watch out for the 'No suits, please'.

▼ DREAMBAGSJAGUARSHOES

☎ 7729 5830; 34-36 Kingsland Rd E2; ⏱ 5pm-1am; ⊖ Old St
A perfect barometer of the latest ugly-1980s dots-and-stripes Hoxton fashion – and more importantly the latest mussed-up, diagonally cut or dyed hairstyle – this tiny, artfully shabby bar takes its name from the two former shop spaces it occupies. Check out the graffiti wall downstairs.

▼ FAVELA CHIC

☎ 7613 5228; www.favelachic.com; 91 Great Eastern St E N1; ⏱ from 6pm Tue-Sun; ⊖ Old St
The 'poverty chic' is more self-conscious and forced than at the Foundry, diagonally opposite, and the shantytown theme has raised some eyebrows. But if you're a fan of all things Brazilian you just might be able to forgive the staff's high-handedness and the slight naffness of this massively well-publicised place.

▼ FOUNDRY

☎ 7739 6900; www.foundry.tv; 84-6 Great Eastern St EC2; ⏱ 4.30-11pm Tue-Fri, from 2.30pm Sat & Sun; ⊖ Old St
The eccentric Foundry so genuinely doesn't give a hoot about being hip that it manages to be impossibly hip and welcoming to all simultaneously. The ramshackle furniture, makeshift bar, graffitied toilets, cheap beer and arty 'happenings' are reminiscent of an illegal squat bar in Eastern Europe or New York's Meatpacking District. Seminal.

▼ GEORGE & DRAGON

☎ 7012 1100; 2 Hackney Rd E2; ⏱ 5-11pm; ⊖ Old St
One of the most popular gay destinations in Hoxton also has a large straight following, probably for the way highlife and lowlife also converge here. Good-looking staff, minor celebs, fashionistas and locals come for the DJs and fun and hedonistic atmosphere. Weekend nights, especially Sunday, are heaving, hectic and legendary. It's quieter during the week.

▼ GOLDEN HEART

☎ 7247 2158; 110 Commercial St E1; ⊖ Liverpool St
The 'Britart' pub is patronised by Tracey Emin and the Chapman Bros and is also famous for its

charmingly, eccentric landlady Sandra. Sadly, sunny markets days are the worst time to visit, when all the chairs are pulled onto the footpath. At other times, the beaded curtains and solid wooden seats create a comfy living-room feel.

▼ HAWKSMOOR
☎ 7247 7392; 157 Commercial St E1; 🕑 6pm-1am Mon-Sat; ⊖ Liverpool St
Unique-sounding and amazing-tasting cocktails are described in intriguing detail, mixed by one of London's best bartenders and served in interesting glasses here. What more could you want for a great evening out? Oh, the steaks are renowned, too.

▼ LOUNGELOVER
☎ 7012 1234; 1 Whitby St E1; 🕑 6pm-midnight, to 1am Fri & Sat; ⊖ Liverpool St
With the same sparkly 'junk shop rearranged by gay stylist' look of its sister establishment Les Trois Garçons (p130), trendy Loungelover was the original maximalist

London bar and is still the best. The mishmash of chandeliers, antiques, street lanterns and comfy lounge chairs materialise just seconds away from the run-down streets outside.

▼ TEN BELLS
☎ 7366 1721; 84 Commercial St E1; 🕑 11am-midnight, to 1am Thu-Sat; ⊖ Liverpool St
With a delightfully scruffy historic sign, flock wallpaper and tiles, this Jack the Ripper pub has been taken over by trendy Spitalfielders since banning tour groups.

▼ VIBE BAR
☎ 7377 2899; Truman Brewery, 91-95 Brick Lane E1; 🕑 11am-11.30pm, to 1am Fri-Sat; ⊖ Liverpool St
This longstanding bar-club has settled into a comfortable routine, and is best in warmer months for the barbecues and food stall in its fairy-lit courtyard. Or enjoy an early evening drink in the bar (which has arcade games and computer terminals) before moving on.

STRIKING CABARET GOLD
It's funny how a place with a dowdy name like the Bethnal Green Working Men's Club and resembling a school hall became London's hottest club. But debt is the underlying reason. Like many WMCs across the country – established as the name suggests as a hub of working-class communities in the Victorian era – Bethnal Green had seen its membership decline and owed the breweries some £40,000. Then along came club promoter Warren Dent and offered a cabaret solution. The old regulars haven't been kicked out; they're just enjoying themselves in the basement.

PLAY

⭐ 93 FEET EAST

☎ 7247 3293; www.93feeteast.co.uk;
150 Brick Lane E2; ⌚ bar 11am-11pm,
to 2am Fri & Sat; club 8pm-2am Thu-Sat;
⊖ Liverpool St or Aldgate East

Probably the most popular club
in Shoreditch, 93 Feet East runs
some top music nights and is a
regular home for the monthly
Rock 'n' Roll Cinema (www.myspace.com
/rocknrollcinema). The venue itself
is appealing too: there's a courtyard, three good-sized rooms
packed with a typically cool East
London crowd, and an outdoor
terrace.

⭐ 333

☎ 7739 5949; www.333mother.com;
333 Old St EC1; ⌚ 8pm-midnight Wed &
Thu, 10pm-5am Fri & Sat, 10pm-4am Sun;
⊖ Old St

It was once at the forefront of the
Shoreditch scene, but today's 333
attracts a less preening crowd
and fewer lengthy queues. But
this three-storey venue's interior
has always been determinedly
down to earth and that hasn't
changed, with everything from
drum-and-bass to electro, indie
guitar music, new wave and
techno – and there are even
Polish nights.

⭐ BETHNAL GREEN WORKING MEN'S CLUB

☎ 7739 2727; www.workersplaytime
.net; 42 Pollard Row E2; ⌚ 8pm-2am
Thu-Sat, 7pm-midnight Sun, tea-dances
usually from 4pm; ⊖ Bethnal Green

London's club of the moment
mines a rich vein of postmodern irony, with its heart
of lights on stage and events
like 1950s tea-dances (girls on
rollerskates serving tea around
trestle-tables laden with cakes),
lounge-meisters The Karminsky
Experience, cabaret evening Toot-
Sweet, the Goth Hellfire Club,
Dolly Parton evenings and more.
Although claimed by the 'cabaret'
crowd, you don't really find much
burlesque here; it's more relaxed.
Most dress up in vintage apparel,
but it's not a massive problem if
you don't.

⭐ CARGO

☎ 7739 3440; www.cargo-london
.com; 83 Rivington St EC2; ⌚ noon-1am
Mon-Thu, noon-3am Fri, 6pm-3am Sat,
noon-midnight Sun; ⊖ Old St

Spread over three different spaces
under brick railway arches, Cargo
is best known for its imaginative
music policy, with a rolling programme of Latin house, nu-jazz,
funk, groove and soul, DJs, global
(particularly Latin) bands, up-and-
coming bands, demos and rare
grooves.

NEIGHBOURHOODS

HOXTON, SHOREDITCH & SPITALFIELDS

>SOUTH BANK

No place better represents London's recent reinvention than South Bank. In around a decade, it's gone from slightly seedy underbelly to trim, taut and terrific middle. Two of 21st-century London's major landmarks have come to be located here. The London Eye has been raised across the water from the neo-Gothic parliament at Westminster, while the disused Bankside Power Station has morphed into Tate Modern.

This is where new London faces off old London, and both come out winners. And if you follow the Silver Jubilee Walkway and the Thames Path along the southern riverbank you're in pole position to see it.

In the late 1990s celebrity chef Jamie Oliver's decision to shop at Borough Market was considered avant-garde. Now that same market is one of the city's most popular. With new restaurants, bars, offices and flats springing up, this neighbourhood just keeps on getting better.

SOUTH BANK

◎ SEE
BFI Southbank		(see 38)
City Hall	1	G2
County Hall	2	B3
Design Museum	3	H3
Fashion & Textile Museum	4	G3
Hayward Gallery	5	B2
Imperial War Museum	6	C4
London Eye	7	B3
Millenium Bridge	8	D1
Old Operating Theatre Museum & Herb Garret	9	F2
RIB London Voyages	10	A3
Shakespeare's Globe	11	E2
Tate Modern	12	D2

🛍 SHOP
Borough Market	13	F2
Cockfighter of Bermondsey	14	G3
Konditor & Cook	15	E2
Oxo Tower	16	C1

🍴 EAT
Anchor & Hope	17	C3
Baltic	18	D3
Bermondsey Kitchen	19	G4
BluePrint Café		(see 3)
Champor-Champor	20	F3
Garrison	21	G3
Roast		(see 13)
Table	22	D2
Tapas Brindisa	23	F2
Tas Borough	24	E2
Tas Ev	25	C2
Tas Pide	26	E2
Village East	27	G3

🍷 DRINK
George Inn	28	F2
King's Arms	29	C2
Laughing Gravy	30	D3
Monmouth Coffee Company	31	E2
Wine Wharf	32	E2

★ PLAY
Crash	33	A6
Ministry of Sound	34	D4
National Film Theatre		(see 37)
National Theatre	35	B2
Old Vic	36	C3
Shakespeare's Globe		(see 11)
South Bank Centre	37	B2
Young Vic	38	C3

Please see over for map

SEE

◉ BFI SOUTHBANK

☎ 7928 3232; www.bfi.org.uk; South Bank SE1; Mediatheque & gallery admission free; ☷ 11am-11pm, Mediatheque 11am-9pm, last session 8.15pm; ✆ Waterloo or Embankment

Opened around February 2007, BFI Southbank not only encompasses the cinemas of the National Film Theatre (p148), a shop and bars, but also a 'Mediatheque' where you can watch historic or other British film clips, as well as a gallery showing contemporary video and film art.

◉ CITY HALL

☎ 7983 4100; www.london.gov.uk; The Queen's Walk SE1; admission free; ☷ 8am-8pm Mon-Fri, plus occasional weekends; ✆ Tower Hill or London Bridge

London's City Hall is by the architect who designed Berlin's famous Bundestag (parliament) dome, and it shows. Sir Norman Foster has even recreated the spiral walkway inside this globular-shaped glass construction. Is it a wonky egg, a testicle on a spaceman's helmet? You decide. Although the bits regularly open to the public aren't that interesting, the walkway and top-floor viewing gallery are open on occasional weekends (check the website).

SOUTH BANK REFURBISHMENT

Built between the 1950s and the 1970s, the South Bank Centre arts complex near Waterloo has always been an unapologetic exponent of concrete brutalism. It never much appealed to most Londoners, and since 2003 it's been getting a softening facelift.

Firstly the new BFI centre is coming out of wraps. Then the Royal Festival Hall, generally the least offensive of the buildings, built in Portland stone in 1951, should be unveiled in mid-2007. After this, landscaping and more work will continue to improve the place's utility.

◉ COUNTY HALL

Westminster Bridge Rd SE1; ✆ Waterloo or Westminster

This magnificent building, with curved façade and colonnades, is an older city hall – home to Greater London Council before PM Margaret Thatcher temporarily abolished local government for London in 1986. (Local government was reinstated in 2000.) Today County Hall boasts two hotels, a few restaurants and entirely missable attractions including the London Aquarium and the Dalí Experience.

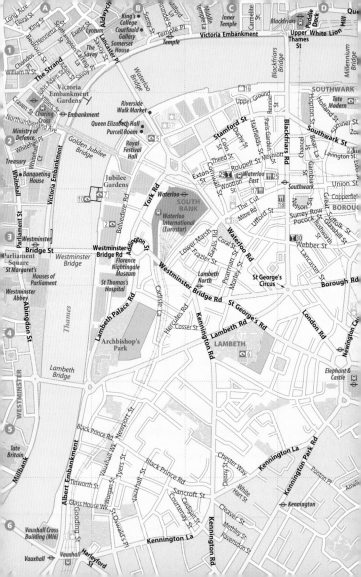

⬛ DESIGN MUSEUM

☎ 7940 8790; www.designmuseum
.org; 28 Shad Thames SE1; admission
varies; ⏲ 10am-5.45pm Sat-Thu, last
entry 5.15pm; ⊖ Tower Hill or London
Bridge

In this minimalist white building, you'll find an interesting
programme of temporary shows,
taking a wide interpretation of
the word 'design'. The Design
Museum's great shop is also a
constant, with lavish coffee-table
books on design and architecture,
plus things that the design-
conscious homebody wants and
needs.

⬛ HAYWARD GALLERY

☎ information 7960 5226, bookings
0870 169 1000; www.hayward.org.uk;
Belvedere Rd SE1; adult/student/senior
£9/5/6, but can vary, Mon half-price;
⏲ 10am-6pm, to 8pm Tue & Wed, to
9pm Fri; ⊖ Waterloo

Although tarted up with a new
foyer a few years ago, this remains
the ugliest of the stone-and-
concrete hulks that comprise the
South Bank Centre (p149). Still, the
spacious interior makes a great exhibition space for the programme
of contemporary art exhibitions
(check listings) – proving that
brutal modernism is at least good
for something.

⬛ IMPERIAL WAR MUSEUM

☎ 7416 5320, 09001 600140; www.iwm
.org.uk; Lambeth Rd SE1; admission free;
⏲ 10am-6pm; ⊖ Lambeth North or
Waterloo

Even committed pacifists appreciate the Imperial War Museum.
That's because, alongside its
internationally famous collection
of planes, tanks and other military
hardware, it provides a telling les-
son in modern history. Highlights
include a re-created WWI trench
and bomb shelter and a Holocaust
exhibition.

⬛ LONDON EYE

☎ 0870 500 0600; www.londoneye.com;
Jubilee Gardens SE1; adult/child/senior
flight £13/6.50/10, discovery flight
£15/7.50/11; ⏲ 10am-8pm, to 9pm Jun-
Sep, closed Jan; ⊖ Waterloo

Still going strong years after it
was supposed to be dismantled,
the world's largest Ferris wheel
takes you on a gentle, 30-minute
ride looking down on London's
rooftops. There's usually no
commentary, but it makes a huge
difference to know what you're
seeing, so at least grab an in-flight
miniguide (£4.50) before boarding.
Discovery Flights do have commentary, but the standard seems
to vary wildly. Finally, don't book
too far ahead, to keep abreast of
that changeable weather.

SPEED ALONG THE THAMES

Traditionally, River Thames cruises have been genteel affairs, with ships pootling along at some seven to eight nautical knots. But after a traditional guided tour down to Canary Wharf, the new services from **RIB London Voyages** (☎ 7928 2350; www .londonribvoyages; London Eye, Waterloo Millennium Pier, Westminster Bridge Rd SE1; adult/child £26/16; ⏰ hourly 11.15am-4.15pm year-round) roar back up the river at 30 to 35 knots. These rigid inflatable boats are the best choice for thrill-seekers, who want to make likes James Bond on the Thames. For other operators, see p223.

◖ MILLENNIUM BRIDGE
Bankside SE1; ⊖ Southwark, Mansion House or St Paul's
Forever doomed to be known as the 'wobbly' bridge, although it's been perfectly stable for many years, the Millennium Bridge has become a much-admired feature of the 21st-century London skyline. It now carries some 10,000 people a day…and unfortunately they all seem to be on it the same time as you! Don't forget to look at St Paul's Cathedral through the Perspex decking at the bridge's southern end.

◖ OLD OPERATING THEATRE MUSEUM & HERB GARRET
☎ 7188 2679; www.thegarret.org.uk; 9a St Thomas St SE1; adult/child/concession/family £4.75/2.95/3.95/12.50; ⏰ 10.30am-5pm; ⊖ London Bridge
This is not one of the area's big-ticket attractions, but it's a true gem nonetheless; this former Victorian surgical theatre is more of a visceral thrill than the lame London Dungeon nearby. Just take a look at the gallbladder-removal instruments and the old wooden operating theatre used in Victorian times, or ask the attendants to explain about speed surgery – when doctors whipped off patients' limbs without antiseptic or anaesthetic in less than a minute. You'll never complain about your own doctor again! (Note this museum is reached by a steep and winding spiral staircase only.)

◖ SHAKESPEARE'S GLOBE
☎ 7902 1500; www.shakespeares-globe .org; 21 New Globe Walk SE1; exhibition & tour adult/child/concession/family £9/6.50/7.50/25; ⏰ 9am-5pm May-Sep, 10am-5pm Oct-Apr, tours every 30min until noon, tours of nearby Rose Theatre after noon; ⊖ London Bridge
This is an authentic replica of the Globe Theatre where Shakespeare worked, which finally closed down in 1642. While

seeing a performance (see p149) is the best way to appreciate the bawdy interaction between actors and audience during the Elizabethan era, there are also instructive tours and an exhibition if you don't have time or can't get tickets.

Tate Modern

 TATE MODERN
☎ recorded information 7887 8008, tickets 7887 8888; www.tate.org.uk; Bankside SE1; admission free, £3 donation requested, prices vary for special exhibitions; ⏰ 10am-6pm Sun-Thu, 10am-10pm Fri & Sat; ⊖ Southwark

The world's most successful contemporary art gallery hasn't always been about the art, but more about the building, location and views. So the rearrangement of its permanent works (see p12) is a refreshing bonus, rather than a vital reinvention before the new planned building extension. Plus it has had some stunning temporary exhibitions recently. The Tate boat service powers to Tate Britain every 40 minutes (£4.30, Travelcard holders £2.85).

🛍 SHOP

🛍 **BOROUGH MARKET**
☎ 7407 1002; www.boroughmarket .org.uk; Borough High St SE1; ⏰ 11am-5pm Thu, noon-6pm Fri, 9am-4pm Sat; ⊖ London Bridge

Borough is the market *du jour* among Londoners, who with all the conviction of the born-again believer have become obsessive foodies. Crowds weave between stalls selling fresh produce and speciality takeaway foods – making 'London's Larder' a heady

Borough Market

sociological, visual, olfactory and taste experience. Meanwhile a community of food shops has sprung up along surrounding streets. Saturday is madly busy, but the market opens on Friday and now Thursday too.

KONDITOR & COOK
☎ 7407 5100; www.konditorandcook
.com; 10 Stoney St SE1; 🕙 7.30am-6pm
Mon-Fri, 8am-2.30pm Sat; ⊖ London
Bridge
There aren't many places we'd happily pay £2.75 for a fairy (or 'magic') cake but – for a special treat – the confections this bakery turns out really do taste and look that good. Brightly iced ginger-bread men, treacle pie, seasonal

German Stollen and mince pies are among the other offerings.

OXO TOWER
☎ 7401 2255; www.oxotower.co.uk;
Bargehouse St SE1; ⊖ Southwark,
London Bridge or Blackfriars
With the name O-X-O spelled out in lights down its tower, this Art Deco building looks fantastic. However, its major appeal is…no, not the overpriced restaurant on the 8th floor or even the viewing platform on the same level, but the small designer boutiques with-in. There's interesting fine china at Bodo Sperlein, quirky household objects at Black + Blum and more to browse through, including a small art gallery.

EAT

Don't forget to also peruse the gastropubs and restaurants in Bermondsey (see the boxed text, p148).

🍴 ANCHOR & HOPE
Gastropub   ££
☎ 7928 9898; The Cut SE1; 🕑 lunch Tue-Sat, dinner Mon-Sat; ⊖ Southwark
An award-winning gastropub certain to delight carnivores but probably terrify vegetarians, the

Anchor & Hope specialises in gutsy dishes like snails, pink lamb's neck, pig's heart and pigeon. No advance bookings are taken, so arrive early or late. Alternatively, wait in the adjoining bar.

🍴 BALTIC
Polish/Eastern European   ££-£££
☎ 7928 1111; 74 Blackfriars Rd SE1; 🕑 lunch & dinner Mon-Sat, dinner Sun; ⊖ Southwark
The swish, shiny bar lined with amber and vodkas tends to attract a buttoned-up after-work crowd, but the food in the high-ceilinged restaurant is excellent, taking Polish to the mainstream, with excellent renditions of blini, herrings, *pierogi* and caviar, black pudding and smoked eel.

🍴 BLUEPRINT CAFÉ
International   £££-££££
☎ 7378 7031; Design Museum, Butler's Wharf SE1; 🕑 lunch daily, dinner Mon-Sat; ⊖ Tower Hill
Really you come to the BluePrint Café for the views of the Gherkin and Tower Bridge, which are spectacular – much better than anywhere else along this strip and enhanced by the tiny blue binoculars on each table. The food isn't bad at all, and has some un-usual touches, like nettle soup, but prices are unquestionably inflated by the privileged outlook.

🍴 ROAST British £££-££££

☎ 7940 1300; www.roast-restaurant
.com; 1st fl, Borough Market, Borough
High St SE1; ⏱ breakfast, lunch & dinner
Mon-Sat, lunch Sun; ⊖ London Bridge

In a steel-and-glass building above Borough Market, with a view of St Paul's Cathedral, Roast has a wonderful atmosphere, especially at night. The food is a little more hit-and-miss, even though it only aims for seriously upmarket comfort food, with roast beef or chicken, suckling pig etc accompanied by seasonal vegetables. You can't fault the breakfasts though.

🍴 TABLE British £

☎ 7401 2760; 83 Southwark St SE1;
⏱ 8am-6pm Mon-Thu, to 11pm Fri;
⊖ Southwark or London Bridge

A handy canteen-style place for a bite to eat after a visit to Tate Modern, albeit you're swapping the river views for casual dishes made from fresh Borough Market ingredients.

🍴 TAPAS BRINDISA
Spanish ££-£££

☎ 7357 8880; www.brindisa.com; 18-20
Southwark St SE1; ⏱ lunch & dinner
Mon-Thu, breakfast, lunch & dinner Fri &
Sat; ⊖ London Bridge

Brindisa offers authentic and mouthwatering tapas at slightly eye-watering prices. But as ever in London, quality comes at

---

RIVERSIDE PINTS

Nothing beats enjoying a pint along with a view of the River Thames. The following places are located a bit further out of central London.
Grapes (☎ 7987 4396; 76 Narrow St E14; 🚇 Westferry)
Mayflower (☎ 7237 4088; 117 Rotherhithe St SE16; ⊖ Rotherhithe)
Prospect of Whitby (☎ 7481 1095; 57 Wapping Wall E1; ⊖ Wapping)

---

a price. There's a no-booking policy, so arrive early (around 6pm). Part of the joy of the place anyway is the buzz of perching on a pivotal corner leading to the busy Borough Market.

🍴 TAS EV Turkish ££

☎ 7620 6191; www.tasrestaurant.com;
The Arches, 97-99 Isabella St SE1; ⏱ lunch
& dinner Mon-Sat; ⊖ Southwark

The small chain of Tas restaurants is known for its tasty, reasonably priced stews and grills (not earth-shattering or sexy but very enjoyable) rather than its décor. This is a little different, being under the railway arches, atmospherically low-lit and with some Turkish fittings. **Tas Pide** (☎ 7928 3300; 20-22 New Globe Walk SE1; ⊖ London Bridge) also distinguishes itself with lower, carved chairs and tables and Turkish pizzas, while **Tas Waterloo** (☎ 7928 2111; 33 The Cut SE1; ⊖ Southwark) and

Tas Borough (☎ 7403 7200; 72 Borough High St SE1; ⊖ London Bridge) branches typify the usual modern and bland variant. All the outlets are quite buzzing and noisy though.

DRINK

There are plenty of obvious places to drink along Waterloo Rd, the Cut and the riverbank, but for something a little more special, try the following.

▾ GEORGE INN
☎ 7407 2056; Talbot Yard, 77 Borough High St SE1; ⊖ London Bridge
Despite being London's last surviving galleried coaching inn, the Heritage-listed George Inn is far from

a touristy museum piece. With its low-ceilinged, dark-panelled and wonky rooms full of enthusiastic punters, one imagines it brims with as much atmosphere as in the 17th century, when it was built. The courtyard is mobbed in summer.

▾ KING'S ARMS
☎ 7207 0784; 25 Roupell St SE1;
⊖ Waterloo
The sort of pub locals never want to see in a guidebook (yeah, sorry about that), this hidden-away winter-warmer boozer is full of character, with a traditional bar area serving up a good selection of ales and bitters in front. Out back, there's a conservatory bedecked in junk-store exotica.

Monmouth coffee drinkers at Columbia Road Flower Market (p127)

LAUGHING GRAVY
☎ 7721 7055; 154 Blackfriars Rd SE1;
⊕ Southwark

Vintage ad posters, bright paintings, potted plants and a large sauce-bottle collection make this delightful place feel a bit like a bohemian 1940s living room. As well as beer, there's a nice range of wine and, of course, some 'laughing gravy' or whisky (in this case even Scotch single malt).

MONMOUTH COFFEE COMPANY
☎ 7645 3585; www.monmouthcoffee
.co.uk; 2 Park St SE1; ⏰ 7.30am-6pm
Mon-Sat; ⊕ London Bridge

Monmouth's coffee – specifically its latte – is a top contender for the best cup in London, thanks to a variety of carefully chosen and freshly ground beans. The bare-board surroundings aren't particularly good-looking and you'll have to clamber for a seat, but who cares when it tastes this good? See p58 for the Covent Garden branch.

WINE WHARF
☎ 7940 8335; www.winewharf.co.uk;
Stoney St SE1; ⊕ London Bridge

No-one's missing anything by skipping the adjacent Vinopolis exhibition, but well-heeled wine lovers will be suitably impressed by the huge range on offer – to taste, drink or buy – here.

PLAY

CRASH
☎ 7793 9262; www.crashlondon.co.uk;
66 Goding St SE11; ⏰ every 2nd Sat;
⊕ Vauxhall

Vauxhall is generally one of London's newer gay hangouts, and Crash is its Muscle Mary heaven, with two dance floors churning

---

WORTH A TRIP FURTHER SOUTH: BRIXTON

Not everyone will get to Brixton, one of London's edgy but brilliant multicultural districts, but if you're heading south on the Victoria Line, these are the three best things it offers.

Brixton Academy (☎ 7771 2000; www.brixton-academy.co.uk; 211 Stockwell Rd SW9; ⊕ Brixton) Scuzzy but lovely former theatre, with good sightlines and a great range of gigs for a 4000-strong crowd.

Brixton Market (Reliance & Granville Arcades, Market Row, Electric Lane & Electric Ave SW9; ⏰ 8am-6pm Mon, Tue & Thu-Sat, 8am-3pm Wed; ⊕ Brixton) A wonderful melting pot of African, Caribbean and South American foodstuffs, clothes and trinkets.

Brockwell Park Lido (☎ 7274 3088; Dulwich Rd SE24; 🚇 Herne Hill) A beautifully designed 1930s number, Brockwell is one of London's best outdoor swimming pools. Call ahead, as it was due to open again in 2007 after refurbishment.

out hard beats, four bars and even a few go-go dancers.

⭐ MINISTRY OF SOUND
☎ 0870 060 0100; www.ministryofsound.com; 103 Gaunt St SE1; ⏲ 10pm-3am Wed, 10.30pm-6am Fri, midnight-9am Sat; ⊖ Elephant & Castle
More than 15 years on, this is no mere club, but an enormous global brand no longer at the cutting edge of the whole London scene. All

the same, it remains a quality act, with big-name DJs, a great sound system and, especially since a 2003 overhaul, an impressive main room.

⭐ NATIONAL FILM THEATRE
☎ 7928 3232; www.bfi.org.uk/nft; South Bank SE1; ⊖ Waterloo or Embankment
Britain's national repository of film is a magnet for cinephiles, whether it's inviting directors and stars to introduce their new releases,

BERMONDSEY
Bermondsey has been billed as 'the new Hoxton', thanks to its growing creative community living in loft warehouses. Truthfully though, it still revolves mainly around one street. Only five minutes' walk from Borough Market and London Bridge, Bermondsey St SE1 lands you in a whole other, more authentically local scene. Highlights include the following:
Bermondsey Kitchen (☎ 7407 5719; 194 Bermondsey St SE1; ⏲ lunch & dinner Mon-Sat, brunch Sun; ⊖ Borough or London Bridge) Big open-plan bistro, with hearty, filling Mediterranean meals.
Champor-Champor (☎ 7403 4600; www.champor-champor.com; 62 Weston St SE1; ⏲ dinner Mon-Sat; ⊖ London Bridge) This quirkily decorated, upmarket Malaysian restaurant serves singularly delicious fusion food. Our favourite place for a neighbourhood splurge.
Cockfighter of Bermondsey (☎ 7357 6482; www.cockfighter.co.uk; 96 Bermondsey St SE1; ⏲ 11am-7pm Tue-Fri, noon-6pm Sat; ⊖ London Bridge) T-shirts with attitude are found in this small boutique popular with DJs and pop stars.
Fashion & Textile Museum (☎ 7407 8664; www.ftmlondon.org; 83 Bermondsey St SE1; ⊖ London Bridge) Now part of Newham College, this has occasional public exhibitions. Ring ahead, and check the website or newspaper listings for the latest.
Garrison (☎ 7089 9355; 99 Bermondsey St SE1; ⏲ breakfast, lunch & dinner, plus brunch Sat & Sun; ⊖ London Bridge) Great gastropub with an old-fashioned green-tiled, vaguely beach-shack interior and fresh Mediterranean food. The best local eatery for every day.
Village East (☎ 0870 780 8271; www.villageeast.co.uk; 171 Bermondsey St SE1; ⏲ lunch & dinner; ⊖ London Bridge) A more chi-chi venue from the Garrison's owners, this place feels as New York as its name implies. Tasty food ranges from blini and tempura oysters to monkfish and lamb.

premiering hits during the London Film Festival (p36) or dusting off golden oldies for retrospectives.

⭐ NATIONAL THEATRE
☎ 7452 3000; www.nationaltheatre.org.uk; South Bank SE1; ⊖ Waterloo

The National Theatre's renaissance, which began when Nicholas Hytner took over as artistic director, is a long way from petering out yet. Audiences still keep packing out the three auditoria – the Olivier, Lyttleton and Cottesloe – for Hytner's adventurous mix of classic and modern. With the mega-successful History Boys, the theatre can even boast it's kickstarted a film.

⭐ OLD VIC
☎ 0870 060 6628; www.oldvictheatre.com, www.theambassadors.com; Waterloo Rd SE1; ⊖ Waterloo

Hollywood star Kevin Spacey's tenure as the Old Vic's artistic director hasn't lived up to expectations, but the tide seems to be turning and a good rule of thumb is this: don't miss Spacey acting in anything by Eugene O'Neill, or Ian McKellen in drag in the Christmas pantomime. For everything else, carefully peruse reviews before booking.

⭐ SHAKESPEARE'S GLOBE
☎ 7401 9919; www.shakespeares-globe.org; 21 New Globe Walk SE1; ⊖ London Bridge

Even if the production you attend comes across a bit 'theme-park Shakespeare' – and they occasionally do – you'll never forget being in an open-roofed theatre in the round that harks back to the Bard's era. 'Groundlings' with £5 tickets will need the stamina to stand all evening, as fire regulations prohibit sitting on the ground and ushers will prod you if you try! Even those with seats should bring something comfy (jacket, cushion) to prevent an aching bottom.

⭐ SOUTH BANK CENTRE
☎ 0870 380 4300; Belvedere Rd SE1; ⊖ Waterloo

Following a two-year renovation, the flagship Royal Festival Hall is back in business as a major concert venue from June 2007, taking its place alongside the smaller Queen Elizabeth Hall and Purcell Room.

⭐ YOUNG VIC
☎ 7928 6363; www.youngvic.org; 66 The Cut SE1; ⊖ Waterloo

This funky young theatre troupe has returned to its refurbished home, after several years as itinerant performers wandering the West End from theatre to theatre, leaving a wake of hits. Outside there's an eye-catching mesh façade, but the spruced-up interior leaves the auditorium as intimate as it ever was.

>GREENWICH

With maritime and regal connections dating back to the Middle Ages, Greenwich is pretty grand for a self-proclaimed 'village'. White neoclassical buildings are laid out in wonderful symmetry across Greenwich Park, while the famous Royal Observatory marks the world's Prime Meridian of time and longitude.

A couple of legendary designers are responsible for this look. In the early 17th century, Inigo Jones designed the existing Queen's House, one of England's first classical renaissance homes. Later, Sir Christopher Wren arrived to build the observatory (1675) and the Royal Hospital for Seaman (1692).

However, Greenwich is right to boast of its village atmosphere. From the hilltop near the Royal Observatory you have excellent views of the skyscrapers of Docklands, but you feel remote and protected from the stresses of the city. People picnic in the park or rummage in the second-hand bookshops and retro clothes stores. A couple of highly recommended restaurants and pubs overlooking the River Thames cap off an always pleasant interlude.

GREENWICH

◉ SEE
Cutty Sark 1 C5
Greenwich Foot Tunnel ... 2 C5
Museum in Docklands 3 B1
National Maritime
Museum 4 D5
Queen's House 5 D5
Royal Navy College 6 C5
Royal Naval College
Chapel 7 D5

Royal Naval College
Painted Hall 8 C5
Royal Observatory 9 D6

◻ SHOP
Flying Duck
Enterprises 10 C5
Greenwich Market 11 C5
Joy 12 C5

⊪ EAT
Gun 13 C2
Inside 14 C6
Plateau 15 B1
Royal Teas 16 C6
SE10 Restaurant & Bar ... 17 C5

▼ DRINK
Trafalgar Tavern 18 D5

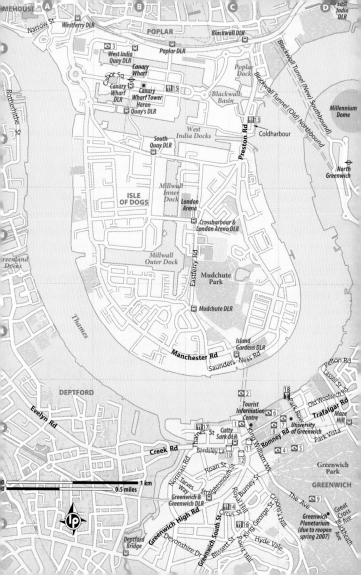

SEE
CUTTY SARK

☎ 8858 3445; www.cuttysark.org.uk;
Cutty Sark Gardens SE10; adult/child/
student/family £4/2.75/2.90/10,
hard-hat tours £8 extra; ☒ 10am-5pm;
🚇 Cutty Sark
Until October 2008, when
onboard repairs should be complete, you can't visit this one-time
great tea clipper in the usual
manner. Instead you can spy on
the renovation work via CCTV
cameras mounted in the temporary pavilion alongside, and learn
about conservation techniques.
Only occasional hard-hat tours
will venture onto the ship itself.

National Maritime Museum

☉ GREENWICH FOOT TUNNEL

Cutty Sark Gardens SE10; ☺ **via stairs 24hr, lifts 7am-7pm Mon-Sat, 10am-5.30pm Sun;** 🚇 **Cutty Sark**
Looked at objectively, this is just a pedestrian tunnel, built in 1902. But it's made quite thrilling by virtue of crossing beneath the River Thames. The echoing footsteps create a certain frisson and, thanks to the tunnel's slope, you see oncoming pedestrians' feet before their faces are revealed. (Although there's CCTV security, those prone to claustrophobia probably won't enjoy the experience.)

☉ NATIONAL MARITIME MUSEUM

☎ **8312 6565; www.nmm.ac.uk; Romney Rd SE10; admission free, prices vary for special exhibitions;** ☺ **10am-6pm Apr-Sep, 10am-5pm Oct-Mar;** 🚇 **Cutty Sark**
Even if you're not interested in the blokey deep-sea diving suits, legendary explorer's lifeboats and the whole science bit at this superlative museum, the gilded royal barge and the re-created cabins of luxury ocean liners may well seduce you. The uniform worn by Admiral Horatio Nelson when fatally shot is the most famous

TO GREENWICH, VIA DOCKLANDS

En route to Greenwich by tube and DLR, it's worth sparing a few minutes to glance around the strange sci-fi neighbourhood of Docklands. A financial district, created during the 1980s Thatcher era on the site of former docks and to rival the City, it's only now starting to live up to its promise. Sir Norman Foster's sleek Canary Wharf Underground station is monumental, while Cesar Pelli's 244m Canary Wharf Tower dominates the landscape. There's also:
Gun (☎ 7515 5222; www.thegundocklands.com; 27 Coldharbour E14; 🚇 Blackwall or Canary Wharf) This restored dockers' pub has Georgian fireplaces and a riverside terrace with front-seat views of the Millennium Dome. Modern British fare is on the menu.
Museum in Docklands (☎ 0870 444 3857; www.museumindocklands.org.uk; Warehouse No 1, West India Quay E14; adult/senior/student or under 16 yr £5/3/free; ☺ 10am-5.30pm; 🚇 West India Quay) The only formal Docklands attraction, this mostly appeals to kids with its hands-on displays and re-creation of 19th-century streets.
Plateau (☎ 7719 7800; 34 Westferry Circus E14; ☎ lunch & dinner Mon-Sat, dinner Sun; 🚇 Canary Wharf) Treat yourself to a delicious meal among Canary Wharf's corporate crowd, in a room with striking Finnish chairs and glass walls.

If you're feeling adventurous as you continue to Greenwich, alight at the Island Gardens DLR and walk under the river through the Greenwich Foot Tunnel (above).

Royal Observatory

exhibit, and it's now accompanied by a computerised display of his masterful strategy at the 1805 Battle of Trafalgar.

QUEEN'S HOUSE

8858 4422; www.nmm.ac.uk; Romney Rd SE10; admission free; 10am-5pm early Sep-May, 10am-6pm Jun-early Sep; Cutty Sark

Its spiral Tulip Staircase is this Palladian house's defining feature, twisting up from the cubical Great Hall to the 1st-floor gallery of old-fashioned paintings (a minor attraction). A rare surviving design by Inigo Jones, the house was built in 1616–35 after the architect returned from Renaissance Italy. The original client – Anne, wife of James I – never lived in it.

ROYAL NAVAL COLLEGE

8269 4747, 0800 389 3341; King William Walk SE10; admission free; 10am-5pm Mon-Sat, 12.30-5pm Sun; Cutty Sark

Now used mainly by the University of Greenwich, the college's two public rooms are in separate buildings, split by architect Christopher Wren so as not to interrupt the views from the Queen's House behind. The western wing's rococo chapel is less spectacular than the east's Painted Hall, which is covered in 'allegorical baroque' murals and is quite a sight indeed.

ROYAL OBSERVATORY

☎ 8312 6565; www.nmm.ac.uk; Greenwich Park SE19; admission free; ⏲ 10am-5pm Oct-May, 10am-6pm Apr-Sep; 🚇 Cutty Sark

Standing with one foot in the world's western hemisphere and the other in the east: that's the Royal Observatory's cheap thrill. But there's also an absorbing tale of how the observatory's astronomers battled to accurately measure longitude – and help improve maritime navigation – only to be beaten to the prize by determined watchmaker John Harrison.

THE MERIDIAN BY NIGHT

Did you know the Prime Meridian of longitude is not just marked by a line on the ground at the Royal Observatory? A green laser also cuts a swathe through London's night sky, outlining the path of the meridian. The diode laser is magnified by two mirrors and beamed from an opening in the observatory's domed roof. On a clear night it's visible for some 15km, as far north as Chingford.

Greenwich was named the Prime Meridian in 1884 anyway, and its astronomical legacy is commemorated in its new planetarium, open from spring 2007.

SHOP

Shopping in Greenwich is largely about secondhand goods – books, household objects and clothes. Here's the best place to come if you're into retro style, too; just wandering between the handful listed, you'll encounter more.

FLYING DUCK ENTERPRISES

☎ 8858 1964; www.flying-duck.com; 320-322 Creek Rd SE10; ⏲ 11am-6pm Tue-Fri, 10.30am-6pm Sat & Sun; 🚇 Cutty Sark

This is a little grotto of kitsch, absolutely crammed with two small rooms mainly lit by retro lamps and jam-packed with everything from snow domes and Bakelite telephones to Vladimir Tretchikoff paintings of exotic women and '70s cocktail kits – new and 'pre-loved'.

GREENWICH MARKET

☎ 8293 3110; www.greenwich-market .co.uk; College Approach SE10; ⏲ 7.30am-5.30pm Thu, 9.30am-5.30pm Fri-Sun; 🚇 Cutty Sark

None of its arts and crafts, antiques or collectables are

particularly earth-shattering, and this is probably not the sort of market you should race to Greenwich for. However, while you're here it's pointless not to have a quick browse, including in the speciality stores around the boundary.

📷 JOY

☎ 8293 7979; www.joythestore.com; 9 Nelson Rd SE10; 🕐 10am-7.30pm; 🚇 Cutty Sark

This spacious 'urban lifestyle' shop is aptly named; it truly is a delight. And although its menswear and womenswear is new and trendy, its saucy, quirky homewares fit right into the Greenwich scene.

Greenwich Market (p155)

EAT

Plenty of unremarkable restaurants cluster around the *Cutty Sark* and central Greenwich. While the following are slightly off the beaten track, they are local favourites.

INSIDE
Modern European £££

☎ 8265 5060; www.insiderestaurant .co.uk; 19 Greenwich South St SE10; ◷ brunch Sat & Sun, lunch Wed-Sun, dinner Mon-Sat; 🚉 Cutty Sark

Inside is more than just the best restaurant in Greenwich; it's one of the best neighbourhood restaurants in London, with a simple and unfussy interior and fresh-tasting Modern European cuisine. Pea-and-mint soup seems to have survived regular menu changes for years; dishes like roast lamb with *puy* lentils, crisp pork belly or Cornish crab with *pappardelle* come and go more frequently.

ROYAL TEAS
Vegetarian £

☎ 8691 7240; www.royalteascafe .co.uk; 76 Royal Hill SE10; ◷ 10am-6pm; 🚉 Cutty Sark

American breakfasts, superb ginger cake for morning tea, baguettes, soups and stews all combine to make this delightful tiny café the perfect daytime option. Skip the crowds around the *Cutty Sark* by popping up here.

SE10 RESTAURANT & BAR
Modern British ££

☎ 8858 9764; www.se10restaurant .co.uk; 62 Thames St SE10; ◷ lunch Mon-Sat, dinner Tue-Sat, brunch Sun; 🚉 Cutty Sark

This restaurant-bar is well off the tourist trail and displays a pleasing eclecticism, with yellow walls, old-fashioned bird paintings and sparkling glasses laid on white tablecloths in the restaurant section at the back. The food, while not as superb as Inside's, is still quite decent for the price and some of the cheapish wines, including the Tortoiseshell Bay, are excellent.

DRINK

TRAFALGAR TAVERN

☎ 8858 2437; www.trafalgartavern .co.uk; Park Row SE10; 🚉 Cutty Sark

The celebrated whitebait now comes with fancy-pants paprika mayo and the rest of the menu has gone upmarket (and become over-priced) too, while the spectacular views of the river and Millennium Dome remain uncharged, as do the honest ales and pretty touristy atmosphere in this dark-wood Victorian pub.

>KING'S CROSS, EUSTON & ISLINGTON

King's Cross is never going to charm anyone in particular. However, the new Eurostar terminus is scheduled to open in 2007, and a cluster of clubs has exploited the urban landscape for added edginess.

The new Eurostar terminus will bring Continental passengers directly into northern London. However, even before it was conceived, this ugly-duckling district did boast two architectural jewels – the Victorian Gothic St Pancras Chambers and the much younger British Library. With street prostitution, crime, drug abuse and drunkenness all regular King's Cross features, visitors should be relatively cautious here at night. However, none of that deters clubbers enjoying themselves at leading London venues.

Meanwhile, minutes away lies the altogether more salubrious Islington. The main thoroughfare, Upper St, hasn't been immune to the generic chains that have invaded most parts of London. However, it still offers good shopping, some excellent restaurants, a handful of hip bars and, in the Almeida, one of London's most innovative and exciting small theatres.

KING'S CROSS, EUSTON & ISLINGTON

◎ SEE
British Library 1 A4
St Pancras Chambers......2 A4

⬠ SHOP
Aria.................................3 D2
Diverse .... (see 7)
Haggle Vinyl.................4 D2

ⵌ EAT
Almeida...........................5 D2
Gallipoli.........................6 D3
Ottolenghi.....................7 D2

▼ DRINK
Elk in the Woods 8 C3
Embassy 9 D2

★ PLAY
Almeida Theatre 10 D2
Cross 11 A3
Egg 12 A2
Scala 13 B4

◉ SEE

◉ BRITISH LIBRARY

☎ visitor services 7412 7332, switchboard 0870 444 1500; www.bl.uk;
96 Euston Rd NW1; admission free;
⏲ 9.30am-6pm Mon & Wed-Fri, to 8pm
Tue, 9.30am-5pm Sat, 9am-5pm Sun,
tours 3pm Mon, Wed & Fri, 10.30am &
3pm Sat; ⊖ King's Cross/St Pancras
Even a parliamentary commit-
tee has called this building's
exterior ugly, but you couldn't
say that about the white, light-
filled interior. Opened in 1998
to replace the former library in
the British Museum, it's got lots
of eye-catching features, from
its quirky sculptures and huge
glass well of historic books to
the Magna Carta and Da Vinci
notebook. There are audio and
guided tours.

◉ ST PANCRAS CHAMBERS

Euston Rd; ⊖ King's Cross/St Pancras
Its current rundown surroundings
make it tempting to describe this
Victorian Gothic masterpiece as
the poor cousin of the Houses of

British Library

BEHIND CLOSED DOORS

Libraries – they're staid, boring places, right? Not the British Library, if the press is to be believed. First, the *Spectator* magazine described it as 'buzzing with sexual tension', with readers (ie users) who supposedly eyed one another up getting into illicit clinches. Then travel writer William Dalrymple nominated the third-floor Oriental and India section as having the best lookers. Later, the library staff stunned newspapers by voting the Sex Pistols' *Never Mind the Bollocks* as their favourite album. In truth, the place's cutting-edge reputation is overblown, but you do see some famous faces around and it's a charming urban myth.

Parliament. But it's an unusual building nonetheless. Today it constitutes part of St Pancras' train station and with the adjacent Eurostar Terminal due to open in late 2007, it's partly being redeveloped into the same thing George Gilbert Scott built it for in 1876 – a hotel.

 SHOP

Islington's Upper St is a very good shopping thoroughfare, although it's best to just amble along and see what takes your fancy. Camden Passage, at the southeastern

end, used to be full of antique stores, but they are increasingly being joined by lifestyle stores. Don't overlook Cross St or Essex Rd, either, if you're looking for clothes or retro furnishings.

 ARIA
☎ 7704 1999; www.aria-shop.co.uk; 295-966 Upper St N1; 🕙 10am-7pm Mon-Fri, 10am-6.30pm Sat, noon-5pm Sun; ⊖ Angel
The crowded window displays will draw you in for a browse of this large household store, which is packed with loads of covetable mugs, plates, toasters, kitchen equipment and furniture.

🗋 DIVERSE
☎ 7359 0081; www.diverseclothing .com; 286 Upper St N1; 🕙 10am-6pm Mon-Sat; ⊖ Angel or Highbury & Islington
One of London's coolest streetwear boutiques for men, this has has jeans, shirts and tees from Italy and New York arranged around a fairly minimalist interior. Jeans labels include Blue Blood, Indigo Form, Rogan and Paper Denim.

🗋 HAGGLE VINYL
☎ 7354 4666; www.haggle.freeserve .co.uk; 114 Essex Rd N1; 🕙 9am-7pm Mon-Sat, 10am-5.30pm Sun; ⊖ Angel
Vintage vinyl records of varying musical flavours are crammed

NEIGHBOURHOODS

KING'S CROSS, EUSTON & ISLINGTON

into the shelves and into boxes on the floor in this cult record store.

EAT

🍴 **ALMEIDA** *French* £££
☎ 7354 4777; 30 Almeida St N1;
🕐 lunch & dinner; ⊖ Angel
Opposite the Islington playhouse of the same name (see p165), this has proven a big success for more than pre-theatre dinners. The staff hit the right balance between Gallic perfectionism and

---

LET THEM EAT CAKE

The original among London's latest 1950s tea-dances, the irrepressible Viva Cake began life at the Bethnal Green WMC (see p135), but has since taken up a residency at the red-brick **St Aloysius Social Club** (20 Phoenix Rd NW1) near Euston train station, as well as making appearances at events like Rock 'n' Roll Cinema (see 93 Feet East, p135).

An evening with the self-declared **Viva Cake Bitches** (www.myspace .com/vivacakebitches) usually kicks off in the late afternoon with tea, cake and sandwiches served by girls on rollerskates. Other diversions include dominos, knitting, baking and, if plans come off, a beauty bar, before the evening steps it up a gear with classic rock 'n' roll bands and jive-dancing. Remember to raid the dressing-up box for some vintage wear before you turn up.

---

chatty friendliness, while the classic French menu is excellent, albeit entirely in French.

🍴 **CHUTNEY'S** *Indian* £
☎ 7388 0604; 124 Drummond St;
⊖ Warren St or Euston Sq
Although, like those in Brick Lane, the South Indian restaurants along Drummond St have seen a decline in standards, the drop is not so pronounced, and Chutney's continues to provide good, cheap all-you-can-eat vegetarian buffets.

🍴 **GALLIPOLI** *Turkish* £
☎ 7359 0630; 102 Upper St N1;
🕐 11am-11pm; ⊖ Angel or Highbury & Islington
For a delightful cheap meal, don't go past this crammed, popular, cheek-by-jowl den. Its funky decorations are accompanied by tasty food, from meze to spicy vegetarian moussaka. There's an overspill restaurant, Gallipoli Again at No 120.

🍴 **OTTOLENGHI** *Mediterranean* ££
☎ 7288 1454; www.ottolenghi.co.uk; 287 Upper St N1; 🕐 8am-11pm Mon-Sat; 9am-7pm Sun; ⊖ Angel or Highbury & Islington
Forced to name just one Islington eatery, we'd choose Ottolenghi. Behind the seductive display of

huge meringues, it's a long white minimalist streak with one communal and several private tables. It's casual enough for a relaxed breakfast and chic enough for a night out. Meals are usually composed of two or three servings of delicious modern Mediterranean dishes. There's also a branch in Notting Hill (p181).

 # DRINK

Upper St is also lined with drinking holes, but many of them appeal to lairy groups of lads out on the piss. We've listed just two of the best you might not otherwise spot.

Gallipoli restaurant

NEIGHBOURHOODS

KING'S CROSS, EUSTON & ISLINGTON

☎ ELK IN THE WOODS

☎ 7226 3535; 39 Camden Passage N1;
⊖ Angel

Part Laura Ashley, part East London
hip, this place has such a lovely
interior, you're inclined to forgive
any shortcomings in the service
department. Its old mirrors, stuffed
deer head and large table up the
back just hit the right quirky note.

☎ EMBASSY

☎ 7359 7882; 119 Essex Rd N1; ⏰ from
5pm; ⊖ Angel

Behind those black walls and smoky
windows, cool muso and media
types quaff beer in the comfy sofas
or enjoy the DJs in the street-level
bar and more recent basement. The
buzz about the street-cred Embassy
has grown, so it's now one of Is-

Arsenal Emirates Stadium

lington's premier venues; there's a cover charge (£3) on weekends.

 # PLAY

★ ALMEIDA THEATRE

☎ 7359 4404; www.almeida.co.uk; Almeida St N1; ⊖ Angel

Small though it is, this theatre's stage has been graced by the likes of Gael Garcia Bernal, Ralph Fiennes and Kevin Spacey. And with a solid reputation for imaginative, challenging plays and staging, it's always worth checking to see what's on here.

★ ARSENAL EMIRATES STADIUM

☎ 7704 4040; www.arsenal.com; Ashburton Grove N7; ⊖ Arsenal, Holloway Rd or Highbury & Islington

Arsene Wenger's team seemed to have a little trouble settling into the bigger pitch of their brand-new stadium, with a home win seeming elusive at the start of the 2006 season. Still, for the spectator the 60,000 new seats are more luxurious and the extra capacity makes it more likely you might actually snaffle one of them.

★ CROSS

☎ 7837 0828; www.the-cross.co.uk; Goods Way Depot, York Way N1; ⊙ 10.30pm-5am Fri & Sat, 10.30am-4pm Sun; ⊖ King's Cross/St Pancras

This is one of London's best venues, comprising several low brick rooms built under railway arches hidden in the wasteland off York Way. There's soul, funk and garage, and a lot of Continental-style clubbing, as well as a great outdoor terrace for the summer months too.

★ EGG

☎ 7609 8364; www.egglondon.net; 200 York Way N1; ⊙ 10pm-6am Fri & Sun, 10pm-2pm Sat; ⊖ King's Cross/St Pancras

Egg and the other cluster of clubs in the neighbourhood have pumped a little luxury into this industrial wasteland. A glam crowd comes for a range of dance music (minimal house, deep house, funk electro etc) spun by the likes of Norman Jay, Mylo and Goldie…but most of all for the courtyard garden and roof terraces with hammocks.

★ SCALA

☎ 7833 2022; www.scala-london.co.uk; 275 Pentonville Rd N1; ⊙ 10pm-5am Fri, plus other one-off events; ⊖ King's Cross/St Pancras

With a glass bar at its centre overlooking the stage but insulated from the noise, this former cinema is a great multipurpose venue. The most regular club night is Friday's gay indie Popstarz event, while live-music acts have included Gomez and the Scissor Sisters.

>CAMDEN, HAMPSTEAD & PRIMROSE HILL

Were it not for the grunginess of neighbouring Camden Town, the districts of Hampstead and Primrose Hill might seem a little staid. But these areas all feed off each other, allowing residents and visitors to easily combine very different experiences.

Camden is best known for its weekend market. But its status as north London's nightlife hub has been confirmed in recent years by the success of places such as the revamped Koko (formerly Camden Palace) and the reopening of the legendary Roundhouse.

Leafy, cultured and well-heeled, but left-leaning and liberal with it, Hampstead is a different proposition. While boasting some decent pubs, restaurants and shops, its centrepiece is its fantastic heath – 320 acres of semi-wilderness, with views of London's skyline from Parliament Hill.

In between lies Primrose Hill, a small but perfectly formed inner-city village. There's no particularly compelling reason to come here, other than that the hillside park offers a pleasant stroll and, with the area's luvvie population, there are some good star-spotting opportunities.

CAMDEN, HAMPSTEAD & PRIMROSE HILL

☉ SEE
Freud Museum 1 A5
Highgate Cemetery
Entrance 2 D2
Keats House 3 B4
Kenwood House 4 B1

🏠 SHOP
Camden Market 5 D6
Rosslyn Delicatessen 6 A4

🍴 EAT
Gilgamesh 7 D5
Haché 8 D6
Jin Kichi 9 A3
Lansdowne 10 C5
Mango Room 11 D6
Manna 12 C5
Trojka 13 C5
Wells 14 A3

▼ DRINK
At Proud 15 C5
Boogaloo 16 D1
Hollybush 17 A3
Lock Tavern 18 D5

⭐ PLAY
Barfly @ The Monarch .. 19 C5
Jazz Café 20 D6
Koko 21 D6
Roundhouse 22 C5

NEIGHBOURHOODS

CAMDEN, HAMPSTEAD & PRIMROSE HILL

 SEE

☉ FREUD MUSEUM
☎ 7435 2002; www.freud.org.uk; 20
Maresfield Gardens NW3; adult/under-
12/concession £5/free/3; ☽ noon-5pm
Wed-Sun; ⊖ Finchley Rd
See the original psychoanalyst's
couch in the home Sigmund Freud
made for his family after fleeing
Nazi-occupied Vienna in 1938.

☉ HAMPSTEAD HEATH
☎ 7485 4491; ⊖ Hampstead,
🚇 Gospel Oak or Hampstead Heath,
🚌 214 or C2 to Parliament Hill Fields
Only 4 miles (6.4km) from the
City of London, this enormous
bit of heath is a world unto itself.
Throttle back by joining the many
summer picnickers. Alternatively,
come to see the view from Parliament Hill, for a walk or a swim. See
p24 for further details.

☉ HIGHGATE CEMETERY
☎ 8340 1834; www.highgate-cemetery
.org; Swain's Lane N6; admission £2,
tours £3, plus £1 per camera; ☽ 10am-
5pm Mon-Fri, 11am-5pm Sat & Sun Apr-
Oct, 10am-4pm Mon-Fri, 11am-4pm Sat &
Sun Nov-Mar, tours 2pm Mon-Fri & every
hour 11am-4pm Sat-Sun; ⊖ Highgate
Karl Marx is one of several nota-
bles buried in the eastern section
of this Victorian Valhalla, but it's
the wildly overgrown and Gothic
western section that makes this

BLADE RUNNERS
London recently seems to have developed a fetish for ice-skating in winter.
It all started soon after Somerset House
opened in 2000 and turned its courtyard
into a temporary rink – a fantastic enclosed space to do it. Now other many
places are joining the gang, including the
following:
> Royal Naval College (www.green
  wichicerink.com; p154) – fabulous
  views
> Hampstead Heath (www.hamp
  steadheathicerink.com; below left) –
  on Parliament Hill Fields
> Kew Gardens (www.kewgardens
  icerink.com; boxed text, p84) – huge
  rink, near the greenhouse
> Natural History Museum (www
  .nhmskating.com; p20) – near the
  main entrance
> Tower of London (www.towerof
  londonicerink.com; p19) – away
  from the river, towards Tower Hill

one of the capital's fascinating
places of rest. With its maze of
winding paths, this half is accessible only by tour (call ahead to
book; no bookings Sunday).

☉ KEATS HOUSE
☎ 7435 2062; www.keatshouse.org
.uk; Wentworth Pl, Keats Grove NW3;
adult/child/concession £3.50/free/1.75;
☽ 1-5pm; ⊖ Hampstead
There's something about Hampstead – all that communing with

nature probably – that can bring out the romantic in us all. And that's just the right mood for visiting the former home of John Keats, where he composed the celebrated poem *Ode to a Nightingale*.

 KENWOOD HOUSE
☎ 8348 1286; www.english-heritage.org.uk; Hampstead Lane NW3; admission free; ☼ house 11am-5pm Apr-Oct, 11am-4pm Nov-Mar, the Suffolk Collection (upstairs) 11am-4.30pm Thu-Sun; ⊖ Archway or Golders Green, then bus 210
This magnificent neoclassical mansion by architect Robert Adam could be from a Jane Austen novel and has indeed been used as a backdrop in Austen films. Inside there's the Iveagh Bequest, a small but very fine collection of paintings by artists including Gainsborough, Reynolds, Turner, Hals, Vermeer and Van Dyck. In summer, classical concerts are performed on the lawn, while the attached Brew House Café is open all year.

SHOP
CAMDEN MARKET
Camden High St NW1; ☼ **9am-5.30pm Thu-Sun;** ⊖ **Camden Town**
Visited by millions each year, Camden Market has made an art form of (and a mint from) packaging and selling 'alternative' culture. Bondage-style trousers, stripy off-the-shoulder sweatshirts, thigh-high wedge boots, batik throws, scented candles, knitted hats, purple Goth wigs are all quite novel initially, but the love affair

Camden High St

rarely lasts that long among these rubbish-strewn streets.

ROSSLYN DELICATESSEN
☎ 7794 9210; www.delirosslyn.co.uk; 56 Rosslyn Hill NW3; ⌚ 8.30am-8.30pm Mon-Sat, 8.30am-8pm Sun; ⊖ Hampstead or Belsize Park

This award-winning deli is the perfect pit stop for a few picnic provisions en route to the Heath, with all the usual sorts of baked goods, olives etc, as well as some more unusual offerings to take home, like damson jam and mulberry salad dressing.

EAT

GILGAMESH
Pan-Asian   £££-££££

☎ 7482 5757; www.gilgameshbar.com; Stables Market, Chalk Farm Rd NW1; ⌚ lunch & dinner Mon-Fri, noon-midnight Sat & Sun; ⊖ Camden Town

It's a rude shock finding bouncers and a dress code right in the heart of Goth-and-grungy Camden Market and, despite some high-profile fawning reviews, therein lies the problem with Gilgamesh. You'll either love the over-the-top Babylonian décor or think it's a monstrosity, but unless it gets over itself and improves its service this currently star-studded spot might eventually struggle. On the food front, the dim sum and sushi are best.

HACHÉ *American*   £-££
☎ 7485 9100; www.hacheburgers.com; 24 Inverness St NW1; ⌚ noon-10.30pm, to 10pm Sun; ⊖ Camden Town

This family-run place is renowned for using the best-quality meat in its excellent burgers – some of the best in London. It also makes an effort to come up with different varieties on its menu, like Catalan, Canadian and even 'Forest' (mushroom and pesto). Only the side orders are sometimes disappointing.

JIN KICHI *Japanese*   ££
☎ 7794 6158; 73 Heath St NW3; ⌚ lunch Sat & Sun, dinner daily; ⊖ Hampstead

The number of Japanese people who eat at this slightly shabby and cramped little place is a seal of approval for its cooking. It's a particularly good bet for grilled meats and other nonstandard Japanese flavours, none of which you'll be able to enjoy unless you book.

LANSDOWNE
Gastropub   ££-£££

☎ 7722 0950; 90 Gloucester Ave NW1; ⊖ Chalk Farm

Many locals have always preferred the Lansdowne, but now even former fans of the fast-deteriorating Engineer down the road agree: the Landowne's food is better, plus it's hipper and less stuffy. Come for stone-baked pizza and an ever-changing blackboard menu of Mediterranean delights. Downstairs is buzzing and full of the trendy beautiful young things who've scootered in. The upstairs restaurant is quieter.

🍴 MANGO ROOM
Caribbean   £££

☎ 7482 5065; www.mangoroom.co.uk; 10 Kentish Town Rd NW1; ⊖ Camden Town

This swish Caribbean restaurant fell off the cool-o-meter a while back, but that has actually been to its benefit. Revamped in darker maroon tones, it's now obviously concentrating on delivering the gastronomic goods, with things like saltfish and *ackee,* and banana-and-mango *crème brûlée,* on the menu.

🍴 MANNA
Vegetarian   £££

☎ 7722 8082; www.manna-veg .com; 4 Erskine Rd NW1; ⊖ Chalk Farm

Tucked away on a side street in London's most glamorous inner-city village, this gorgeous little place does a brisk trade in inventive vegetarian

Mango Room restaurant

Trojka

cooking, featuring mouthwatering dishes. Prices are not low – this is Primrose Hill after all – but Manna is often heavenly.

THE PRIMROSE HILL SET

A leafy and privileged part of town, Primrose Hill has become a byword for trendy luvvies, but remember that Jude (Law) has moved out, Sadie (Frost) lives on the edge of the 'village' and Kate (Moss) actually has her home in St John's Wood. Keep your star-spotting radar alert all the same, though, because residents do include Gwen Stefani and Gavin Rossdale, Daniel Craig (the new James Bond), chef Jamie Oliver, *Little Britain* actor David Walliams, Bob Hoskins, and a whole host of fashionistas, writers, media personalities and politicians.

🍴 TROJKA
Eastern European　　　　££
☎ 7483 3765; www.trojka.co.uk; 101 Regent's Park Rd NW1; ⊖ Chalk Farm
This Primrose Village place serves Eastern European/Russian dishes such as herrings with dill sauce and Russian salad, Polish *bigosz* (a cabbage 'stew' with mixed meats) and salt beef in an attractive, sky-lit restaurant frequented by local bohos.

🍴 WELLS
Gastropub　　　　££-£££
☎ 7794 3785; 30 Well Walk NW3;
🕐 lunch & dinner; ⊖ Hampstead
Posh but extremely pleasant with it, the Wells is a colourful, taste-

fully decorated place just minutes from Hampstead Heath. On a sunny day, its ground floor and outdoor terraces overflow with punters of all ages, but plumping for the Modern European menu in the upstairs restaurant gives you a better chance of getting a seat.

 # DRINK

AT PROUD

☎ 7482 3867; The Gin House, Stables Market, Chalk Farm Rd NW1; ⏱ 10am-1am Mon-Sat, noon-11pm Sun; ⊖ Camden Town

Sit on Pete Doherty's face – his mugshot and that of other iconic musicians adorn the canvas chairs here. On the concrete terrace of the Proud photography gallery, floating above the Camden Market melee, this casually flung together, Berlin-like establishment also has mattresses you can lounge on, under the watchful eye of a horse statue and the railway line. There are also some DJ eves.

BOOGALOO

☎ 8340 2928; www.theboogaloo.co.uk; 312 Archway Rd N6; ⊖ Highgate

Better yet, try to get a sighting of the real Pete Doherty, whose appearances in this seminal musos' pub have given it extra cachet, as if it needed it. Slightly more self-

consciously cool these days place, it has a popular Tuesday-night music quiz and a jukebox regularly reprogrammed by celebrity musicians

HOLLYBUSH

☎ 7435 2892; 22 Holly Mount NW3; ⊖ Hampstead

A beautiful pub that makes you envy the privileged residents of Hampstead, Hollybush has an antique Victorian interior, a lovely secluded hilltop location (above Heath St, reached via Holly Bush Steps), open fires in winter and a knack for making you stay longer than you had intended at any time of the year.

OTHER TOP BURGERS

Gourmet burgers are certainly having a moment in London. Check the websites for the nearest outlet of the following chains:

Gourmet Burger Kitchen (www.gbkinfo.co.uk) This is the best of the bunch, using lip-smackingly fresh ingredients.

Hamburger Union (www.hamburgerunion.com) Pretty good burgers, with organic meat; only a few outlets in Soho and Islington.

Ultimate Burger (www.ultimateburger.co.uk) Our experience has always been good, though we know people who say otherwise. Nice diner environment.

Lorna Clarke,
Festival Director, BBC Electric Proms

Electric Proms is... A new festival bringing together completely different musicians – classical, jazz, rock, guitar to Asian, established and unsigned. In 2006 at Camden's Roundhouse (p175) and Barfly (p175), we had everyone from the Who to Nitin Sawhney, including Damon Albarn's The Good, the Bad and the Queen. **What's on this year** Check www.bbc.co.uk/electric proms. **Best thing about London music** Lots and lots of choice, whatever your taste – from folk to dance music. **Top tip** Don't write off small pub bands. It's easy to find out about big concerts; just pick up a paper. But there's something quintessentially London about watching a band over a pint in a sticky venue. **Best for new music** Barfly (p175) is second to none. If you're a fan of brand-new music, particularly guitar music, you'll see future stars. **Other favourites** The open-air theatre in Regent's Park (p73) in summer and the **Halfmoon Putney** (www.halfmoon.co.uk). **Bush Hall** (www.bushhallmusic.co.uk) is this really sweet music hall – Victorian-style and very atmospheric.

☒ LOCK TAVERN

☎ 7482 7163; www.lock-tavern.co.uk; 35 Chalk Farm Rd NW1; ☒ from noon; ☒ Camden Town or Chalk Farm

Trustafarian Notting Hill cool comes to Camden in the shape of this black-walled pub, with great tunes, a nicely relaxed atmosphere, fashionable fellow punters and an upstairs roof terrace.

PLAY

☒ BARFLY @ THE MONARCH

☎ 7691 4244; www.barflyclub.com; Monarch, 49 Chalk Farm Rd NW1; ☒ from 7.30pm ☒ Chalk Farm or Camden Town

This typically grungy and sweaty, although not unpleasant, Camden pub is full of small-time artists looking for their big break. (Some of them like the Kaiser Chiefs have even made it.) Guitar-led thrash and rock is the order of the day in this seminal London venue.

☒ JAZZ CAFÉ

☎ standing reservations 0870 060 3777, restaurant 7534 6955; www.jazzcafe .co.uk; 5 Parkway NW1; ☒ from 7pm; ☒ Camden Town

The club that's really made the most of jazz's crossover to the mainstream, this trendy industrial-style restaurant takes a very broad interpretation of the genre, mixing it with Afro, funk, hip, R&B and soul styles. Unknowns and big-name acts perform to a faithful bohemian Camden crowd. Booking necessary.

☒ KOKO

☎ 0870 432 5527; www.koko.uk.com; 1a Camden High St NW1; ☒ from 10pm Fri & Sat, plus special events; ☒ Mornington Cres

Formerly the Camden Palace, and before that a theatre, Koko is one of the best London venues right now, hosting regular NME music evenings as well as the so-bad-it's-good strains of Guilty Pleasures. Big names, even Madonna launching *Confessions on a Dance Floor,* have played, and it's surfing the cabaret wave with some burlesque evenings, for which its multilevel cherry-red interior is very well suited.

☒ ROUNDHOUSE

☎ 0870 389 1846; www.roundhouse .org.uk; Chalk Farm Rd NW1; ☒ Chalk Farm or Camden Town

This former railway-engine shed and then 1960s counterculture magnet is back – not for the first time, but this time hopefully for good. As the name suggests, the auditorium is round, making it just as good for circus/dance performers like Fuerzabruta as it is, after rearrangement, for eyes-forward musical concerts.

>NOTTING HILL

Few London districts have been so bound up in urban legend as Notting Hill. Its recent history dates from the 1950s when Caribbean immigrants of the *Windrush* generation came to Britain to fill a post-war jobs gap. Artists and rock stars followed, and the area began trading off a reputation for multiculturalism and general dope-smoking liberalism.

But for decades now, the neighbourhood has been subject to creeping gentrification. Rastafarians were joined by trustafarians (bohemians with secret trust funds), the race riots discussed in the book *Absolute Beginners* gave way to the solipsism of *Bridget Jones's Diary* and the chick-lit *Notting Hell*.

But while *Times'* columnists write that Notting Hill is becoming 'anaesthetised by its own popularity', and others lament the commercialisation of the famous Notting Hill Carnival, there's life in the old girl yet. Portobello Rd and its market still reel the shoppers in. The area continues to display its underlying multiculturalism; and on any given night, a good time is guaranteed in the bars and restaurants that pepper the district.

NOTTING HILL

🏠 SHOP
Lisboa Patisserie	1	A2
Portobello Road Market	2	B4
Rellick	3	B1
Rough Trade	4	B3
Travel Bookshop	5	B4

🍴 EAT
Bumpkin	6	C3
Cow	7	C3
Crazy Homies	8	C3
E&O	9	B4
Electric Brasserie	(see 14)	
Ledbury	10	C3
Ottolenghi	11	C4

🍸 DRINK
Earl of Lonsdale	12	B4
Lonsdale	13	B4

⭐ PLAY
Electric Cinema	14	B4
Notting Hill Arts Club	15	D5

SHOP

Notting Hill has several shopping thoroughfares. If you alight at Notting Hill Gate tube station, you'll pass a handful of trendy fashion stores even before you hit the beginning of Portobello Rd Market. For something a little more exclusive and totally unaffordable, turn off Portobello Rd into the local 'Rodeo Drive' of Westbourne Grove.

LISBOA PATISSERIE

☎ 8968 5242; 57 Golborne Rd W10; 🕙 8am-8pm, to 7pm Sun; ⊖ Westbourne Park or Ladbroke Grove

We've listed this as a shopping option, because the *pasteis de nata* (Portuguese custard tarts) are divine, but the café is really too small to be conducive. Grab a takeaway.

PORTOBELLO ROAD MARKET

Portobello Rd W10; 🕙 8am-6pm Mon-Wed, 9am-1pm Thu, 7am-7pm Fri & Sat; ⊖ Notting Hill Gate or Ladbroke Grove

Like Camden Market, Portobello Market is several rolled into one, stretching virtually from Notting Hill Gate tube station to the heart of Ladbroke Grove, and it's best approached by a wander

Portobello Road Market

Rough Trade

from one end to the other. From Notting Hill Gate, you begin by passing antiques, homewares and bric-a-brac stores and stalls, moving on through food to clothing – both young designer and secondhand. This place is established enough to mean that you're not going to find any super bargains here. Saturday is the main market day.

RELLICK
☎ 8962 0089; www.relliklondon.co.uk; 8 Golborne Rd W10; ⏲ 10am-6pm Tue-Sat; ⬡ Westbourne Park
One of London's most lauded retro clothing stores, this place is not cheap, but there is a chance of unearthing secondhand designer labels, including from the likes of Vivienne Westwood, Zandra Rhodes and even 1960s icon Ossie Clark. While you're here, have a look at Trellick Tower opposite – another love-or-hate London building.

ROUGH TRADE
☎ 7229 8541; www.roughtrade.com; 130 Talbot Rd W11; ⬡ Ladbroke Grove or Notting Hill Gate
With its underground, alternative and vintage rarities at a premium, this home of the seminal punk-

music label remains a haven for older vinyl junkies who get all misty-eyed about the days before CDs (also on sale) and MP3 players.

☐ TRAVEL BOOKSHOP

☎ 7229 5260; www.thetravelbookshop.co.uk; 13-15 Blenheim Cres W11; ⏱ 10am-6pm Mon-Sat, noon-5pm Sun; ⊖ Ladbroke Grove

Such a landmark as to have become a cliché, this is the store on which Hugh Grant's was based (it was a copy) in the film *Notting Hill*. Still, visiting it will bring you to Blenheim Cres, where there are a couple of other browsable shops.

 # EAT

☐ BUMPKIN
Gastropub ££-£££

☎ 7243 9818; 209 Westbourne Park Rd W11; ⏱ lunch & dinner Mon-Sat, noon-5pm Sun; ⊖ Westbourne Park or Ladbroke Grove

This faux rustic outfit – with its designer floral wallpaper and 'You're not from around here' staff T-shirts – is good for an unpretentious helping of old-fashioned comfort food. Wash down everything, from dorset crab bruschetta to beef pie and huge steaks, with a glass of Guinness, Adnam's or some very unusual

whisky cocktails. The cooking's not particularly fancy or skillful, but – despite the occasionally high noise levels downstairs – there's something uncomplicatedly pleasant about the whole experience.

☐ COW *Gastropub* ££-£££

☎ 7221 5400; www.thecowlondon.co.uk; 89 Westbourne Park Rd W2; ⊖ Westbourne Park or Royal Oak

Owned by Tom Conran, the son of renowned restaurateur Sir Terence, this gastropub has a vintage top-floor dining room that has long maintained its reputation as one of the best in west London. Fresh oysters with Guinness are a speciality. Despite its fair share of trust-funded Notting Hillbillies, it's still a great hangout.

☐ CRAZY HOMIES
Mexican ££

☎ 7727 6771; www.crazyhomieslondon.co.uk; 127 Westbourne Park Rd W2; ⏱ 6-11pm Mon-Fri, noon-11pm Sat & Sun; ⊖ Westbourne Park

It's tiny, with just a handful of tables and a no-booking policy, so this funky, bohemian Mexican is certainly somewhere you need to arrive at early to guarantee getting a seat. It's worth it though, as the food here is authentically hot, spicy, delicious and excellent value. Diners rave about the pork dishes, the guacamole, the desserts, the tacos, the margaritas, and, hell, even the chips.

E&O *Asian* £££
☎ 7229 5454; www.rickerrestaurants .com; 14 Blenheim Cres W11; ⊖ Notting Hill Gate or Ladbroke Grove

This hot-spot is about the best (certainly about the trendiest) of a notable neighbourhood. The Eastern & Oriental presents fusion fare in a stark and minimalist room, but you'd better appreciate it at lunch because the evenings are mental. You can dim sum at the bar if a table is unavailable.

ELECTRIC BRASSERIE
Brasserie ££
☎ 7908 9696; www.electricbrasserie .com; 191 Portobello Rd W11; ⏱ 8am-midnight, to 1am Thu-Sun; ⊖ Ladbroke Grove

The name comes from the next-door cinema, but it's possible to believe that it's a comment on the atmosphere here too, as this place never seems to stop buzzing. Whether it's for brunch over the weekend, a hearty lunch or a full dinner, the Electric certainly draws a trendy, loquacious and sometimes celebrity Notting Hill crowd with its British-European menu.

LEDBURY
French ££££
☎ 7792 9090; www.theledbury.com; 127 Ledbury Rd W11; ⏱ lunch & dinner; ⊖ Westbourne Park

Within a year or so of opening, this tastefully minimalist restaurant lassoed in a Michelin star to the Notting Hill neighbourhood. Not only has Ledbury been garnering awards for Australian chef Brett Graham's clean, crisp flavours, its discreet and efficient service and wine list are also much acclaimed. Well-heeled trendies come here for the see-and-be-seen atmosphere.

OTTOLENGHI
Mediterranean ££
☎ 7727 1121; www.ottolenghi.co.uk; 63 Ledbury Rd W11; ⏱ 8am-8pm Mon-Fri, 8am-7pm Sat, 8.30am-6pm Sun; ⊖ Westbourne Park or Notting Hill Gate

Although the newer Islington branch (p162) nowadays gets a little bit more attention, chef Ottam Ottolenghi's original venue is just as good for delicious Mediterranean cuisine.

DRINK
EARL OF LONSDALE
☎ 7727 6335; 277-81 Portobello Rd W11; ⊖ Notting Hill Gate or Westbourne Park

This renovated traditional gin pal-

Electric Cinema

ace is a convivial change of pace for an area of ultra-cool cocktail lounges and bustling boozers. The large bar is split up into booths where you can enjoy intimate conversation, Sam Smiths ales are served up and there's a fantastic smoke-free back saloon, complete with huge leather armchairs to sink into.

▼ LONSDALE

☎ 7727 4080; www.thelonsdale.co.uk; 48 Lonsdale Rd W11; ⏱ to midnight Mon-Sat, to 11.30pm Sun; ⊖ Notting Hill Gate or Westbourne Park

The super-slick Lonsdale looks like Buck Rogers' pad, with its bumpy space-aged walls that are suffused in purple light and given a traditional touch with tiny red candles beneath a stunning oval skylight. The cocktails are what people come to this place for, although there are also beers and wines.

★ PLAY

★ ELECTRIC CINEMA

☎ 7908 9696, 7229 8688; www.electric cinema.co.uk; 191 Portobello Rd W1; ⊖ Ladbroke Grove or Notting Hill Gate

A night out at this Rolls Royce of cinemas is no ordinary evening at the pictures. The Edwardian-era picture house has been

TOP LONDON FILMS

> *The Ladykillers* (1955) – watch the last great Ealing comedy in its original; ignore the Coen Brothers' remake
> *The Ipcress File* (1965) – brilliant London-centric period piece starring Michael Caine
> *My Beautiful Laundrette* (1985) – an interesting vignette from the Thatcher years which launched Daniel Day-Lewis' career
> *Vera Drake* (2005) – bleak, touching and tragic, Mike Leigh's Oscar-nominated movie re-creates the post-war East End to perfection
> *Children of Men* (2006) – mixed opinions on the dystopian, sci-fi storyline, but atmospheric use of London backdrops

luxuriously fitted out with leather armchairs and footstools. There are tables for food and drink in the auditorium, and an upmarket brasserie. Of course, such pampering comes at a slightly higher cost; on full-price nights the seats are £12.50, or £30 for a two-seater sofa.

★ NOTTING HILL ARTS CLUB

NHAC; ☎ 7460 4459; www.notting hillartsclub.com; 21 Notting Hill Gate W11; ⏰ 6pm-1am Tue-Thu, 6pm-2am Fri & Sat, 4pm-11pm Sun; ⊖ Notting Hill Gate

'Eclectic' seems to be the catchphrase of the subterranean NHAC, with a range of different nights playing funk to hip-hop to indie – hell, there are even knitting evenings! – plus an equally diverse crowd of dreadlocked students and the occasional celebrity. The best-known nights include indie/punk Death Disco and boogie/soul YoYo. Arrive early.

★ SHEPHERD'S BUSH EMPIRE

☎ 7771 2000; www.shepherds -bush-empire.co.uk; Shepherd's Bush Green W12; ⊖ Shepherd's Bush

The 2000-capacity Empire is certainly one of the cleanest and most civilised midsized music venues in the capital, with a slightly older, chilled but still hip crowd. A former BBC recording theatre, its ground floor is irritatingly flat (meaning views of the stage are tricky from up the back), but its acoustics are nonetheless good.

London's a multi-faceted city. Whether your interests lie in architecture or music, whether you're into shopping or art galleries, if you're here for the clubbing or the gay scene, this city has an almost unparalleled breadth and depth of options to let you to indulge your passions to the full.

>Accommodation	186
>Architecture	188
>Food	190
>Galleries	192
>Cabaret	194
>Clubs	195
>Gay & Lesbian	196
>Music	197
>Pubs	198
>Riverside London	199
>Shopping	200
>Theatre	201
>Views	202

Inside County Hall (p137)

ACCOMMODATION

Location, location, location? That scarcely matters a damn in London, where booking a hotel room is more about price, price, price.

The bad news is that at a wallet-pinching £110 nightly average per room, only those wishing to be near local friends can really afford to be too fussy about the neighbourhood in which they stay. The good news is that, as with the city's restaurants, London hotels have raised their game dramatically. Plus, a mini-boom has resulted in more evenly distributed accommodation choices throughout the city, including in reborn districts like Hoxton, Marylebone and the South Bank.

A decade ago, Swedish furniture chain Ikea pleaded with British households to 'chuck out your chintz', and it seems London's fusty hotels have *finally* got the message. Not only have grande dames like Browns adopted a more contemporary look, scores of midrange hotels and B&Bs have ditched the doilies, floral curtains and patterned carpets, too.

Upmarket boutique hotels have brought a real sense of style to the city's digs, while chains have found a niche providing boringly functional but affordable rooms. Most heartening of all, however, has been the recent trend – right down the middle – for 'budget boutique' hotels with a pinch of chic at a reasonable price.

This hotel revolution has permeated the traditional accommodation enclaves. Earl's Court now boasts trendy lodgings like the Mayflower and Base2Stay, as well as the tasteless but cheap easyHotel. B+B Belgravia leads the way around Victoria. The choices around Bloomsbury are also improved.

haystack.lonelyplanet.com

Need a place to stay? Find and book it at lonelyplanet .com. More than 60 properties are featured for London – each personally visited, thoroughly reviewed and happily recommended by a Lonely Planet author. From hostels to high-end hotels, we've hunted out the places that will bring you unique and special experiences. Read independent reviews by authors and other travellers, and get practical information including amenities, maps and photos. Then reserve your room simply and securely via Haystack – our online booking service. It's all at www.lonelyplanet.com/accommodation.

Hotels are now also springing up where they never previously existed. The Southwark Rose Hotel joins chain outlets from Holiday Inn Express and Premier Travel Inn on the South Bank. Clerkenwell's Zetter and the Hoxton Hotel have made inroads in the east.

Of course, you still shouldn't expect anywhere near the same value for money in London as in other world cities. But if you choose carefully you might find the situation far better than the city's reputation would suggest.

As well as generic online booking sites, read Lonely Planet's own accommodation reviews at www.lonelyplanet.com/accommodation. Local booking engines like www.hotelconnect.co.uk might also be useful, while the official tourist site, www.visitlondon.com, frequently has good last-minute bargains.

BEST GRAND HOTELS
> Brown's (www.brownshotel.com)
> Claridge's (www.claridges.co.uk)
> Dorchester (www.dorchesterhotel.com)

BEST DESIGNER DENS
> Charlotte Street Hotel (www.firmdale.com)
> Sanderson (www.morganhotels.com)
> Mandeville (www.mandeville.co.uk)
> Soho Hotel (www.firmdale.com)
> Zetter (www.thezetter.com)

BEST BUDGET CHAINS
> Express by Holiday Inn (www.holidayinn.co.uk)
> Ibis (www.ibishotel.com)
> Premier Travel Inn (www.premiertravelinn.com)
> Travelodge (www.travelodge.co.uk)

BEST HOMEY LODGINGS
> Hampstead Village Guesthouse (www.hampsteadguesthouse.com)
> Vancouver Studios (www.vancouverstudios.co.uk)

BEST STYLE ON A BUDGET
> Base2Stay (www.base2stay.com)
> B+B Belgravia (www.bb-belgravia.com)
> Hoxton Hotel (www.hoxtonhotels.com)
> Mayflower (www.mayflowerhotel.co.uk)
> Southwark Rose Hotel (www.southwarkrosehotel.co.uk)

BEST HOSTEL
> Generator (www.the-generator.co.uk)

MOST RIDICULOUSLY ORANGE (BUT CHEAP-ISH) ROOMS
> easyHotel (www.easyhotel.com)

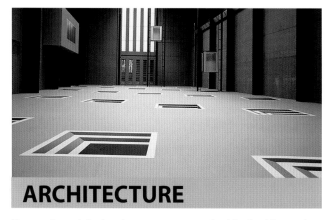

ARCHITECTURE

Never a planned city, London presents a merry jumble of architectural styles – from the Norman core of the Tower of London to the space-age Norman Foster creation of the 'Gherkin'.

A handful of early structures do survive, including the Tower and Westminster Abbey, but really only a small proportion predates 1666, when the Great Fire of London razed 80% of buildings. The great architect Sir Christopher Wren was commissioned to oversee reconstruction, but his grand scheme for broad, symmetrical avenues never came to pass. Instead, his main legacy comprises St Paul's Cathedral, the Monument (to the fire), a brace of impressive churches and the Royal Naval College at Greenwich – the last taking its place beside Inigo Jones's unscathed neoclassical, or Palladian, masterpieces.

Wren acolyte Nicholas Hawksmoor joined contemporary James Gibb in pursuing a style known as English Baroque, with churches like Christ Church Spitalfields and St Martin-in-the-Fields. However, remnants of Inigo Jones's classicism endured, morphing into neo-Palladianism in the Georgian era.

Like Wren before him, Georgian architect John Nash fancied imposing a bit of symmetry on unruly London, and was slightly more successful in developing the Mall, Trafalgar Sq and the western end of the Strand, although his plans for a linear Regent's street (now a crescent) obviously involved compromise.

The following generation, the Victorians, rebelled against their parents' fondness for clean lines with 'neo-Gothic' (or 'Gothick') buildings, iced like wedding cakes with perpendicular towers, ornate turrets and pointed arches.

Suburban terraces and Dickensian slums followed, but few individual buildings of enduring note were erected until Admiralty Arch and County Hall went up in the early 20th century.

A brief flirtation with Art Deco before WWII was followed by functional modernism after it, as large swathes of London again needed to be rebuilt. The 1990s postmodernist enclave of Docklands languished for nearly a decade before finding success. By then the city had embarked on an unexpectedly successful millennial facelift, producing several new London icons, such as the London Eye and Tate Modern.

Perhaps emboldened by the popularity of the 'Gherkin', mayor Ken Livingstone has since been enthusing about the need for more skyscrapers on the London skyline. Unesco, guardian of World Heritage sites like the Tower of London, is less certain about such plans.

BEST MEDIEVAL MASTERPIECES
> Tower of London (p114)
> Westminster Abbey (p86)

BEST ART DECO DELIGHT
> Former penguin pool at the London Zoo (p72)

BEST VICTORIAN CONFECTIONS
> Albert Memorial (p95)
> Leadenhall Market (p109)
> Houses of Parliament (p82)
> Natural History Museum (p99)
> St Pancras Chambers (p160)

BEST MODERNIST MONOLITHS
> Barbican (p119)
> South Bank Centre (p149)

BEST NEOCLASSICAL DESIGN
> Queen's House (p154)

BEST GORGEOUS GEORGIANS
> Bank of England façade (p109)
> Institute of Contemporary Arts (p83)
> Kenwood House (p169)
> Somerset House (p50)

BEST 21ST-CENTURY ICONS
> City Hall (p137)
> Gherkin (p114)
> London Eye (p140)
> Tate Modern (p142)

BEST FOR ENGLISH ECCENTRICITY
> Sir John Soane's Museum (p112)

Top left Tate Modern (p142)

FOOD

The dining scene in London has improved immeasurably in the past decade, as discussed on p26, but there are two other points in its favour. Firstly, vegetarians will find it no trouble to eat here. Secondly, the city offers a truly international range of cuisines.

In the neighbourhoods, we've listed several exclusively vegetarian establishments, including Eat & Two Veg (p76), Manna (p171) and Mildred's (p57), close to the centre. In truth, though, London's best veggie restaurant is off the map for most short-stay visitors: it's the Gate (www .gateveg.co.uk), way out in Hammersmith, should you be interested.

In any case, herbivores will find most gastropubs and restaurants have a few meat-free options on the menu. The few exceptions are those venues concentrating on new British cuisine, including the Gordon Ramsay signature restaurants and St John, which specialises in so-called nose-to-tail eating.

When it comes to different varieties of cuisine, London offers much more than French, Italian, Indian, Spanish and Thai. Afghani, Brazilian, Cuban, Eritrean, Jewish, Korean, Malaysian, Turkish – you could name pretty well any ethnic cuisine and find it somewhere in the city.

Sometimes restaurants cluster. Lebanese establishments line Edgeware Rd (Map p71, A5), north of Marble Arch. Portuguese is the flavour around Stockwell Rd and tube station. A couple of Argentine *parillas*, or grills, nestle along Broadway Market in Hackney (see the boxed text, p131).

However, other varieties of cuisine are spreading across London. With the restaurant influx of Polish and other Eastern European immigrants, long-standing favourites like Daquise (p105) and Trojka (p172) are set to gain plenty more competition.

One cuisine we continue to find disappointing, although many tied-to-London critics think otherwise, is the city's take on Vietnamese. It adheres perhaps a little too closely to its Chinese cousin and will probably disappoint anyone who's eaten Vietnamese outside the UK. However, if you want to try for yourself, head to the southern end of Kingsland Rd (Map p122-3, F3) in Hoxton.

BEST GASTROPUBS
> Anchor & Hope (p144)
> Gun (p153)
> Princess (p130)
> Wells (p172)

BEST FOR INDIAN
> Amaya (p104)
> Kastoori (p128)
> New Tayyab (p130)
> Painted Heron (p106)

BEST CHAINS
> Busaba Eathai (p56 & p66)
> Giraffe (p130)
> Gourmet Burger Kitchen (p173)
> Tas (p145)

BEST FOR ITALIAN
> Locanda Locatelli (p77)

BEST FOR FRENCH
> Almeida (p162)
> Club Gascon (p115)

BEST FOR SEAFOOD
> J Sheekey (p56)

BEST FOR CHINESE
> Hakkasan (p66)
> Yauatcha (p57)

BEST DÉCOR
> Les Trois Garçons (p130)
> Wolseley (p92)

Top left Boxwood Café (p105)

GALLERIES

London has fallen in love with the blockbuster art exhibition, and taken the genre to a whole new level recently. While there's nothing new about huge, highly publicised art 'events' – nor are they without critics – they've been all the rage in the English capital in the past several years.

London has upped the ante, and broken box-office records, by inventing previously unheard-of combinations, like Turner Whistler & Monet (all studying the Thames) at Tate Britain. It's thrown new light on Old Masters, with Caravaggio and Velázquez shows at the National Gallery, and presented jaw-dropping beauty at the Royal Academy of Arts' 'Turks'. And it's provoked debate about modernism and opened Leonardo da Vinci's sketchbooks at the Victoria & Albert Museum.

With the necessary prestige and gravitas to persuade overseas museums to lend them priceless masterpieces, the city's galleries are in a good position to marry these to their own impressive holdings. They often have little-seen gems tucked away in their vaults, as well. So it's even worthwhile planning an entire visit around an exhibition; check sites such as www.visitlondon.com, www.thisislondon.co.uk, www.guardian .co.uk and www.timeout.com for listings.

Of course, crowd-pleasers always come with crowds, and if the prospect of wading through rows of people for a glimpse of a favourite painting doesn't entice you, there's always the opposite extreme. With so many public and private galleries, London offers an unusually broad range of styles and genres. It's not shocked by the new, it's not afraid to experiment or provoke, and it's willing to gamble on the up-and-coming or fringe.

That's demonstrated not just by smaller galleries like the Serpentine and Whitechapel, but also by the Britart movement of the 1990s. Once considered outrageous, the works of Damien Hirst, Tracey Emin and the Chapman Brothers have now entered the mainstream, and you'll find some in Tate Britain.

Meanwhile, adman Charles Saatchi, the art collector who most nurtured that movement, is set to make a permanent comeback in 2007. After a warehouse fire and a disagreement that saw his previous collection leave County Hall, Saatchi's new gallery is near Sloane Sq. Don't come expecting more of the same Britart theme, though. Saatchi has moved on and is now concentrating on post-9/11 US painting.

BEST BLOCKBUSTER TEMPORARY EXHIBITIONS
> National Gallery (p47)
> Royal Academy of Arts (p84)
> Tate Britain (p85)
> Victoria & Albert Museum (p101)

BEST BRITART
> Tate Britain (p85)
> White Cube Gallery (p87)

BEST CUTTING-EDGE ART
> Institute of Contemporary Arts (p83)
> Photographers' Gallery (p47)
> Serpentine Gallery (p100)
> Whitechapel Art Gallery (p125)
> White Cube Gallery (p87)

PHOENIX-LIKE RESURRECTION
> Saatchi Gallery (p100)

Top left Tate Modern (p142)

CABARET

Doubtless an earnest student somewhere is already penning a thesis on the sociological underpinnings and implications of London's cabaret boom – leaving residents and visitors simply to revel in this strange, nostalgic phenomenon. It's not quite Berlin in the 1930s, as there are varying degrees of commercialism and postmodern irony knitted into contemporary London's mix of burlesque and vaudeville. It attracts its fair share of hen nights. However, the city's latest, headline-grabbing nightlife trend is usually intriguingly different.

'Cabaret', as loosely defined in the capital, runs the gamut of nightlife from impresario Vince Power's very grown-up Pigalle supper club, where guests enjoy 'variety' shows over dinner, to the playful, good-time 'happenings' at the Bethnal Green Working Men's Club.

There's a strong vein of camp, gay culture at Bistrotheque and on certain nights at Madame Jo Jo's, while the Volupté Lounge takes a more risqué tone with feather dancers and striptease.

Think of Dita von Teese – Marilyn Manson's wife and a regular in the UK papers – as the poster girl for this entertainment revolution. Her inaugural UK appearance at music venue Koko apparently created an even bigger stir than Madonna's most recent star-studded performance.

BEST FOR…
Good ole-fashioned fun Bethnal Green Working Men's Club (p135)
Cabaret meets indie rock Koko (p175)
Tranny showgirls Madame Jo Jo's (p61)
Camping it up with cocktails Bistrotheque (p129)
Afternoon tea served by waiters on rollerskates Viva Cake, St Aloysius Social Club (see the boxed text, p162); Bethnal Green Working Men's Club (p135)
Maids' uniforms, nipple tassles & striptease Volupté Lounge (p119)

CLUBS

Few cities can rival London for its number of club venues, and none can rival it for its sheer variety of club evenings. Disco, boogie, funk, punk, R&B, drum and bass, hip-hop, electro, electro-clash, techno, deep house, rave – hell, even Polish pop and more – are played here. And all that happens pretty well every night of the week. In fact, one of the city's best regulars is Monday's Trash at the End, a punk-electronic-punk-indie mash-up, with excellent bands who've included Bloc Party, Scissor Sisters and the Yeah, Yeah, Yeahs.

Perhaps one of the reasons for this is that in the West End, on the weekend, things can be a bit rowdy and messy – it's a binge-drinking thing. But if you head to the nightlife hub of Hoxton, an enjoyable time is almost guaranteed. Good individual venues are found in Camden, Clerkenwell and Notting Hill, while there's a cluster of clubs in the industrial wastelands north of King's Cross, for that gritty, urban feeling.

Dress fashionably, but not too smart, to get past the frequently attitudinal door staff. London is awash in giveaway daily newspapers at the moment and the cost-free *londonpaper* (www.thelondonpaper.com), if it survives, has comprehensive listings to rival *Time Out's* (www.timeout .com; £2.50). Also try www.dontstayin.com.

BEST...
Super-club to end all super-clubs Fabric (p119)
Sound system Ministry of Sound (p148)
Big-name DJs End (p60); Fabric (p119)
Open-minded music policy Cargo (p135)
Relaxed door scene (usually) 333 (p135); Cargo (p135)
Outdoor terrace Cross (p165); 93 Feet East (p135)
After-party Egg (p165)
Indie sounds Club NME, Koko (p175)
Wee hours pit-stop Bar Italia (p58); Brick Lane Beigel Bake (p121)
Sunday comedown Big Chill Bar (p131)

GAY & LESBIAN

The pink pound certainly flexes its muscle in London. Some local gay men and lesbians even complain that the scene is too commercial. The upside is that it's out and proud. Discrimination is a rare thing here.

The homosexual visitor to London could do much worse than making a beeline for Soho's Old Compton St (Map p48, D3). Night and day, this is the queer community's meeting point, lined with gay bars and shops, and full of good-looking, preening customers. Here you'll be sure to find gay freesheets like *Boyz* and *QX*, and be able to buy copies of *Attitude*, *Gay Times* or *Diva*.

London's most famous – and certainly its most central – gay club is Heaven (p61). However, there's also a cluster of small but essential clubs south of the river in the so-called 'Vauxhall Village'. Here you'll not only find Muscle-Mary nirvana Crash (p147), but also Horse Meat Disco (www .horsemeatdisco.co.uk) and legendary kitsch cabaret evening Duckie (www.duckie.co.uk).

Finally, London's scene – whatever the moans about commercialism – is quite a broad church. It doesn't just cater for buff fans of mainstream techno. Connoisseurs of indie, alternative and even grunge are catered for with venues ranging from the Scala (p165) and Ghetto (p160) to the sweaty Astoria (p59).

BEST…

Warm-up drinks Trash Palace (www.trashpalace.co.uk)
Girl bar Candy Bar (www.candybar.co.uk)
Six-packs on display Crash (p147); Saturday night, Heaven (p61)
Polysexual clubbing DPTM, Fabric (p119); Fiction, Cross (p165)
Cheesy camp fun G-A-Y Camp Attack, Astoria (p59)
Sweaty, electroclash evenings Nag, Nag, Nag, Ghetto (p60)
Indie kicks Popstarz, Scala (p165); Miss-shapes, Ghetto (p60)
Decadent dining Les Trois Garçons (p130)
Cocktail hour Bistrotheque (p129); Loungelover (p134)

MUSIC

London moves to any number of different beats, from the patriotic strains of Elgar on the last night of the Proms (p35), to the spiky strummings of a wannabe guitar band, fronted by a Russell Brand lookalike with kohl eyeliner, spiky hair and skinny jeans.

The classical music scene has been in some flux of late, with the premier venue – the Royal Festival Hall – only due to reopen after refurbishment in 2007, plus public debate about whether the Proms in 2006 managed to put sufficient bums on seats.

By contrast, the rock scene is healthier than ever. Fuelled by the re-emergence of guitar rock half a decade ago, it's developed quite a DIY ethos, coupled with a willingness to dabble in other genres, that's injected greater diversity. See www.xfm.co.uk or www.irlondon.co.uk to swot up on the scene.

Jazz has been happily burbling on underneath, meanwhile, although it, too, has received a shot in the arm, with the revamp and reopening of the world-famous Ronnie Scott's.

JAZZ
> Jazz Café (p175)
> Ronnie Scott's (p61)

GRUNGIER GIGS
> Barfly @ the Monarch (p175)
> Boogaloo (p173)

CHART-TOPPERS WITH CRED
> Brixton Academy (p147)
> Koko (p175)
> Shepherd's Bush Empire (p183)

CROSS-OVER GENRES
> Barbican (p119)
> Jazz Café (p175)
> Roundhouse (p175)

BEST FOR CLASSICAL PERFORMANCES
> Barbican (p119)
> Royal Albert Hall (pictured above; p107)
> South Bank Centre (p149)

PUBS

They can't quite compete with Dublin's, but London's pubs nevertheless remain a much-loved social institution. One or two historic examples date from the 16th and 17th centuries. However, more are from the Victorian era, the city's greatest pub-building period. (Even more are Victorian fakes, but we're ignoring those here.)

Despite dire predictions, a change of licensing laws in late 2005 has not brought rampaging hordes of drunken yobbos and anarchy to London's streets – well, no more than previously. The traditional closing time of 11pm lives on in some venues, although those in the centre now tend to serve at least half an hour later during the week and until midnight on Friday and Saturday.

In this guide, we've reviewed historic pubs that the short-term visitor might easily get to. In reality, though, many of London's best pubs are further out, or off the traditional tourist trail. If you're a pub connoisseur check out websites like www.fancyapint.co.uk or www.beerintheevening.com. We don't agree with their every review, but they're certainly comprehensive.

BEST FOR A QUICK PRE-THEATRE GAWP
> Salisbury (p58)

BEST FOR CONVIVIAL NURSING OF A PINT
> George Inn (pictured above; p146)
> Lamb (p67)

BEST FOR ROWDY CAROUSING
> Lamb & Flag (p58)

BEST FOR HISTORIC SETTINGS
> George Inn (p146)
> Lamb & Flag (p58)
> Princess Louise (p68), Salisbury (p58)
> Ye Olde Mitre (p118)

RIVERSIDE LONDON

Historically, the River Thames has been London's *raison d'être* and lifeblood. Without it, the Romans would never have founded Londinium, nor would the city have become such a successful trading hub (see the boxed text, p205).

Yet the 21st-century Thames is relatively underused. Modern container ships are too large to come far upriver and most unload their cargo outside its mouth. Meanwhile, of the two million people who take to its waters each year, most are sightseers. (There have been calls for increased commuter services by 2012, although the mayor has declared river travel relatively uneconomic.)

For decades, the riverbank also lay neglected. Unused docks fell into disrepair in the 1960s and '70s, and it was only in the 1990s that the refurbishment of buildings like the Oxo Tower, and areas such as Butler's Wharf around the Design Museum, heralded its rediscovery. This move was subsequently sealed by the millennial projects of the London Eye, Millennium Bridge and Tate Modern, and has continued around City Hall.

Today, London has definitely fallen in love with the Thames again, with the stretch from Waterloo Bridge to Butler's Wharf one of the city's most popular districts.

BEST FOR...
The whole city in an instant Waterloo Bridge (pictured above; p11)
That Parisian left-bank feeling Riverside Walk, near the South Bank Centre (p149)
Quintesssential London views Through the windows of Tate Modern (p142)
Looking both ways up the river Top level of Tower Bridge (p114)
A rear view of Docklands From near the Royal Observatory (p155)
Travel in style The Tate boat (p142)
An adrenaline rush An RIB voyage (p141)
Table with a view BluePrint Café (p144)

SHOPPING

No-one would want to miss a little retail therapy in London, one of the world's unrivalled shopping experiences.

The over-the-top emporium Harrods and the antiques of Portobello Rd Market are part of London's identity. However, the city's major retail strength is its fashion. Its range of streetwear is unrivalled, as is its ability to quickly and cheaply bring catwalk trends to the ordinary consumer. While chains increasingly line the High St, one of the capital's delights remains its independent boutiques. For every classic Savile Row tailor, there are a dozen funky young designer outlets in Hoxton. Vintage clothes shops pepper the landscape from Notting Hill to Spitalfields, traditional British brands like Burberry and Mulberry have radically reinvented themselves, and young British designers, such as Stella McCartney and Matthew Williamson, maintain lavish outlets just worth a look.

It's true that some central shopping districts are dirty, littered and crowded. But the city is always compensating with interesting shopping hubs spinning off elsewhere every few years.

Even if you've no money to spend, visiting one of London's markets offers a perfect insight into the city. Camden is almost exclusively the preserve of tourists. See p25 for the best starting points.

BEST DEPARTMENT STORES
> Harrods (p102)
> Selfridges (p76)

BEST FOR AFFORDABLE NEW TRENDS
> Topshop (p66)

BEST FOR QUICKLY GAUGING HOXTON STREET STYLE
> Laden Showrooms (p127)
> Spitalfields Market (p128)
> Sunday Up Market (p125)

BEST FOR WELL-PRICED CDS & DVDS
> Fopp (p51 & p65)

BEST FOR VINTAGE CLOTHES
> Absolute Vintage (p126)
> Beyond Retro (p127)
> Rellick (p179)

BEST NOSTALGIC SHOPFRONT
> A Gold (p126)

BEST QUIRKY KNICK-KNACKS
> Oxo Tower (p143)

BEST FASHION MAG FAVOURITES
> Alfie's Antiques Market (p74)
> Dover Street Market (p88)
> Shop at Bluebird (p102)
> Tatty Devine (p128)

THEATRE

From the time of Shakespeare, London has enjoyed a formidable reputation for theatre, and its current scene is thoroughly deserving of the Bard's legacy. The English language's most esteemed playwright was essentially a crowd-pleaser – as you'll appreciate watching one of his works bawdily staged in the reconstructed Globe Theatre. In the same way, the contemporary London stage has reaped huge rewards by blurring the lines between the serious and the feel-good.

Highbrow theatres have begun staging more vibrant and timely productions to woo new audiences. At the same time, the West End has shown a greater tendency to take risks. (Take the example of the esteemed National Theatre acting as a springboard to catapult the controversial *Jerry Springer: The Opera* from the fringe to the West End.)

The resulting excitement has attracted major movie names, and left critics remarkably uncritical. One local listings magazine recently declared theatre the new rock 'n' roll, while even the worthy *Independent* has enthused about the quality of current West End musicals, from *Billy Elliot* and *Dirty Dancing* to *Spamalot*. (Although they are, also, starting to get worried about musicals dominating the West End.) For comprehensive listings, visit www.officiallondontheatre.co.uk.

BEST FOR...
Plays in the news National Theatre (p149)
Intimacy and experimentation Almeida Theatre (p165); Donmar Warehouse (p59); Young Vic (p149)
New pieces from angry young playwrights Royal Court Theatre (p107)
Authentic Shakespearean surrounds Shakespeare's Globe (p149)
Seeing Kevin Spacey Old Vic (p149)

VIEWS

From above, you really start to appreciate London's grandeur and size. Even from the London Eye, you can't quite discern the capital's outer reaches.

Strangely, for a city with relatively few skyscrapers, London has at least a dozen publicly accessible outlook points. Some, like St Paul's Cathedral and the Monument, date back to the 17th century. However, a good many weren't here a mere decade ago, including the Eye, the Oxo Tower and Tate Modern.

With restaurants like Portrait at the National Portrait Gallery and Galvin @ Windows opening in just the last few years, it seems contemporary London is happy to continue with a little navel-gazing. For visitors, it's simply fun to admire London's historical landscape and work out which are the various buildings.

BEST FOR AN OVERVIEW
> Dome of St Paul's Cathedral (p114)
> London Eye (pictured above; p140)
> Parliament Hill, Hampstead Heath (p24)

A DIFFERENT PERSPECTIVE
> Portrait Restaurant, National Portrait Gallery (p47)
> Top-floor café, Waterstone's (p88)

RIVER VIEWS
> Oxo Tower (p143)
> Tate Modern (p142)
> Tower Bridge (p114)

TWILIGHT COCKTAILS
> Vertigo 42 (p118)
> Restaurant on 7th floor, Tate Modern (p142)

A LONG CLIMB
> Dome of St Paul's Cathedral (p114)
> Monument (p112)

AN EASY RIDE
> London Eye (p140)
> Tower Bridge (p114)
> Westminster Cathedral (p86)

SPYING ON THE QUEEN
> Galvin @ Windows (p90)

>BACKGROUND

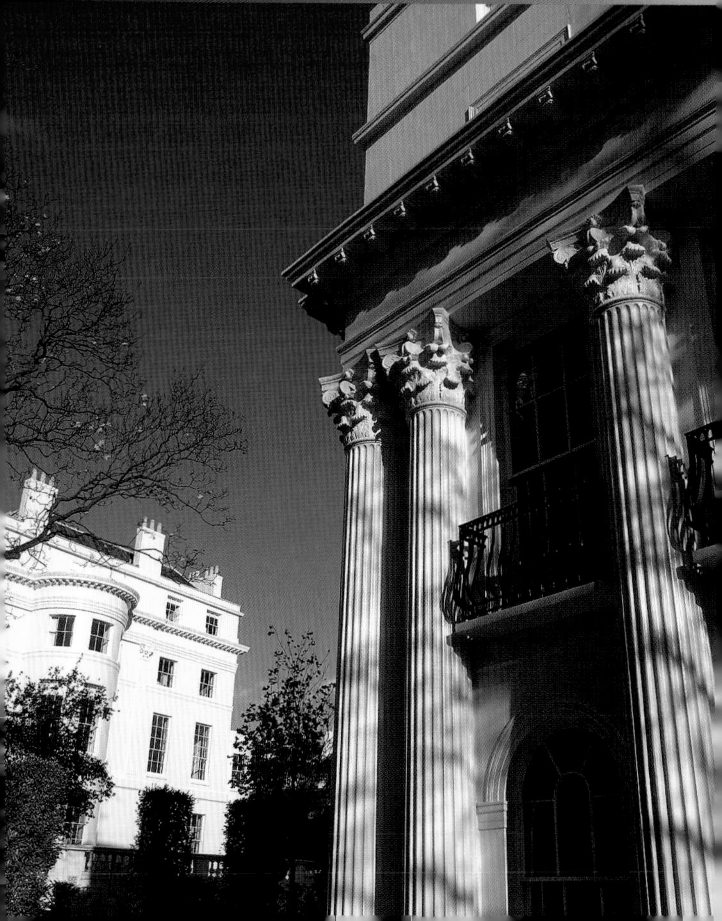

BACKGROUND
HISTORY
THE CELTS & ROMANS

Today's diverse, exciting metropolis had its genesis in the walled Roman city of Londinium, which was established in AD 43 on the northern bank of the River Thames in the area that's now the City or financial district. The Romans built a bridge across the river and managed to establish an important port and trade hub, before their empire crumbled and Londinium was abandoned in AD 410.

THE SAXONS & DANES

After this, a series of Saxons (northern Teutonic tribes) moved into the area west of the walled city, around today's Aldwych and Charing Cross. Danish Vikings took an interest in Saxon London, attacking it sporadically between 842 and the early 11th century, at which point Danish King Canute briefly ruled England. However, it was Edward the Confessor who left an indelible mark on London. By moving his court to Westminster after taking the throne in 1042, and there founding Westminster Abbey (p86), he gave the capital two distinct hubs – political (Westminster) and commercial (the City).

LONDON'S LIFEBLOOD

The River Thames has played a pivotal role in London's evolution.
>   The Romans founded Londinium here in AD 43 because of the river
>   It made the city a wealthy trading centre, as ships brought in global riches
>   It froze over in medieval winters and was used for 'frost fayres' (fairs) and ice-skating
>   London Bridge was the only crossing until Westminster Bridge opened in 1750
>   Industrial traffic declined substantially when the British empire began to crumble after 1945. Docks became offices; container ships now unload outside the Barrier.
>   Biologically dead in 1957, the river now sustains 122 fish species; in 2006 a poor whale even strayed into its slipstream
>   Some 2 million people go on the river annually, mainly for pleasure

Top left The City from the north bank of the Thames **Top right** Westminster Abbey (p86) **Bottom** A tube station

THE NORMANS

After Edward, the Normans invaded from northern France and William the Conqueror gained control of the city in 1066. William's distrust of the 'fierce populace' led him to build several strongholds, including the White Tower, at the core of the Tower of London (p114).

TUDOR LONDON

London thrived during the Middle Ages, but it was under the Tudors in the 16th century that it really created waves. Not only did their reign coincide with the discovery of the Americas and thriving world trade, Henry VIII's desire to divorce the first of his six wives also led him to break with the Catholic church and establish the Church of England in 1534. Henry's move obviously had global implications, but it also transformed London's own landscape, as he went about annexing church property and turning some of it into the royal hunting grounds that would later become Hyde Park (p98) and Regent's Park (p73). Imprisoning opponents (and wives), Henry also did much to give the give the Tower of London its bloody reputation.

Henry's powerful daughter Elizabeth I (r 1558–1603) died without an heir, and the weak rule of her relatives James I and Charles I (the descendants of her Catholic cousin Mary, Queen of Scots) loosened the monarchy's grip on the country.

During the English Civil War (1642–49), Oliver Cromwell's Roundheads (a coalition of Puritans, Parliamentarians and merchants) wrested complete control of the country from the king in 1646. Parliament restored the monarchy in 1660, but the English monarchy had already ceased to be absolute.

London suffered a major setback when the Great Fire of 1666 razed 80% of its buildings. But the inferno wasn't without its silver linings: it took few lives, wiped away the last vestiges of the 1665 plague (which had killed 100,000) and gave Christopher Wren a clean slate upon which to build. Wren's St Paul's Cathedral (p114) remains a major landmark, and he made major contributions at Greenwich (p150), as well as leaving dozens of churches and other buildings throughout London. The memorial to the blaze, the Monument (p112), was another Wren design; when erected in 1677 it was the highest structure in the city.

Actually, London's post-fire building boom continued for several centuries. Soon after the Great Fire, Charles II moved out of Westminster to

St James's, and the surrounding area was taken over by the gentry who built the grand squares and town houses of modern-day Mayfair and St James's. In 1685 some 1500 Huguenot refugees arrived in London fleeing persecution in Catholic France, and turned their hands to the manufacture of luxury goods like silks and silverware in and around the already multicultural districts of Spitalfields and Clerkenwell.

GEORGIAN PERIOD

By 1700 there were 600,000 Londoners and, as focus for a growing empire, the city was becoming ever richer and more important. Georgian architects such as John Nash, the planner of Trafalgar Sq (p51), and Sir John Soane (see Sir John Soane's Museum, p112) erected imposing symmetrical buildings and residential squares.

VICTORIAN AGE

The population really mushroomed during the 19th century. It jumped from just under one million in 1800 to 6.5 million a century later, leading

Trafalgar Sq (p51)

to the creation of vast suburbs during Queen Victoria's 64-year reign and the Industrial Revolution.

As well as building terraced suburban housing, docks in the East End and, crucially, the railways, the Victorians were also partial to 'neo-Gothic' architecture, with perpendicular towers, pointed arches and turrets. The best example of this is the current Palace of Westminster/Houses of Parliament (p82), which was erected by architect Charles Barry and interior designer August Pugin in 1840–60, after the previous parliament burned down. But other Victorian Gothic buildings remain, including architect Alfred Waterhouse's Natural History Museum (1880; p99) and

Natural History Museum (p99)

George Gilbert Scott's St Pancras Chambers (1874; p160).

After Victoria died in 1901, her son Edward's reign saw the introduction of motorised buses, expansion of the nascent Underground train system and the first Olympics in London.

THE WORLD WARS

The Great War (WWI) began in August 1914. During this war, there was a huge loss of British life on Continental battlefields, and aerial raids on London killed 650 people. However, tragic as these deaths were, they were overshadowed by the carnage during WWII. Churchill and his government in the underground Cabinet War Rooms (p79) were powerless to prevent swathes of east London being obliterated during the Blitz of 1940–1. By the time WWII ended in 1945, 32,000 Londoners had been killed and another 50,000 seriously wounded.

After the war, ugly housing and low-cost developments were hastily erected. Indeed, the 'brutal modernist' architectural style that then held sway can still be seen in some high-profile complexes, such as the South Bank Centre (p149) and the Barbican (p119). The Thames docks, once an important economic mainstay, never really recovered; shipping moved east to Tilbury, and the Docklands declined until redevelopment into a financial district in the 1980s and '90s.

The post-war welfare state established by Labour was largely dismantled during 18 years of era-defining Conservative rule from 1979. Privati-

---

DID YOU KNOW?

> Central London population: 7.5 million
> Greater London population: 12.8 million
> Percentage of London residents born outside the UK: 33%
> London's share of UK GDP: 19%
> Average annual household income: £37,073
> Average London house price: £285,434
> Average house price in Kensington and Chelsea: £768,000
> Time a Londoner must work to pay for a Big Mac: 16 minutes
> Unemployment: 7.6%
> Rubbish produced annually: 3.4 million tonnes
> Passengers travelling through Heathrow each year: 67 million
> Overnight stays by tourists in 2005: 25.4 million
> Annual tourist income: £15 billion

sation and deregulation were the mantras of the Thatcher years, leading to a boom in the financial services sector. However, political sleaze and voter disenchantment eventually helped a Labour government to romp in under Prime Minister Tony Blair in 1997.

LONDON TODAY

Initially, Blair's charisma, coupled with a strong economy, won over the capital's citizens, who contributed to Labour's second landslide win in June 2001. But subsequent unpopular decisions by the PM, including UK involvement in the 2003 Iraq war, saw Labour limp home in the 2005 elections with a much reduced majority, while Londoners united slightly more behind their mayor, Ken Livingstone, instead.

A day after winning its bid to host the 2012 Olympics, London became the victim of suicide bombings on its Underground transport system on 7 July 2005 (locally referred to as '7/7'). The understandable sorrow and anger generated by that event was tempered by incredible bravery and stoicism. Since then, life in the capital has pretty much returned to its everyday pace, albeit with greater vigilance and a renewed discussion of multiculturalism.

LIFE AS A LONDONER

With nearly 50 different ethnic groups (33% of the population was born outside the UK) and 300 languages spoken, London is one of the planet's most diverse cities, truly deserving of the accolade 'the world in one city'.

As befits any metropolis, though, this is a fast-moving and often overwhelming place, and Londoners frequently have a love/hate relationship with their 'hometown'. On the one hand, there is an unparalleled range of cultural offerings and things to do, with London attracting the very best talent to its galleries, clubs and theatres. On the other hand, London is dirty, expensive and stressful; it has a workaholic tendency. So many residents

USEFUL WEBSITES

> Official information from the Greater London Authority is available at www.london.gov.uk
> Read up on the latest from the City of London and the Lord Mayor at www.corpoflondon.gov.uk
> The London School of Economics carries out independent research into the government and economy of London; see www.lse.ac.uk/collections/LSELondon

complain of not having the money or time to appreciate the wonderful smorgasbord the city spreads out. It's worth noting, though, that many Londoners have actually chosen to move here from elsewhere, and most usually find the right sort of balance eventually.

Locals have a reputation for being slightly standoffish and unfriendly, and it's true that if you try to strike up a chatty conversation with a stranger on a bus or the tube you might be rebuffed. Probably as a way of coping with the constant crush of people, commuters usually adopt a thousand-yard stare and travel in silence on tubes, buses and trains, so somebody disturbing that equilibrium might even be looked at as if they are a little mad. Don't worry, though; if you're obviously a tourist in need of directions, there won't be a problem.

And underneath it all, Londoners are a liberal and tolerant bunch. It's difficult to offend them, and they're unfazed by outrageous dress or behaviour. (Indeed, they are skilled at ignoring anyone trying to draw attention to themselves.)

However, one relatively minor thing does cause amusingly disproportionate outrage, and is worth noting even on the briefest of city visits. To avoid being sworn at by commuters, stand on the *right* side on tube-station escalators, allowing your hassled and harried fellow passengers to dash by on the left!

GOVERNMENT & POLITICS

London has improved markedly since regaining control of its own affairs in the 21st century. Curiously, this great city – which has a GDP of £150 billion and is the engine of the British economy – was once without a mayor or self-governing authority. After 1986, when Prime Minister Margaret Thatcher abolished the Greater London Council (GLC), the city spent 14 years rudderless. That finally changed when Tony Blair's Labour government established a new Greater London Authority (GLA) and the public elected former GLC leader Ken Livingstone as mayor in May 2000. The GLA has strategic influence over transport, economic development, environmental policy, police, fire brigades, civil defence and culture.

Livingstone's reign started well. He won plaudits for his courage in introducing the world's first 'congestion charge', making car drivers pay to cross the city's central zone, and seemed to be doing well in improving the bus services. And when he was re-elected in 2004, he did so after being welcomed back into the Labour Party that had once expelled him.

However, the mayor hit a few bumps in his second term. After an intemperate discussion with a Jewish journalist, for example, he was handed a brief suspension from office. Londoners were also dismayed by his decision to withdraw the traditional Routemaster double-decker bus (see the boxed text, p88) after he had said one would have to be a moron to do so. However, the mayor did preside over London's successful bid for the 2012 Olympics, galvanised the city after the 7/7 bombings and eventually managed to overturn his suspension on High Court appeal, and began to regain his good reputation.

The mayor of London is separate from the Lord Mayor of the City of London, who is more of an administrative official.

FURTHER READING

Novelists like Charles Dickens have left a sterling legacy of London-oriented fiction, but that has never overawed modern writers such as Martin Amis or Zadie Smith. Writing on the city ranges from the populist to the highbrow, so there's plenty to choose from, including the following:

Absolute Beginners (1959; Colin MacInnes) Brilliantly capturing the youth culture of London in the '50s.

Brick Lane (2003; Monica Ali) An Islamic Bangladeshi woman comes to London after an arranged marriage and initially accepts her lot, before a voyage of self-discovery.

The Buddha of Suburbia (1991; Hanif Kureishi) A raunchy, heartwarming and insightful trawl into the hopes and fears of a group of Asian suburbanites in 1970s London.

The End of the Affair (1951; Graham Greene) A woman is torn between her husband, lover and religion in this emotional classic set in battle-scarred WWII London.

The Jeeves Omnibus (1931; PG Wodehouse) Sending up the upper classes with tales of wealthy Mayfair resident Bertie Wooster and butler Jeeves.

Last Orders (1997; Graham Swift) Four ageing friends reminisce about the East End of wartime London.

London: The Biography (2000; Peter Ackroyd) Widely regarded as the definitive guide, this enormous, meandering tome weaves a fascinating London tapestry.

London: City of Disappearances (2006; Peter Ackroyd) The great London-lover's latest tomes focuses on the changing face of the city, particularly the bits that have been erased or are no longer with us.

London Fields (1989; Martin Amis) A dense but gripping study of London lowlife. 'Dickens plus swearing and sex, minus compassion', wrote one reviewer.

London Orbital (2002; Iain Sinclair) Sinclair circumnavigates the capital on foot around the M25 motorway.

Oliver Twist (1837; Charles Dickens) This tale of a runaway orphan falling in with a gang of thieves isn't Dickens' best novel, but it is a vivid portrayal of Victorian London.

Tunnel Visions: Journeys of an Underground Philosopher (2002; Christopher Ross) Brilliant, funny, light, and often overlooked ruminations by an overqualified tube-station attendant.

White Teeth (2000; Zadie Smith) A funny, poignant, big-hearted book about friendship and cultural differences between three unassimilated families in north London.

FILM

London has never had an auteur to chronicle it in the same way that Woody Allen has New York, although even Allen himself has fallen in love with the city recently, filming *Match Point* and *Scoop* here. And there are a good range of cinematic representations from 1950s Ealing comedies to recent rom-coms, gangster flicks and gritty working-class dramas, including the following:

Breaking and Entering (2006) Anthony Minghella's first London-based drama in many years, starring Jude Law and Juliette Binoche, isn't afraid to show the gritty side of the city.

Bridget Jones's Diary (2001) London is the backdrop to Bridget Jones's relationships dilemmas, as played out by normally skinny Texan Renee Zellweger.

Children of Men (2006) This dystopian sci-fi thriller, set in 2027, isn't always successful, but it does provide an entirely new take on some London icons, portraying places such as the Battersea Power Station, Tate Modern and Millennium Bridge to chilling effect.

Closer (2004) Adapted from Patrick Marber's play about infidelity, with Jude Law, Julia Roberts, Clive Owen and lots of London, including the Aquarium, Smithfield, South Bank, and NPG Restaurant.

The Ipcress File (1965) This moody Michael Caine spy thriller shows off Blackfriars Bridge, the Royal Albert Hall, Trafalgar Sq and the Victoria & Albert Museum.

The Krays (1990) Gary and Martin Kemp (from 1980s New Romantic band Spandau Ballet) play the notorious Kray brothers, Ronnie and Reggie, gangland masters of the 1950s and '60s East End.

The Ladykillers (1955) In the last great Ealing comedy, Alec Guinness is a criminal mastermind unwittingly foiled by his little old King's Cross landlady.

Lock, Stock and Two Smoking Barrels (1998) Guy Ritchie (now Mr Madonna) directs Nick Moran, Jason Statham and others, as they find themselves £500,000 in debt to a scary East End 'ard man.

Notting Hill (1999) The Hugh Grant/Julia Roberts vehicle that launched a thousand clichés about the district of the title.

My Beautiful Laundrette (1985) Daniel Day-Lewis plays a gay punk helping his boyfriend open a neon-lit, music-filled laundrette, in a Hanif Kureishi script exploring racism, sexuality and more.

Secrets & Lies (1996) Hortense, a successful black optician, go in search of her natural – white – mother in this bleak but funny Mike Leigh examinations of working-class British lives.

Vera Drake (2005) Mike Leigh's period piece recreates the post-war East End to perfection, following an ill-fated abortionist who 'helps out' young girls.

28 Days Later (2002) Superb scenes of a desolate London, devoid of all human life after zombies take over the world.

DIRECTORY
TRANSPORT
ARRIVAL & DEPARTURE
AIR

London's airports are scattered around its perimeter, with its major hubs Heathrow, Gatwick and Stansted lying west, south and north respectively.

Heathrow

Heathrow (LHR; ☎ 0870 000 0123; www.heathrowairport.com) is the world's busiest international airport; it has four terminals, with a fifth due to be progressively opened between 2008 and 2011. There are two transport stations: one for Terminals 1, 2 and 3 and one for Terminal 4. When leaving London, remember to check which terminal you need.

Gatwick

There are two terminals – north and south – at **Gatwick** (LGW; ☎ 0870 000 2468; www.gatwickairport.com), which are linked by a two-minute monorail service. The train station is in the south terminal.

Stansted

Low-cost airlines have turned **Stansted** (STN; ☎ 0870 000 0303; www.stanstedairport.com) into London's fastest-growing airport.

London City

London City Airport (LCY; ☎ 7646 0000; www.londoncityairport.com) is a smaller, business-orientated airport in the city's east.

The **Docklands Light Railway** (☎ 7222 1234; www.tfl.gov.uk/dlr) has services running between Bank tube/DLR station and London City Airport, taking 30 minutes. Trains run from 5.30am

---

CLIMATE CHANGE & TRAVEL

Travel – especially air travel – is a significant contributor to global climate change. At Lonely Planet, we believe that all who travel have a responsibility to limit their personal impact. As a result, we have teamed with Rough Guides and other concerned industry partners to support Climate Care, which allows people to offset the greenhouse gases they are responsible for with contributions to energy-saving projects and other climate-friendly initiatives in the developing world. Lonely Planet offsets all staff and author travel.

For more information, turn to the responsible travel pages on www.lonelyplanet.com. For details on offsetting your carbon emissions and a carbon calculator, go to www.climatecare.org.

DIRECTORY

Travel to/from Heathrow

	Piccadilly Line tube	Heathrow Express train	Bus	Taxi
Going to	King's Cross/St Pancras	Paddington	Victoria Coach Station	Central London
Duration	1hr to Leicester Sq	15min	45-70min	1hr (rush hour 1½hr)
Cost	one-way £4 (with Oyster Card £3.50)	one-way/return £13.50/26	one-way/return from £4/8	black cab £55-60, service cab £35-45
Other	every 5-10min 5am-11.45pm Mon-Sat, 5.50am-10.50pm Sun	every 15min, from Heathrow 5.05am-11.45pm, reduced Sun service, from Paddington 5.10am-11.25pm	buses 032, 035, 050, 403 & 412 every 30-60min, from Heathrow 5am-9.30pm, from Victoria Coach Station 7.15am-11.30pm	
Contact	☎ 7222 1234; www.tfl.gov.uk	☎ 0845 600 1515; www.heathrowexpress.co.uk	☎ 0870 580 8080; www.nationalexpress.com	☎ black cab 7253 5000, 7908 0207, service cab 7272 2222, 8888 4444

Travel to/from Gatwick

	Gatwick Express train	Southern train	Thameslink train	Bus	Taxi
Going to	Victoria rail station	Victoria rail station	London Bridge, Farringdon, King's Cross	Victoria Coach Station	Central London
Duration	30min	45min	1hr to King's Cross	65-95min	1½hr
Cost	one-way/return £14/25	one-way/return £8/16	one-way/return £10/20	one-way/return from £6.60/12.20	black cab £90-95, service cab £55
Other	every 15min, from Gatwick 5.50am-12.35am, from Victoria 5am-11.45pm; some overnight services	every 15-30min, hourly midnight-4am	every 30min, 24hr	bus 025 hourly, from Gatwick 5.15am-10.15pm, from Victoria 7am-11.30pm	
Contact	☎ 0845 850 1530; www.gatwickexpress.co.uk	☎ 0845 748 4950; www.southernrailway.com	☎ 0845 748 4950; www.thameslink.co.uk	☎ 0870 580 8080; www.nationalexpress.com	☎ black cab 7253 5000, 7908 0207, service cab 7272 2222, 8888 4444

Travel to/from Stansted

	Stansted Express train & night bus	National Express bus	Terravision bus	Taxi
Going to	Liverpool St station	Victoria Coach Station	Victoria Coach Station	Central London
Duration	45-50min	65-95min	1¼hr	80min
Cost	one-way/return £15/25 £10/16	one-way/return £8/14 service cab £50	one-way/return	black cab £105,
Other	every 15min, from airport 6am-midnight, to 12.30am Sat & Sun, from Liverpool St 4.55am-10.55pm, to 11.25pm Sat & Sun; overnight buses every 30min, from airport midnight-4am, from Liverpool St 2.30-4.30am	every 20min 10am-11pm, overnight buses A6 & A4 24hr	every 30min, from airport (coach bay 26) 7.15am-1am; from Victoria 2.40am-11.10pm	
Contact	☎ 0845 748 4950; www.stanstedexpress .com	☎ 0870 580 8080; www.nationalexpress .com	☎ 01279 680 028; www.lowcostcoach .com	☎ black cab 7253 5000, 7908 0207; service cab 7272 2222, 8888 4444

to 12.30am Monday to Saturday, and 7.30am to 11pm Sunday. The journey costs £4 (£2.50 for Oyster Card holders).

Otherwise a **black cab** (☎ 7253 5000, 7908 0207) will cost £25 to £30 to/from central London.

Luton

Another smaller airport is **Luton** (LTN; ☎ 01582 405100; www.london -luton.co.uk), which is roughly 35 miles (56km) north of central London.

Thameslink (☎ national rail enquiries 0845 748 4950; www.thameslink .co.uk; off-peak one-way/return £11.70/11.90) trains run from King's Cross/St Pancras station and

other central London stations to Luton Airport Parkway station (30 to 40 minutes, every six to 15 minutes from 7am to 10pm), and from there an airport shuttle bus will take you to Luton Airport in eight minutes.

Green Link (☎ 0870 608 7261; www .greenline.co.uk; one-way/return £9.50/11) operates bus 757, which runs between Luton and Buckingham Palace Rd, Victoria (one hour). Services are round the clock, with half-hourly buses between 3.30am and 11.30pm.

A black cab to/from central London costs £95 to £100.

BUS

Within the UK & to Europe

Bus travellers arrive at and depart from **Victoria Coach Station** (☎ information 7730 3466, booking 7730 3499; 164 Buckingham Palace Rd SW1; ☺ booking office 8.30am-7pm Mon-Fri, 8.30am-3.30pm Sat). **National Express** (☎ 0870 580 8080; www.national express.com) is the largest bus operator, affiliated to **Eurolines** (www .eurolines.com). Eurolines handles all international buses, which also arrive at and leave from Victoria Coach Station.

TRAIN

Within the UK

Train services to the north tend to leave from King's Cross/St Pancras or Euston stations, services to the southwest leave from Waterloo, services to the south leave from London Bridge and services to the west leave from Paddington, but contact **National Rail Enquiries** (☎ 0845 748 4950; www.rail.co.uk) for exact details.

Continental Europe

For European train enquiries contact **Rail Europe** (☎ 0870 584 8848; www.raileurope.com).

Eurostar (☎ 0870 518 6186; www .eurostar.com) links London with the Gare du Nord in Paris (2¾ hours, up to 25 a day) and Brussels' international terminal (2½

LET THE TRAIN TAKE THE STRAIN

Getting into London from its major airports – London City excluded – often takes as long as an entire flight from mainland Europe. But if you catch the Eurostar train from the Continent, you'll not only be plumping for a more eco-friendly form of transport, you'll be saving yourself an enormous amount of hassle, too. Travelling by train from Paris, Brussels or Lille, you skip the schlep to the airport and check-in, plus you'll find yourself arriving at Waterloo, or, from the end of 2007, King's Cross, immediately in the central part of the city. Coming overland from Paris or Brussels also gives you the wonderful opportunity to explore Europe.

hours, up to 12 a day). Until late 2007, all services will continue to terminate at London's Waterloo station (Map pp138–9, B3). From November 2007, they will arrive at the new King's Cross terminal (Map p159, A4), which will cut these journey times by about 25 to 35 minutes.

Le Shuttle (☎ 0870 535 3535; www .eurotunnel.com) is a train that transports motor vehicles and bicycles to the Continent; see the website for details.

GETTING AROUND

Despite its somewhat decrepit state, the Underground, or tube, is still the best way to traverse this enormous city, because it avoids road traffic and so is usually faster than anything else. **Transport for London** (☎ 7222 1234; www.tfl.gov.uk) has information about the Underground, buses, Docklands Light Railway (DLR) or local trains. For up-to-the-moment news of how services are running, call **Travelcheck** (☎ 7222 1200). In this book, the nearest tube station is noted after the ⊖ in each listing.

TRAVEL PASSES

Prices are deliberately structured to make a smart-card Oyster Card the cheapest way of paying for public transport, as well as the most convenient. Costing £3 initially, the electronic Oyster Card can be credited with 'pre-pay' single fares, deducted each time your card is placed on a card reader at the entry to tube stations and on buses. Alter-

Recommended Modes of Transport

	Covent Garden	Piccadilly Circus	South Kensington	Westminster
Covent Garden	n/a	walk 10min	tube 10min	tube 15min, walk 25min
Piccadilly Circus	walk 10min	n/a	tube 8min	tube 8min, walk 20min
South Kensington	tube 10min	tube 8min	n/a	tube 8min
Westminster	tube 15min, walk 25min	tube 8min; walk 20min	tube 8min	n/a
Waterloo	tube 11min, walk 20min	tube 5min	tube 15min	tube 2min, walk 15min
London Bridge	tube 20min	tube 12min	tube 20min	tube 5min
Tower Hill	tube 20min	tube 15min	tube 20min	tube 10min
Liverpool St	tube 15min, walk 25min	tube 20min	tube 20min	tube 20min, bus 25min
Notting Hill	tube 20-25min	tube 15min	tube 8min	tube 15min

natively, you can load it with a weekly Travelcard for all London transport – eg paying £23.20 for Zones 1 and 2. The Oyster Card can be purchased at train and Underground stations and on online; go to www.tfl.gov.uk or www.oystercard.com.

Old-fashioned paper Travelcards are still available too. A daily Travelcard for Zones 1 and 2 costs £6.60, for example, or £5.10 for an off-peak Travelcard, which can be used all day on weekends and after 9.30am weekdays.

UNDERGROUND

Underground services run from 5.30am (7am on Sunday) to roughly midnight. However, a timetable change from May 2007 will see trains running half an hour later on Friday and Saturday nights, and starting a half-hour later on Saturday and Sunday mornings.

The Underground and London rail services are divided into six concentric zones. If you pay by cash, a single fare anywhere within Zones 1 to 6 is £4. Oyster

Waterloo	London Bridge	Tower Hill	Liverpool St	Notting Hill
tube 11min, walk 20min	tube 20min	tube 20min	tube 20min	tube 20-25min
tube 5min	tube 12min	tube 15min	tube 20min	tube 15min
tube 15min	tube 20min	tube 20min	tube 25min	tube 8min
tube 15min	tube 5min	tube 10min	tube 20min, bus 25min	tube 15min
n/a	tube 4min	tube 15min	tube 10min	tube 20min
tube 4min	n/a	bus 25min; walk 20min	tube 10min, bus 15min	tube 25min
tube 15min	tube 10min, walk 20min	n/a	tube 10min	tube 30min
tube 10min	tube 10min, bus 15min	tube 10min	n/a	tube 20min
tube 20min	tube 25min	tube 30min	tube 20min	n/a

Card fares are much cheaper, at £1.50/2/2.50/2.50/3.50/3.50 for Zones 1/2/3/4/5/6. No matter how much you travel during a day within Zones 1 and 2 with an Oyster Card, a maximum of £6.10 (off-peak £4.60) will be charged to your card – less than the cost of a Travelcard. See www.tfl.gov.uk /oyster for more details.

BUS
Buses run regularly between 7am and midnight; less frequent night buses (prefixed with the letter 'N') take over between midnight and 7am.

Single-journey bus tickets (valid for two hours) cost £2/1 cash/Oyster Card and bus-only day passes are £3.50/3 cash/Oyster Card. In central London at stops with yellow signs you must buy your ticket *before* boarding from the automatic machine (or have an Oyster Card). Elsewhere, you can purchase your ticket on the bus. Under-16s (with ID, including a valid Oyster photocard for 14- to15-year-olds) are entitled to free bus travel.

Trafalgar Sq, Tottenham Court Rd and Oxford Circus are the main terminals for night buses.

CAR
If you want to bring your car to London, note that the city has a groundbreaking 'congestion charge', and it will cost you £8 a day to drive into the centre or western suburbs. See www.cclondon .com for details.

DLR & TRAIN
The **Docklands Light Railway** (DLR; www .tfl.gov.uk/dlr) links the City at Bank and Tower Gateway at Tower Hill with services to Stratford and London City Airport to the east and the Docklands and Greenwich to the south. The DLR runs from 5.30am to 12.30am Monday to Saturday, and 7.30am to 11pm Sunday.

Suburban passenger trains are operated by **Silverlink** (North London Line; ☎ 0845 601 4867; www .silverlink-trains.com), which connects Richmond in the southwest with North Woolwich in the southeast; and **Thameslink** (☎ 0845 748 4950; www.thameslink.co.uk), running from London Bridge through the City to King's Cross and Luton.

Fares for the DLR and suburban trains are as for the tube (see p219).

TAXI
Licensed black cabs are reliable but expensive; minicabs are cheaper, but their drivers will not have undergone the same extensive training as black-cab drivers to obtain 'the knowledge' of every central London street (although this is increasingly less important in the days of in-car GPS).

Black cabs are available for hire when the yellow light above the windscreen is lit. Fares are metered, with flag fall at £2.20 and each successive kilometre costing £1.20. To order a black cab by phone, try **Dial-a-Cab** (☎ 7253 5000) or **Computer Cabs** (☎ 7908 0207). It's more costly to call them, though, with up to £6.20 in flag fall and booking fee.

Minicabs can only be hired by phone or from a minicab office; every neighbourhood and high street has one. Minicabs often don't have meters, so get a quote before you start.

Small companies are based in particular areas, or try a large 24-hour operator: ☎ 7387 8888, 7272 2222/3322 or 8888 4444.

PRACTICALITIES
BUSINESS HOURS
London is not a 24-hour city, but it does have generous shopping hours, and pubs and bars are now able to apply for 24-hour licences, although few have. Otherwise, use the following as a rule of thumb.
Banks 9.30am to 5.30pm Monday to Friday
Offices 9am to 5pm, 9.30am to 5.30pm or 10am to 6pm Monday to Friday
Pubs 11am to 11pm Sunday to Thursday, 11am to midnight Friday and Saturday, to 3am or 4am in nightlife districts like Shoreditch
Restaurants Noon to 11pm, last orders 10pm, many close Sunday or Monday

Shops 9am or 10am to 6pm Monday to Saturday, many also noon to 6pm Sun; late-night shopping 9am or 10am to 8pm Thursday, plus sometimes Wednesday in the West End

DISCOUNTS
Most attractions offer discounts to children (ask at each venue for age limits), youth cardholders under 25 (or 26), students with ISIC cards (age limits may apply), those over 60 (or 65; sometimes lower for women), disabled visitors and families.

The **London Pass** (☎ 0870 242 9988; www.londonpass.com) allows free admission to over 55 attractions in the capital, but it is slanted towards those wishing to visit places like the Tower of London and London Zoo rather than galleries and museums (most of which are free anyway). For adults the pass costs £32/55/71/110 for one/two/three/six days including transport (and £32/42/52/72 without transport).

EMERGENCIES
London is remarkably safe considering its size and uneven wealth. Generally, be careful at night and in crowded places such as the tube, where pickpockets and bag snatchers operate. Even following a recent upsurge, there is still minimal gun crime.

EU citizens, and those from Iceland, Liechtenstein, Norway or Switzerland, are entitled to free emergency treatment if they have an EHIC (European Health Insurance Card), as are some other nationals whose countries have reciprocal agreements with the UK. However, because of the limits of EHIC and similar cover, you should always have travel insurance.

For emergencies, call **Ambulance, Fire & Police** (☎ 999).

A&E (accident and emergency) departments operating 24 hours:
Chelsea & Westminster Hospital (Map pp96-7, B5; ☎ 8746 8000; 369 Fulham Rd SW10; ✦ Earl's Ct or Fulham Broadway)
Royal Free Hospital (Map p167, B4; ☎ 7794 0500; www.royalfree.org.uk; Pond St NW3; ✦ Belsize Park)
Royal London Hospital (☎ 7377 7000; Whitechapel Rd E1; ✦ Whitechapel)
St Thomas' Hospital (Map pp138-9, B3; ☎ 7188 7188; Lambeth Palace Rd SE1; ✦ Waterloo)
University College Hospital (Map p63, B4; ☎ 0845 155 5000; 253 Euston Rd NW1; ✦ Warren St or Euston Sq)

Late-opening chemists:
Boots (Map pp80-1, C5; ☎ 7734 6126; www.boots.com; 44-46 Regent St W1; ☯ 9am-8pm; ✦ Piccadilly Circus)
Pharmacentre (Map p71, B5; ☎ 7723 2336, 0808 108 7521; www.hhm.com /pharmacentre; 149 Edgware Rd; ☯ 9am-midnight; ✦ Edgware Rd or Marble Arch)

HOLIDAYS
New Year's Day 1 January
Good Friday Late March/April
Easter Monday Late March/April
May Day Bank Holiday First Monday in May
Spring Bank Holiday Last Monday in May
Summer Bank Holiday Last Monday in August
Christmas Day 25 December
Boxing Day 26 December

INTERNET
London is chock-a-block with cybercafés. The largest chain is **easyEverthing** (www.easyeverything .com). Meanwhile, useful websites include the following:
BBC London (www.bbc.co.uk/London)
Evening Standard (www.thisislondon .co.uk)
Streetmap (www.streetmap.co.uk)
Time Out (www.timeout.com)
UK Weather (www.met-office.gov.uk)

MONEY
London is one of the world's most expensive cities, and it would be no problem to go through several hundred pounds a day here. For a comfortable time, not pinching the pennies, bank on £50 to £75 a day spending money, on top of your hotel bill, and more if you're planning on a shopping spree. If you're on a tight budget, you might get away with £30 per day on top of your hotel bill.

The easiest way to access your money is via ATMS; almost all in London are international compatible. There are also numerous banks, *bureaux de change* and travel agencies all competing for business. London banks are usually open 9.30am to 5.30pm Monday to Friday.

For currency exchange rates, see the inside front cover of this book.

ORGANISED TOURS

You'll find many guided bus tours circulating the city; places such as Marble Arch and near Trafalgar Sq are good starting points if you're keen.

RIVER CRUISES

During daylight hours, you can simply catch a boat along the Thames by heading for the nearest pier – found at Westminster, Embankment, Waterloo (London Eye), Bankside (Tate Modern), Tower and Greenwich, among others. Fares cost about £4 to £8 one way (there are some discounts for Travelcard/Oyster Card holders).

Only dinner cruises, RIB London Voyages (see the boxed text p141) or journeys to the Thames Flood Barrier, Kew and Hampton Court (see the boxed text, p84) really require much planning.

Operators include the following:
Bateaux London – Catamaran Cruisers (☎ 7987 1185, 7925 2215; www.bateauxlondon.com)

City Cruises (☎ 7740 0400; www.citycruises.com)

Crown River Cruises (☎ 7936 2033; www.crownriver.com)

Thames River Boats (☎ 7930 2062; www.wpsa.co.uk) Formerly Westminster Passenger Services Association.

Thames River Services (☎ 7930 4097; www.westminsterpier.co.uk)

SPECIALIST TOURS

London Duck Tours (☎ 7928 3132; www.londonducktours.co.uk; adult/child/concession/family £17.50/12/14/53) has a different take on the river, using amphibious craft, based on D-Day landing vehicles, to cruise the streets of central London before making a dramatic descent into the Thames at Vauxhall. Tours depart from outside the County Hall (p137).

CANAL TOURS

To see a different side of the city entirely, try the **London Waterbus Company** (Map p167, D6; ☎ information 7482 2660, bookings 7482 2550; www.londonwaterbus.com; 2 Middle Yard, Camden Lock NW1; adult/child one-way £4.80/3.10, return £6.20/4; ⏲ 10am-5pm Mon-Sun Apr-Oct, 10am-3pm or 4pm Sat & Sun Nov-Mar; ⊖ Camden Town). It runs 90-minute trips on Regent's Canal in an enclosed barge between Camden Lock and Little Venice, passing through Regent's Park and London Zoo. Services run every hour (every 30 minutes on Sunday) from April to October.

TELEPHONE

The UK uses the GSM 900 mobile phone network, compatible with phones from Continental Europe, Australia and New Zealand, but not North American GSM 1900 or Japanese systems (some North Americans have GSM 1900/900 phones that do work here). Make sure your phone has a 'roaming' capability before you leave home. Otherwise, there are public phones, either coin or phonecard operated (phonecards are available at newsagents).

COUNTRY & CITY CODES

London (☎ 020)
UK (☎ 44)

USEFUL NUMBERS

Directory enquiries (☎ 118 118, 118 500)
International dialling code (☎ 00)
International directory (☎ 118 661)
Local & national operator (☎ 100)
Reverse-charge/collect calls (☎ 155)
Time (☎ 123)
Weathercall (☎ 0906 850 0401) Premium-rate call.

TIPPING

Porters Around £2 per bag.
Restaurants From 10% to 15% (usually included in the bill).
Taxis Round up to nearest pound.

TOURIST INFORMATION

You can get information or book hotels through **Visit London** (☎ 0870 156 6366, 7932 5800; www.visitlondon .com).

TRAVELLERS WITH DISABILITIES

London isn't the easiest city for travellers with impaired movement. Access to the Underground is pretty limited, while uneven pavements and crowding make things even more difficult. However, newer buses sometimes have ramps that lower for easier access, and there are two dedicated bus services offering disabled access from 6am to midnight: bus 205 runs from Paddington to Whitechapel (every 12 minutes); bus 705 runs from Victoria to Waterloo and London Bridge (every half hour).

For more details, contact Transport for London's **Access & Mobility for Disabled Passengers** (☎ 7222 1234, textphone 7918 3015) or the **Royal Association for Disability and Rehabilitation** (RADAR; ☎ 7250 3222; www.radar .org.uk).

INDEX

>INDEX

See also separate subindexes for See (p235), Shop (p236), Eat (p237), Drink (p239) and Play (p239).

7/7 bombings 210
30 St Mary Axe 114

A
accommodation 186-7
    internet resources 186
Adam, Robert 169
afternoon teas 91
air travel 214-16
Albert Memorial 95
Ali, Monica 121
ambulance 222
antiques 74-5, 103
architecture 65, 188-9
arts, *see* galleries
ATMS 223

B
ballet 61
Bank of England 109
Barbican 65
Barry, Charles 208
Battersea Power
    Station 98
BBC Electric Proms 174
Bermondsey 148
Bethnal Green 131
Bethnal Green Museum of
    Childhood 131
BFI Southbank 137

Big Ben 14, 82
Blair, Tony 210
Bloomsbury 62-9, **63**
Bonfire Night 36
books 212-13
Borough Market 25, 142-3
bowling 69
breweries 125, *see also*
    gastropubs
Brick Lane 121
British Library 160
British Museum 17, 64-5
Brixton 147
Brixton Market 147
Broadway Market 131
Brockwell Park Lido 147
BT Tower 65
Buckingham Palace 79
bus travel 217, 220
    Routemaster 88
business hours 221

C
cabaret 134, 194, *see also*
    Play *subindex*
    Bethnal Green 129, 135
    Camden 175
    Holborn 119
    St James's 93
    Soho 61
Cabinet War Rooms &
    Churchill Museum 79
Camden 166-75, **167**

Camden Market 169-70
Canute, King 205
car travel 220
Caribbean Showcase 35
Carols in Trafalgar Sq 36
castles 19, 114-15
cathedrals, *see* See *subindex*
celebrities 90, 172
cell phones 224
Celts, the 205
cemeteries 168
Centre Point 65
Changing of the Guard 79
Chelsea 94-107, **96-7**
Chelsea Flower Show 33
Chelsea Physic Garden 95
chemists 222
children, attractions for, *see*
    See *subindex*
Chinese New Year 32
Christ Church Spitalfields 125
churches, *see* See *subindex*
Churchill, Winston 79, 209
cinema, *see* film
cinemas, *see also* Play
    subindex
    Bloomsbury 69
    City, the 119
    Notting Hill 182-3
    St James's 83
    Soho 59
    South Bank 148-9
circuses 175

000 map pages

City, the 108-19, **110-11**
City Hall 137
Clerkenwell 108-19, **110-11**
clubbing 195, *see also* Play
    subindex
    City, the 119
    Clerkenwell 119
    Convent Garden 60-1
    King's Cross 165
    Shoreditch 30, 135
    Soho 60-1
    South Bank 148
cocktail bars 58, 129, 130,
    134, 182, *see also* Drink
    subindex
comedy 59
Conran, Terence 102
Corrigan, Richard 56
costs 222
County Hall 137
Courtauld Institute of
    Art 50
Covent Garden 46-61, **48-9**
cricket 72
Cromwell, Oliver 206
cruises 22, 84-5, 141, 223
curry houses 27, 121, 128,
    see also Eat *subindex*
Cutty Sark 152

D

dance 61, 119
    festivals 36
Dance Umbrella 36
Danes, the 205
Dennis Severs' House 121
Design Museum 140
Diana, Princess of Wales
    Memorial Fountain 95-8

disabilities, travellers
    with 224
Docklands 153
Docklands Light Railway 220
drinking 198, *see also* Drink
    subindex
    Bloomsbury 67
    Camden 173
    City, the 118
    Clerkenwell 118
    Covent Garden 58-9
    Fitzrovia 67
    Greenwich 157
    Hampstead 173
    Holborn 118
    Hoxton 131
    Islington 163-5
    Mayfair 93
    Notting Hill 181-2
    Primrose Hill 173
    Shoreditch 131
    Soho 58-9
    South Bank 146
    Spitalfields 131
drugstores 222

E

economy 210
Edward the Confessor 205
emergency 221-2
English Civil War 206
entertainment
    Camden 175
    City, the 119
    Clerkenwell 119
    Covent Garden 59-61
    Euston 165
    Holborn 119
    Hoxton 135

Islington 165
King's Cross 165
Mayfair 93
Notting Hill 182-3
Shoreditch 135
Soho 59-61
South Bank 147-9
Spitalfields 135
environmental issues 214
Euston 158-65, **159**
events 31-6
exchange rates *see inside
    front cover*

F

FA Cup Final 33
Fashion & Textile
    Museum 148
festivals 31-6
    dance 36
    film 36
    gay & lesbian 35
    music 34
film 183, 213
    festivals 36
fire services 222
Fitzrovia 62-9, **63**
food 26, 27, 190-1, *see
    also* Eat *subindex*
    Bloomsbury 66-7
    Camden 170
    Chelsea 104
    City 115
    Clerkenwell 115
    Covent Garden 55-8
    Euston 162
    Fitzrovia 66-7
    Greenwich 157
    Hampstead 170

food *continued*
  Holborn 115
  Hoxton 129
  Islington 162
  King's Cross 162
  Knightsbridge 104
  Marylebone 76-7
  Mayfair 90
  Notting Hill 180-1
  Pimlico 90
  Primrose Hill 170
  Regent's Park 76-7
  reservations 57
  Shoreditch 129
  Soho 55-8
  South Bank 144
  South Kensington 104
  Spitalfields 129
  St James 90
  Westminster 90
football 33, 107, 165
Freud Museum 168
Fruitstock 34
fussball 118

G
galleries 192-3, *see also*
  See *subindex*
gardens, *see* See *subindex*
gastropubs, *see* Eat
  subindex
Gatwick airport 214
gay travellers 196
Geffrye Museum 121-4
Georgian Period 207
Gherkin 114

government 211-12
Graham, Brett 181
Great Fire of London 206
Greenwich 23, 150-7, **151**
Greenwich Foot
  Tunnel 153
Greenwich Market 155-6
Guy Fawkes Night 36

H
Hackney 131
Hampstead 166-75, **167**
Hampstead Heath 24, 168
  festivals 34
Hampton Court Palace 84
Haystack 186
Hayward Gallery 140
Heathrow airport 214
Henderson, Fergus 117
Henry VIII 206
Highgate Cemetery 168
history 205-10
Holborn 108-19, **110-11**
holidays 222
Horse Guards Parade 79-82
hospitals 222
Houses of Parliament 14,
  82-3
Hoxton 120-35, **122-3**
Huguenot silk weavers 121
Hyde Park 15, 98
  festivals 34

I
ice-skating 50, 168
Imperial War Museum 140
Institute of Contemporary
  Arts 83
internet access 222

internet resources 210, 222
  accommodation 186
  car travel 220
  clubbing 195
  music 197
  pubs 198
  theatre 201
Islington 158-65, **159**
itineraries 37-41

J
jazz 61, 175, 197
Jones, Inigo 154

K
Keats House 168-9
Keats, John 168-9
Kensington Gardens 15, 98
Kensington Museums 20-1
Kensington Palace 99
Kenwood House 169
Kenwood Picnic Concerts 34
Kew Gardens 84
Kinetica 124
King's Cross 158-65, **159**
Knightsbridge 94-107,
  96-7

L
Leadenhall Market 109
lesbian travellers 196
Lincoln's Inn 112
Livingstone, Ken 210
Loaded in the Park 34
London City
  Airport 214-16
London Eye 10-11, 140
London Film Festival 36
London Marathon 32
London Open House 36

London Parade 32
London Zoo 72
Lord Mayor's Show 36
Lord's Cricket Ground 72
Lovebox Weekender 34
Luton 216

M
Madame Tussauds 73
markets 25, *see also* Shop subindex
Marylebone 70-7, **71**
Mayfair 78-93, **80-1**
memorials 95-8
Millennium Bridge 141
mobile phones 224
money 222-4
    discounts 221-4
Monument 112
monuments 86, 112
Museum in Docklands 153
Museum of London 112
museums, *see* See subindex
music 197, *see also* Play subindex
    festivals 34, 35
    jazz 61, 175, 197
    opera 60, 61

N
Nash, John 188, 207-13
National Gallery 16, 47
National Maritime Museum 153-4
National Portrait Gallery 16, 47
Natural History Museum 20-1, 99

Nelson's Column 51
nightlife, *see* entertainment, Play subindex
No 10 Downing Street 83
Normans, the 206
Notting Hill 176-83, **177**
Notting Hill Carnival 35

O
observatories 155
Old Operating Theatre Museum & Herb Garret 141
Oliver, Jamie 129, 172
Olympics 209, 210
opera 60, 61
Ottolenghi, Otto 181
Oxford & Cambridge Boat Race 32
Oyster Card 72

P
palaces 79, 84, 99
parks, *see* See subindex
pharmacies 222
Photographers' Gallery 47-50
Pimlico 78-93, **80-1**
plague 206
planning 40, 57
    discounts 221
police 222
politics 211-12
Pollock's Toy Museum 65
pool tables 118
population 209, 210
Portobello Road Market 178-9
Pride 35

Primrose Hill 166-75, **167**
Proms 35
pubs 198, *see also* Drink subindex
Pugin, August 208

Q
Queen's House 154

R
Ramsay, Gordon 91, 92, 105, 106
Raven 115
Reckless Records 54
Regent's Park (area) 70-7, **71**
Regent's Park (park) 73-4
reservations 40
    accommodation 186-7
    restaurants 57
restaurants 26, 27, 190-1, *see also* Eat subindex
Rise 34
River Thames 199, 205
    cruises 22, 84-5, 141, 223
    festivals 36
Robuchon, Joël 56-7
Romans, the 205
Routemaster 88
Royal Academy of Arts 84
Royal Geographical Society 98
Royal Naval College 154-5
Royal Observatory 155
Royal Parks 15
    Hyde Park 34, 98
    Kensington Gardens 98
    St James's Park 84-5

S
Saatchi Gallery 100
St Bartholomew-the-
  Great 113
St James's 78-93, **80-1**
St James's Park 15, 84-5
St Martin-in-the-
  Fields 51
St Pancras Chambers
  160-1
St Paul's Cathedral 18, 114
Saxons, the 205
Science Museum 21, 100
Senate House 65
Serpentine Gallery 100-1
Serpentine Lake 101
7/7 bombings 210
Severs, Dennis 121
Shakespeare 141
Shakespeare's Globe 141-2
shopping 52, 200, see also
  Shop subindex
    Bloomsbury 65
    Camden 169
    Chelsea 102
    Clerkenwell 115
    Covent Garden 51-5
    Fitzrovia 65
    Greenwich 155
    Hampstead 169
    Hoxton 126
    Islington 161
    Knightsbridge 102
    Marylebone 74
    Mayfair 87
    Notting Hill 178-80

000 map pages

Pimlico 87
Regent's Park 74
St James's 87
Shoreditch 126
Soho 51-5
South Bank 142
South Kensington 102
Spitalfields 126
Westminster 87
Shoreditch 30, 120-35,
  122-3
Sir John Soane's
  Museum 112
Soane, Sir John 112, 207
Soho 46-61, **48-9**
Somerset House 50
  festivals 34
Somerset House
  Museums 50
Somerset House Summer
  Series 34
South Bank 10-11, 136-49,
  138-9
South Kensington 94-107,
  96-7
Space NK 54-5
Spitalfields 120-35, **122-3**
Spitalfields Market 25
sporting events, see also
  Play subindex
    FA Cup Final 33
    London Marathon 32
    Oxford & Cambridge
      Boat Race 32
    Wimbledon Lawn Tennis
      Championships 33
Stansted 214
Sunday Up Market 125
swimming pools 147

T
tailors 86
Tate Britain 85
Tate Modern 12-13, 142
Tatty Devine 55
taxis 220-1
tea dances 135, 162
telephone services 224
tennis 33
Thames,
  see River Thames
Thames Festival 36
Thames Flood Barrier 85
theatre 28-9, 61, 201, see
  also Play subindex
    City, the 119
    Convent Garden 59-60
    Islington 165
    South Bank 149
30 St Mary Axe 114
tipping 224
Tooting 128
tourist information 224
tours 223-4
Tower Bridge 114
Tower of London 19,
  114-15
Trafalgar Sq 51
train travel 217, 219-20
travel passes 72, 218-19
Trooping the Colour 33
Truman Brewery 125
tube, the 218, 219-20
Tudors, the 206-7

U
Underground, the 218,
  219-20
unemployment 209

INDEX

V
vacations 222-4
vegetarian travellers 190,
   see also Eat *subindex*
Victoria & Albert Museum
   20, 101-2
Victorian Age 207-9
views 117, 202

W
Wallace Collection 74
Wareing, Marcus 106
Wellington Arch 86
Westminster 14, 78-93,
   80-1
Westminster Abbey 86
Westminster Cathedral 86
White Cube Gallery 87,
   125
Whitechapel Art
   Gallery 125
William the Conqueror 206
Wimbledon Lawn Tennis
   Championships 33
Wireless 34
World Wars 209-10
Wren, Christopher 114, 154,
   188, 206

Y
Yau, Alan 66

Z
zoos 72

SEE
Areas & Streets
BFI Southbank 10-11, 137
Brick Lane 121

Bridges
Millennium Bridge 141
Tower Bridge 114

Castles
Tower of London 19, 114-15

Cemeteries
Highgate Cemetery 168

Churches & Cathedrals
Christ Church Spitalfields 125
St Bartholomew-the-
   Great 113
St Paul's Cathedral 18, 114
Westminster Abbey 14, 86
Westminster Cathedral
   14, 86

Cruises
River Thames 22

Galleries
Courtauld Institute of Art 50
Hayward Gallery 140
Institute of Contemporary
   Arts 83
Kenwood House 169
Kinetica 124
Madame Tussauds 73
National Gallery 16, 47
National Portrait Gallery
   16, 47
Photographers' Gallery
   47-50
Royal Academy of Arts 84
Saatchi Gallery 100
Serpentine Gallery 100-1
Tate Britain 85
Tate Modern 12-13, 142

Wallace Collection 74
White Cube Gallery 125
Whitechapel Art Gallery 125

Lakes
Serpentine Lake 101

London for Children
Bethnal Green Museum of
   Childhood 131
Cutty Sark 152
Kinetica 124
London Eye 10-11, 140
London Zoo 72
Madame Tussauds 73
Monument 112
Museum in Docklands 153
Natural History Museum
   20-1, 99
Pollock's Toy Museum 65
Science Museum 21, 100

Memorials
Albert Memorial 95
Diana, Princess of Wales
   Memorial Fountain 95-8

Monuments
Monument 112
Wellington Arch 86

Museums
Bank of England 109
Bethnal Green Museum of
   Childhood 131
British Museum 17, 64
Cabinet War Rooms &
   Churchill Museum 79
Cutty Sark 152
Dennis Sever's House 121

Design Museum 140
Fashion & Textile
   Museum 148
Freud Museum 168
Geffrye Museum 121-4
Imperial War
   Museum 140
Keats House 168-9
Kensington Museums 20-1
Kinetica 124
Museum in Docklands 153
Museum of London 112
National Maritime Museum
   153-4
Natural History Museum
   20-1, 99
Old Operating Theatre
   Museum & Herb
   Garret 141
Pollock's Toy Museum 65
Science Museum 20-1, 100
Sir John Soane's
   Museum 112
Somerset House
   Museums 50
Victoria & Albert Museum
   20-1, 101-2
Wallace Collection 74

Notable Buildings &
   Structures
30 St Mary Axe 114
Battersea Power Station 98
Big Ben 14, 82
British Library 160
Buckingham Palace 79

City Hall 137
County Hall 137
Gherkin 114
Greenwich Foot Tunnel 153
Horse Guards
   Parade 79-82
Houses of Parliament 14,
   82-3
Kenwood House 169
London Eye 10-11, 140
Millennium Bridge 141
No 10 Downing Street 83
Royal Hospital Chelsea 100
Royal Naval College 154-5
St Pancras Chambers 160-1
St Paul's Cathedral 114
Science Museum 100
Shakespeare's
   Globe 141-2
Somerset House 50
South Bank 10-11
Tower Bridge 114
Tower of London 19, 114-15
Trafalgar Sq 51
Truman Brewery 125
Wellington Arch 86
Westminster Abbey 14, 86
Westminster Cathedral
   14, 86

Observatories
Royal Observatory 155

Palaces
Buckingham Palace 79
Kensington Palace 99
Westminster Abbey 84

Parks & Gardens
Chelsea Physic Garden 95

Hampstead Heath 24, 168
Hyde Park 15, 98
Kensington Gardens 15, 98
Lincoln's Inn 112
Regent's Park 73-4
Royal Parks 15
St James's Park 15, 84-5
Westminster Abbey 84

Sporting Grounds
Lord's Cricket Ground 72

Zoos
London Zoo 72

SHOP
Accessories
Coco de Mer 59
Shop at Bluebird 102-4
Tatty Devine 55, 128-9

Antiques
After Noah 103
Alfie's Antiques Market 74-5
Joanna Booth 103

Arcades
Burlington Arcade 88
Dover Street Market 88
Oxo Tower 143

Books
Forbidden Planet 53
Shop at Bluebird 102-4
Travel Bookshop 180

Clothing
Absolute Vintage 126-7
Alfie's Antiques Market
   74-5

000 map pages

Beyond Retro 127
Blackout II 53
Burberry 87-8
Burberry Factory Shop 131
Cockfighter of
  Bermondsey 148
Diverse 161
Joy 156
Kilgour 86
Laden Showrooms 127-8
Matthew Williamson 89
Mulberry 89-90
Ozwald Boateng 86
Paul Smith 52
Paul Smith Sale Shop 90
Primark 131
Rellick 179
Shop at Bluebird 102-4
Start 128
Steinberg & Tolkien 103
Stella McCartney 90
Topman 66
TopShop 66

Cosmetics
Pout 53
Space NK 54-5

Department Stores
Fortnum & Mason 88-9
Harrods 102
Harvey Nichols 102
Liberty 52
Selfridges 76

Food
A Gold 126
Camden Market 169-70
Cyber Candy 53
Konditor & Cook 143

Lisboa Patisserie 178
Rococo 75, 102
Rosslyn Delicatessen 170

Furniture & Homewares
Alfie's Antiques
  Market 74-5
Aria 161
Flying Duck Enterprises 155
Habitat 52, 65
Heal's 65-6
Joy 156
Shop at Bluebird 102-4

Jewellery
Crazy Pig 53
Lesley Craze Gallery 115
Tatty Devine 55, 128-9

Markets
Borough Market 25,
  142-3
Brixton Market 147
Broadway Market 131
Columbia Road Flower
  Market 127
Dover Street Market 88
Greenwich Market 155-6
Leadenhall Market 109
Portobello Road Market
  178-9
Spitalfields Market
  25, 128
Sunday Up Market 125

Music
Fopp 51, 65
Haggle Vinyl 161-2
Reckless Records 54
Rough Trade 179-80

Shoes
Poste 90
Poste Mistress 52-4
Tracey Neuls 76

Toys
Forbidden Planet 53
Hamleys 52

EAT
American
Gourmet Burger Kitchen 173
Hache 170
Hamburger Union 173
Ultimate Burger 173

Asian
E&O 181
Gilgamesh 170

British
Canteen 129
Electric Brasserie 181
Gordon Ramsay at
  Claridges 91
Ivy 56
Medcalf 116
Roast 145
St John 117
SE10 Restaurant &
  Bar 157
Smiths of Smithfields 117
Table 145

Cafés
Inn the Park 91
Ladurée 104
Maison Bertaux 57
Patisserie Valerie 57

Carribean
Mango Room 171

Chinese
Hakkasan 66
Hunan 91
Yauatcha 57-8

European
Andrew Edmunds 55
Arbutus 56
Boxwood Café 105
Coach & Horses 116
Electric Brasserie 181
Gordon Ramsay 105
Inside 157
Petrus 106
Sketch 92
Wolseley 92-3

Fish & Chips
Golden Hind 77

French
Almeida 162
Bibendum 105
Club Gascon 115-16
Galvin @ Windows 90-1
La Bouchée 103
La Poule au Pot 106
L'Atelier de Joël
   Robuchon 56-7
Le Pain Quotidien 77
Ledbury 181
Les Trois Garçons 130
Racine 106
Sketch 92

Gastropubs
Anchor & Hope 144
Bumpkin 180
Cow 180
Eagle 116
Garrison 148
Lansdowne 170-1
Princess 130
Wells 172-3

Indian
Amaya 104
Café Spice
   Namaste 115
Chutney's 162
Cinnamon Club 90
Kastoori 128
Masaledar 128
New Tayyab 130
Painted Heron 106
Radha Krishna
   Bhavan 128

International
BluePrint Café 144
Plateau 153
Sketch 92
Village East 148

Irish
Lindsay House 56

Italian
Café Mode 53
Fifteen 129
Locanda Locatelli 77

Japanese
Jin Kichi 170
Nobu 92

Malaysian
Champor-Champor 148

Mediterranean
Bermondsey
   Kitchen 148
Eagle 116
Ottolenghi 162-3, 181

Mexican
Crazy Homies 180-1
Green & Red 129

Modern International
Giraffe 130
Maze 92

North African
Moro 117

Polish
Baltic 144
Daquise 105
Trojka 172

Seafood
Golden Hind 77
J Sheekey 56

Spanish
Fino 66
Moro 117
Providores & Tapa
   Room 77
Salt Yard 66-7
Tapas Brindisa 145

Thai
Busaba Eathai 56, 66
Mango Tree 91-2

000 map pages

Turkish
Gallipoli 162
Ozer 77
Tas Borough 146
Tas Ev 145-6
Tas Pide 145
Tas Waterloo 145

Vegetarian
Eat & Two Veg 76-7
Food for Thought 53
Fresh & Wild 53
Manna 171-2
Mildred's 57
Royal Teas 157

DRINK
Bars
All Star Lanes 69
Annexe 3 67
At Proud 173
Bar Italia 58
Big Chill Bar 131
Bistrotheque 129
Blue Bar 107
Bradley's Spanish Bar 67
Bloomsbury Bowling 69
Cafe Kick 118
Dragon Bar 131-3
Dreambagsjaguarshoes 133
Earl of Lonsdale 181-2
Embassy 164-5
Favela Chic 133
Floridita 58
Foundry 133
George & Dragon 133
Hawksmoor 134
Hollybush 173
LAB 58

Londsdale 182
Loungelover 134
Nobu Berkeley 93
Ten Bells 134
Troubadour 103
Vertigo 42 118
Vibe Bar 134
Wine Wharf 147

Cafés
Coffee, Cake & Kink 59
Monmouth Coffee Company
    58, 147
Montparnasse Cafe 103

Cocktail Bars
Annexe 3 67
Bistrotheque 129
Blue Bar 107
Hawksmoor 134
LAB 58
Lonsdale 182
Loungelover 134

Pubs
Boogaloo 173
Elephant & Castle 103
Elk in the Woods 164
French House 132
George Inn 146
Golden Heart 133-4
Grapes 145
Gun 153
Jerusalem Tavern 118
King's Arms 146
Lamb 67-8
Lamb & Flag 58
Laughing Gravy 147
Lock Tavern 175
Mayflower 145

Princess Louise 68
Prospect of Whitby 145
Salisbury 58-9
Scarsdale 103
Trafalgar Tavern 157
Ye Olde Cheshire Cheese 118
Ye Olde Mitre 118-19

PLAY
Ballet & Dance
Roundhouse 175
Royal Ballet 61
Sadler's Wells 119

Bowling
All Star Lanes 69
Bloomsbury Bowling 69

Cabaret
Bethnal Green Working
    Men's Club 134, 135
Bistrotheque 129
Koko 175
Madame Jo Jo's 61
Pigalle 93
Volupté Lounge 119

Cinemas
Barbican 119
Curzon Soho 59
Electric Cinema 182-3
National Film Theatre 148-9

Circus
Roundhouse 175

Clubs
93 Feet East 135
333 135
Astoria 59

Bethnal Green Working
  Men's Club 135
Bosuns 103
Cargo 135
Crash 147-8
Cross 165
Egg 165
End 60
Fabric 119
Ghetto 60
Heaven 61
Madame Jo Jo's 61
Ministry of Sound 148
Notting Hill Arts Club 183
St Aloysius Social Club 162
Scala 165
Turnmills 119

Comedy
Comedy Store 59

Gay Clubs
Astoria 59
Crash 147
Ghetto 60
Heaven 61
Scala 165

Live Music
Astoria 59
Barbican 119
Barfly @ the Monarch 175
Brixton Academy 147
Jazz Café 175
Koko 175
Pigalle 93
Ronnie Scott's 61
Roundhouse 175
Scala 165
Shepherd's Bush Empire 183
South Bank Centre 149

Opera
English National
  Opera 60
Royal Opera House 61

Pool Tables
Elbow Room 118

Sport
Arsenal Emirates
  Stadium 165
Brockwell Park Lido 147

Theatre
Almeida Theatre 165
Barbican 119
Donmar Warehouse 59-60
National Theatre 149
Old Vic 149
Shakespeare's Globe 149
Young Vic 149